You Are
Magnificent!

CONFIDENCE EXPLOSION

For my friend Peggy!

Julian James

UCL
1-pm.
24 Feb.

CONFIDENCE EXPLOSION

Destroy Your Fears & Explode Your Confidence Through the Roof!

JULIAN JAMES

FOREWORD BY PETA HESKELL

Julian James International

Published by: Julian James International
Publishing partner: Paragon Publishing
First published 2011

ISBN 978-1-907611-90-2

Cover design by: Stephen Saha
Photographs by: John Lilley

Book design, layout and production management by Into Print
www.intoprint.net
+44 (0)1604 832149

Printed and bound in UK and USA by Lightning Source

Foreword 9

01 Discovering Your Power 15
02 What Confidence Really Is. 27
03 Confidence: Your Natural State 41
04 Operating from a Solid Foundation 51
05 Your Golden Birthright 63
06 Embracing the Full Bloom of Human Experience 71
07 Give Up the Need for Everyone to Like You 91
08 Finding Comfort Inside of Discomfort 107
09 Absolute Self-Acceptance: Being Totally You – Without Apology! . . 131
10 You Fit In Perfectly 155
11 Authentic Power 167
12 The Magic of Living Without Rejection 181
13 Escaping the Venom of Cultural Conditioning 193
14 Endless Connection to Power 233

About the Author 239

JULIAN JAMES

FOREWARD
By Peta Heskell

As a young girl, growing up in the white picket fence suburban fantasy world of the post WW2 era I did not feel like I fitted in. Somehow I had this innate sense that it was all wrong but didn't know how to fix it, so, like an animal caught in a trap, I struggled with all my might to escape. For that I was labelled a "rebel". I rebelled against everything from my mother's "what will the neighbours say" philosophy to the regulation shoes and stockings they made us wear in my uptight, conservative, private school.

It took me many years of personal exploration to realise that the "rebellion" was not bad. Instead I came to learn that it was my unconscious self crying out to be *me*. The *me* that was so desperate to emerge was not the "me", my parents and the authoritarian figures in my world wanted me to be.

In those days there were no books like *Confidence Explosion*. There was very little counselling for parents and school was all about academic achievement. Anyone who did not fit the "happy dappy" picture of success was labelled a misfit.

As a schoolgirl I was branded a troublemaker. I entertained my fellow students with mimicry of the teachers, and I inspired them to break the rules and have fun. If only they'd seen that these were qualities, not defects, I might have found my path earlier. And that said, I have no regrets and neither should you. Wherever you are today is perfect and the fact that you are reading this means you are ready to take the next step to discovering your confident, authentic self. Congratulations!

My parents and teachers saw me as demonised. I now know that they were wrong. That insistent voice that led me to rebel was not a demon, but an angel, trying to guide me to find my place in this world. Mine was a long journey, which has not ended yet. And the greatest joy in life is knowing that tomorrow we will find yet another facet of ourselves that is *special* and *magical*.

Joseph Cambell, the great mythologist and practical philosopher, emphasises some of the essence of what Julian shares in this wonderful book you're now holding. His philosophy is profound, and one of my favourite Cambell quotes is: "The privilege of a lifetime is being who you are."

Who you truly are is far more than anything anyone else thinks you should be. Teachers and parents train us to be "normal". But what is "normal"? Aldous Huxley remarked that the people who think they are normal are actually abnormal because they spend their lives trying to fit into a standardised "normal" box. The real "normal" people are those who struggle from an early age to be who they are.

As you read this book, I urge you to remember these words and know that if you feel alien, or rejected, or unimportant, it's probably because you have tried to be who you are *not*. Finding yourself should be the first and foremost goal in your life regardless of what anyone else tells you.

I remember the first time, at the age of 32, when I got just how important this is. I wandered into a bookshop in San Francisco, and picked up a book called *Wishcraft*. As I read the opening lines that told me I could live the life I loved and love the work I do, I was awestruck. *This*, I told myself, is what it's all about. I knew then, that the boxes they'd tried to force me into were *their* boxes and not mine. I knew that I could fit in, and I also realised that in order to do so I had to find my personal "box" and that it would be like no other.

After many years of study and working on my personal development, which I repeat, *is* a lifelong journey, I found a niche and began teaching the wonderful stuff I'd learned to others in the guise of flirting workshops. If someone were to ask me what those workshops were really all about, I'd say it was simply *confidence*. Confidence is at the core of our development and without authentic belief in our ability to be magnificent, we will always struggle.

As I watched over and over again, the people coming into the seminar room, fearful and shy, I visualised them with that glow of inner confidence, and my greatest joy was to go down to the bar after the workshop and hear the buzz of animated conversation and the laughter and see the confident body language and ease of interaction.

Without a shadow of a doubt, before anyone can be truly confident in life they have to find out who they are, love themselves and believe that they have a productive part to play in the living jigsaw of humanity.

The first time I ever encountered Julian James was in London, at the *Royal National Hotel* in Russell Square. It was at a private meeting of trainers and hypnotists. I remember seeing him sitting amongst a group of people and thinking how charismatic and mysterious he appeared. I was fascinated. I have a nose for interesting people and was on the lookout for a gifted facilitator to help me in my workshops, so I invited Julian to assist me.

I'm so glad Julian agreed to be a facilitator in my trainings and workshops – he proved to be such an invaluable resource, bringing his charisma and own brand of expertise to the events. On the second day of the workshops, I always invite my facilitators to run small sessions on areas of their own choosing and I watched, with a smile on my face, as many of the students lined up to have a session with Julian because he was so compelling and so very unique. He put what he did into action with powerful exercises that allowed the attendees to really access their inner confidence, and the results spoke for themselves.

In short, Julian knows his place in the universal jigsaw puzzle and, more importantly, he has the ability to facilitate others to have the experience of being authentically confident. I'm therefore so excited that he is about to share his insights with *you*, in this book.

One of the greatest sadnesses of this world is that we are born perfect and from our earliest moments there is a band of well-meaning people who install in us their erroneous ideas of what life is about, leading us away from the jewel of who we truly are. Parents so desperately want their children to have what they didn't have, or follow in their footsteps, or do what they think society will value, regardless of what that child is fascinated by.

I remember asking a Chinese doctor who attended one of my workshops, whether he liked his work and he told me, "Put it this way, in Chinese culture, art is *not* an option." In that moment I felt the pain of all those children, including myself, who were led like sheep and herded into square pens that did not accommodate the many facets of our unique and individual beings.

And, as these well-meaning guardians and educators try to push us into alien boxes, we naturally feel the pressure and we do one of two things. We either rebel, like me, and face the wrath of those who have power over us, or we conform and spend our lives miserably being who we are not, forcing ourselves every day to try and live up to impossible expectations.

The world today is in great chaos economically and politically. More and more people are being ousted from their boxes, feeling a sense of fear, not knowing what to do next as the social structures crumble.

But this is not a disaster; it's a wonderful opportunity for all of us to find our unique place in the world and be who we were destined to be. Every one of us has some gift that we can offer to help make the world a better place. These gifts are not something that we "get", as Julian reminds us, they are already inside us, and we are all capable of waking up to this fact along the journey of discovering our own confident self.

I trust that, as you embrace the ideas inside of *Confidence Explosion*, you will begin to feel that sense of personal power – that jewel that is truly you – and, as Julian puts it, "embrace the full bloom of your human experience". Like that, you will become the confident person you already were but just didn't know it. You will not only feel great but you will find it easy to shine your light on those people around you who have not yet learned to do what Joseph Campbell calls "following your bliss".

The ancient myth of *Indra's Net* sums up what this book is all about: the world is seen as a huge net connected at individual points by jewels. Each jewel represents a human being and each jewel is unique. When everyone discovers the jewel inside and reveals themselves, the world lights up and is indeed a perfect place. Go forth and shine your light, be who you are, and the world will welcome you with open arms.

Peta Heskell
The original *Flirt Coach*

> *If you only realised just how powerful you are – and carried this truth through all the moments of your life – you would never again feel empty, unworthy or afraid.*
>
> –JULIAN JAMES

CHAPTER ONE
Discovering Your Power

"The voyage of discovery is not in seeking new landscapes, but in having new eyes."

–Marcel Proust

There is *magic* inside of discovery.

It's really quite extraordinary how what we expect to generate as particular outcomes for ourselves can sometimes move us into totally fresh domains of experience, gravitating out of a source that not only we couldn't possibly have fathomed, but one that could not have been present without those things that went before them being present to begin with. It's the non-sequential and non-predictive adventure of moving in certain directions and, during the process, finding ourselves being seamlessly pulled and beckoned into *other* avenues and dimensions of experience – experiences that feel *just right* – because they resonate with us completely and intimately. And to arrive at these places sometimes requires the willingness to release the fixations we hold about what we *think* needs to be true in any given moment, in exchange for the reward of simply having the experience of the unfoldment of what's occurring, and being present to it without condition or expectation.

Stephen King's unforgettable film, *Stand By Me*, starring River Phoenix and Corey Feldman, is the perfect portrayal of a journey of discovery that had in store for four 12-year-old boys much more than they ever could have anticipated. This motion picture, a special and timeless narrative, truly encapsulates the essence of adventure and discovery through the course of great challenge, growth, comradeship and courage. It was a captivating voyage of edification and personal trial – at times pleasant and at other times terrifying – that led four inquisitive adolescents so far outside of the comfort and familiarity of their present standpoint that their emergence at the other side of their experience represented an extraordinary and momentous milestone in their lives.

These young men learnt many things, but exactly what they did learn wasn't everything they thought that they had to, or even needed to, but instead, what was perfect and necessary for them to experience in those moments that transpired.

When the boys arrived home, it wasn't possible for them to consider their lives in the same way that they had done before they set off on their journey. So much had taken place. So much had touched and moved them from the very centre of themselves. It was clear that there had been a re-evaluation of who they knew themselves to be. Their expedition had indelibly shaped the very manner in which they looked at the world around them. Their friendships had been strengthened and bonded to a degree that could only have been possible through the sharing of what happened along their adventure, yet there was also an unmistakable sense that it was time to let go – it was time for them to move on and say goodbye.

THE ESSENCE OF ADVENTURE!

I truly believe that considering our lives as an adventure that we are living, shaping and participating in from moment to moment allows us to perceive our experiences from a place of discovery and even wonder, instead of regarding what happens through the lens of fear, which, of course, produces a very different set of personal outcomes. Aligning with this magical nature of exploration allows us to notice the things we wouldn't otherwise notice, and experience the things we wouldn't otherwise experience – and this single distinction is capable of changing the entire scope and direction of our lives.

What's certain is that the freedom to do this will always remain a choice of our own making. Again, this choice often necessitates the *letting go* of the things we think we need to be desperately holding on to. It's only by sometimes releasing the death-grip we have on what we fear we need to be so tightly clinging onto that the doors of possibility open up before us. Doing so reveals to us "hidden treasures" that were before, in a way, invisible.

And so, in digesting the ideas that follow, I encourage you to place aside your current expectations about what you *think* this book is really about. Allow yourself to release any firmly held preconceptions in regard to what you're about to be presented with.

In order for new distinctions to internalise, it's important to embrace the willingness to momentarily place aside our current paradigms long enough to freshly assimilate and appreciate new information (even if that information challenges what we already know!) This is not to devalue or marginalise our own standpoints, but, instead, to become open to the awareness of the possibilities contained inside of what we haven't yet considered. Without the establishment of this frame of consideration, any new information has no choice but to be filtered through the reference point of our existing ideologies. This generates a very different outcome – an outcome which must be coloured by the perceptual filters already in place.

Therefore, give yourself permission to connect to the place within you that allows you to be present to what follows with a pair of fresh eyes, and with the openness for discovery. Lord Thomas Dewar phrased this rather nicely when he proclaimed that, “Minds are like parachutes; they work best when they're open!”

CULTIVATING POSSIBILITIES

Consider these questions: What is it that makes a person truly confident? Where does what we call “confidence” actually come from? Why is it that some people are totally confident in who they are, whilst others seem to have no self-confidence at all? How can we have more confidence? What is the secret to being totally confident and comfortable with ourselves, regardless of the situations and people that we encounter?

If you feel drawn and compelled to explore these questions in considering your *own* sense of personal confidence, there are things in store for you here, that I know you're going to find of tremendous and lasting value, and that will serve to enrich you in endless ways.

One of the fascinating truths about us human creatures is that we're all uniquely able to share the learnings from our lives and the journeys and adventures that we participate in. That's part of the magic of simply being alive – not only do we create and engage in a spectrum of experiences, but we all also have different experiences in relation to the *same* shared experience! That's why two people can watch exactly the same film, yet come away from the cinema with different ideas of what the film was about. And, regardless of our age or background or educational foundation, there will always be distinctive learnings that we can acquire from others, and there will always be our own unique insights that we can bring to the people around us as well, simply by virtue of being who we are. After all, we truly are extraordinary beings. And what we refer to as “learning” sometimes includes being reminded of the things that we already fundamentally know to be true. Often, in fact, essential learning is only really “re-learning” the things that we have simply forgotten or lost touch with.

For instance, if you want to remember what it's like to embrace the world with a sense of total wonderment, you need only to look into the eyes of a baby and observe how that young child is relating to and interacting with the world around him. You will be present to an expression of sheer radiance that is heartening and captivating in every way. Observe this fully and completely – allow the baby's energy to saturate and permeate you – and you'll experience the very sense of this effortless connection babies have to all things. It's a natural relatedness to the universe that we've all at some point lived from, yet a sense that many of us have lost sight of altogether. And this is perhaps one of the very "re-learnings" that, at the very depth of us, we need the most: to simply "re-see" the true wonder in the totality that we are – and in the universe of which we're an integral part – awakening to the exquisite uniqueness of our place in the world.

INTEGRAL CONNECTION

We are not, and never have been, separate and isolated entities. Even though there is so much that makes each and every one of us so very different from each other, there is a fundamental truth that binds us in unity – an unmistakable thread of primal union that weaves inside of all humans. There's no question that, regardless of the things that we decide to do in this lifetime, we are still all having the *same* experience – the *human experience.* And, in the most primordial sense, amidst the wide expanse of all of our many differences in character, belief and behaviour, we are not different at all – *we are in fact one and the same.* We all look different, we all speak differently, we all engage in different activities, yet, we are still all as one, because we're all expressions of the very same "oneness" that brought us into being.

But what do these ideas of "oneness" and "connection" have to do with self-confidence? What's the link between them? Why do these things matter at all? Here's why: because the more we return to the realisation of the connectedness between us all – when we awaken to the awareness that the same divine life force infuses each and every one of us – the more we begin to see that there's actually nothing to be afraid of!

When we live from this truth, all of the lies we have been told about how we *should* be operating in the world, and even how we should be *feeling* in relation to others – the insidious lies that rob so many of their intrinsic confidence and self-assurance – drop away. We discover that there is nothing that keeps us from the total and uninhibited expression of our essential power, other than our investment in the illusions which have been designed to suffocate and suppress us. And when we see these illusions for nothing other than what they are, they lose their hold over us.

From this way of being – connecting to the essential nature of our existence – we're able to view the world and the people that we encounter from an awakened perspective. It destroys the illusion of separation. It's like taking a sledgehammer and smashing to pieces the "House of Mirrors".

We suddenly become able to see with a clarity that wasn't previously possible. It changes and affects everything. It opens our hearts and minds to deep wonder. It draws forth the awareness of our inextricable connection to everything. It allows us to show up as we are, embracing and celebrating the totality of our uniqueness, and unapologetically standing in our own special place – *a place in which absolute inner confidence is natural and effortless.* And this is when true magic really begins! This is when what before caused us to respond with fear now appears only as information that we can do with as we wish. Being *this* way, we embody a personal power that is nothing less than extraordinary.

"Nobody holds a good opinion of a man who has a low opinion of himself."

–Anthony Trollope

Deep self-confidence is something we all desire. The ability for a person to be confident and fully at ease with himself is a capacity that's inspiring to others. It's the internal component that makes someone authentically strong. When it's fully flourishing, people sense it instantly. People also sense when it isn't present. It's the difference between a person that we instinctively trust, and one that we wouldn't dare place our trust in because it's clear that they don't trust or value themselves. After all, we can only see in others what they see in themselves. It's impossible for us to respect a man who has no respect in or for himself. A person such as this becomes a projection of his own perceived limitation. We see a lack of respect, so we respond with a lack of respect in kind. In essence, we have given to him exactly what he has projected from himself into the world. And this is why connecting to that aspect within us that is solid and grounded is the most crucial and powerful position we can hold, because it's the position from which everything else emanates.

> Confidence is not something that exists or can be attained from outside of you; it's something that you recognise and cultivate from within you.

Confidence, at its very essence, is *a way of being*. It's the quality of unshakable certainty and conviction a person exudes. It's about being present to the world, fully and completely, in such a way that feeling inwardly certain, centred and at ease is your most natural state. It's about radiating an autonomous and commanding resonance from within you, that is solid and unchanging and unable to be undermined by external factors, because the very source of this resonance is powerful beyond measure.

And, like this, everything flows so much more effortlessly. We are connected to our deepest truth. We feel an abiding sense of congruence and inner strength. We are immune to insult or criticism. We feel no hesitation in expressing our unique and individual essence. We feel no need to apologise for who we are. And we instinctively know when we're operating from this sense of authentic confidence because there's an aliveness inside that impels us to move with purpose and passion. People interact with and respond to us differently, and we experience much more of the respect that is our entitlement. It's almost as if what needs to be present for us finds us, instead of us having to go looking. This is because we're expressing so much more of who we authentically are, and these things cannot help but to unfold in this way. Our very energy makes it so.

What's true for most of us, however, is that this way of operating comes and goes in fleeting moments. It seems to show us at certain times, and then dissipates. It appears as though we have no direct control over when it'll again come to pass. Yet, there is a way we can connect to our interior power so that it is stable and permanent and unchanging, and this is at the heart of what *Confidence Explosion* is really about.

REAL CONFIDENCE FLOWS FROM THE WELLSPRING OF AUTHENTICITY

Your authentic self is *already* confident.

There is a tremendous distinction between "acting" confident, and actually "being" confident. "Acting" requires you to draw from elements that are outside of you. But "being" draws from your internal reservoir of truth. Genuine confidence is about accessing the way that you are when you're *naturally* powerful, so that no acting or pretending is ever necessary.

Despite the formulation of the letters in the word, there is no "con" in confidence. If you think being confident is about "conning" other people, or conning yourself, you're operating from a belief system that will never satisfy your desire to be authentically strong.

A person who is unable to connect to his true power in a real and authentic way attempts to force or fake this sense of confidence. We've all at some point witnessed this in others. Anyone who attempts this will never internally experience genuine personal command, because the pretence will always serve to block and inhibit any possibility of it being so. This is why real confidence cannot be faked. People try to do just this – to counterfeit that which cannot be counterfeited – and do so both for themselves, and out of the desire to *appear* this way before others in order to satisfy the need to feel significant and be accepted.

Sadly, regardless of whether or not such a "display" convinces others, it will never change the way that person feels on the inside, where it really counts. A person cannot successfully "trick" or "fool" himself into feeling confident, because within the effort of doing so is the awareness of the sense of unworthiness they were trying to shroud and conceal. And even though others might not know this, *they'll* always know, which is why such an undertaking can never be sustainable and deeply satisfying. It is an endeavour that is fundamentally flawed. What's more, what will also be present for this person is the fear that someday someone will find out what they've *really* been up to.

Such an approach is like having a brass ornament gold plated and trying to convince yourself that it's pure solid gold. Your attempt to deceive yourself and others will be present in all that you do. Living from the energy of pretence affects everything. It will be present in the subtle inflections of the words that you speak, and through the way that you carry your body as you move. The truth will reveal itself in some way. It can't not. Our primal energetic projection doesn't lie. Your attempt at this deception will betray you, sooner or later. Sigmund Freud communicated this idea when he said that, "We leak the truth from every pore." We feel what is genuine and true in the very bones and blood of us. It's a visceral, ineffable "knowing" that speaks to us intuitively, and, of course, to others as well.

In the act of pretending, you are actually hindering your ability to have the real experience. For as long as the pretence is being exerted, your true strength has no real way to emerge, because it's being blocked by your struggle to keep up the disguise. What's more, pretending to appear confident requires a tremendous amount of energy and effort in order to sustain it. To try doing this consistently would be utterly exhausting. Yet, when your authentic confidence is allowed to flow from within you, no effort is required at all. What's more, it feels wonderful.

Ultimately then, trying to "appear" to have confidence is not enough. It is simply not a sufficient means to achieving genuine internal stability. After all, who really wants to move through the world pretending? Wouldn't you rather have the *real thing?* How can a person truly sustain any genuine level of grounded inner strength based on the foundation of pretence? Do you see how this approach is fundamentally flawed? Wouldn't you rather learn to generate *real* confidence? Wouldn't you rather feel the emanating force formed from a sense of personal command that is so strong, and so resolute, that no other person could do anything to undermine you?

If you feel drawn towards this idea, you're in the right place.

CONNECTION TO AUTHENTIC POWER

Many people make the mistake of believing *true* confidence to be something totally different from what it actually is. True confidence is not boastful, ostentatious or conceited. True confidence is not the manifestation of outward displays of behaviour designed to generate attention from others. True confidence is not overbearing or pretentious. Rather, it is an eternal inner quietude that is incredibly powerful, yet still. It's a pervasive energy that is solid and unchanging.

How much more confident would you feel inside knowing that you didn't have to posture or pretend to be powerful because you knew that, at your centre – at the deepest part of you – you were that way already?

"Who looks outside, dreams; who looks inside, awakens."

–Carl Jung

This is specifically what I mean when I refer to the idea of *authenticity*: to be so completely and absolutely connected to the source of your intrinsic power that no one else could possibly stand in the way of you being this way. Then, in *this* way, there would be no reason for you to search for methods to veil yourself with pretence. You would already be what others are constantly trying to parrot or imitate. And part of the work that I carry out with my personal clients, towards engendering and sustaining an energy of powerful fearless command, embraces this very standpoint – the realisation of our *given* confidence – the expression of the potency we *already* contain and to which we're *already* endlessly connected.

This book is about getting back in touch with that feeling of worthiness you were born with. It's about bringing you home to the acknowledgement that confidence isn't something you need to "get", because the idea of "getting confidence" is a concept that is predicated on the idea that your value and worthiness exist somewhere *outside* of you. It presumes that you are not already connected to what makes you strong. If you expend your energy "looking for confidence", your striving reinforces the notion that you don't already possess it!

And so, as you'll discover, having real confidence is the result of aligning with a source of strength that is not changing, but *changeless*. When you connect with it – when you embrace your inextricable truth – a warm, pleasurable glow will resonate from inside. It will bring you into harmony with yourself, without needing anything at all from outside of you.

Are you ready to look upon your place in the world with "new eyes"; to harness the power that is already yours and to experience the very nature of your being from a totally refreshed horizon?

T. S. Eliot wrote the poignant words: "We shall not cease from exploration. And the end of all our exploring will be to arrive where we started and know the place for the first time." These words really encapsulate a familiar and pervasive story; a narrative that inevitably unfolds in much the same way for us all. It's the story of looking outside of ourselves for the answers and the resolutions that we strive to attain, and eventually coming to realise that – in spite of all of our frantic searching and striving and struggling – what we've been looking for, and yearning for, has been present within us the entire time. And when we arrive at this deep appreciation of our truest nature – the deepest essence of who we are – we instinctively know this to be the very core of our fundamental strength.

There is *magic* inside of discovery.

"*You shape the world around you by shaping the world within you.*"

–Julian James

CHAPTER TWO
What Confidence Really Is

"Faith is the bird that feels the light and sings when the dawn is still dark."

—RABINDRANATH TAGORE

The word *confidence*, according to its literal translation, means "with faith". The term has its roots in Latin: *con* meaning "with" and *fidence* meaning "faith". Therefore, within this specific meaning, to be confident is to be and act "with faith". And to have faith is to have great certainty. So *self-confidence* is about being and operating in the world with conviction and certainty in oneself.

My own definition of confidence is somewhat more expansive than this. It includes the awareness of our connection to the larger system that contains us. It's pertains to the certainty of knowing that we are fundamentally whole and complete and not lacking in any way. It's about knowing – at the deepest level – that the totality of who we are is a gift, and that we have an unconditional birth-given right to *be* in the world. It's also about the capacity to fearlessly express our uniqueness (Later in this chapter, I expand on my definition of confidence.)

I want you to realise that the kind of solid and unconditional confidence I'm speaking of is ontologically based – it relates to the nature of our *being*. It is not about the behaviours that we enact; rather, it's about the essential ground from which these behaviours emerge. That's why, within my work, I make the distinction between *two* types of confidence: *behavioural confidence* and *integral confidence*.

BEHAVIOURAL CONFIDENCE

The term *behavioural confidence* refers to what we have certainty about *doing*. It relates to our specific skills, behaviours and capabilities, and not necessarily to who we fundamentally are, or the relationship we have to ourselves. As I make distinct throughout this book, we are *not* our behaviours, because we are infinitely more than what we *do*. Whilst it's true that our behaviours can serve as a reflection and an indication of who we are and what we stand for in the world, they are not, in and of themselves, the constituents of our being. Our *being* – our primal and essential nature – is far deeper. It is far more integral. It is changeless. Our being transcends the behaviours that we enact because who we are, at the most essential level, is far greater than our behaviours can ever be.

So, *behavioural confidence* is about the sense of certainty we have about the specific skills we know we're able to carry out well, whatever those skills happen to be. A concert pianist, for example, with twenty years of experience, is able to play his instrument and create music with virtuosity and effortlessness. He can place his hands upon the ebony and ivory keys and produce beautiful mellifluous music; music that touches the hearts and minds of his audience. And this is the nature of *behavioural confidence*: the ability to effectively (even expertly) carry out particular behaviours, tasks or skills, without doubt or hesitation.

But *behavioural confidence*, in any specific area of activity, does not automatically bring with it the promise of *integral confidence*. We know this to be true because we all know people who are exceptionally good at *doing* certain things – chefs, mechanics, dentists, swimmers, doctors, teachers – but who still don't possess that essential core confidence in who they *are*. They still don't live from the total embracement of their uniqueness in the world. They don't operate from their power. They are tremendously talented in their respective fields, but they still don't emanate that distinct aura which bespeaks the resolute and unwavering recognition of unconditional self-worth.

For example, that very same concert pianist that I mentioned, despite his extraordinary talent and dazzling ability, may have trouble making eye contact with others and communicating with certainty and conviction. He may be timid and fearful. He may shy away when people come over to congratulate him on his impeccable performances because his *integral confidence* is not fully actualised. Although he may have developed mastery in playing his instrument of choice, he does not have mastery in his capacity to operate with stable self-assurance. Put another way: he is confident in his musical ability, but he does not have confidence in who he fundamentally *is*. And this distinction is one that is crucial.

In the same way, a woman might feel confident that she can cook the perfect lasagne for her husband – and have every detail of the dish turn out exquisitely – but this doesn't mean that she is necessarily *self-confident*, in a way that is solid and grounded. Another person might feel confident about being able to organise and complete his company accounts successfully, but this doesn't necessarily mean that he feels truly secure within himself. Another person might feel confident that he can bench press five repetitions of 130kg, down at the gym. But the fact of this ability doesn't automatically indicate a deep *integral confidence*. In fact, I have met and interacted with many bodybuilders – gigantic men, rippling with staggering layers of muscle and astonishing physical strength – who are, behind the ostentation of their physique, deeply insecure. And what's interesting is that the reason a lot of people begin bodybuilding in the first place is in an attempt to resolve and reconcile the emptiness they feel internally, thinking that if they get "big" on the outside, they'll somehow get "big" on the inside as well. This is a detrimental and very unsustainable approach to garnering a sense of worth and security, because it's based on the belief that our exterior form holds the key to our self-confidence. But what's on the "outside" is always subject to change. There are no exceptions to this. As we age, our physical form has no choice but to alter. And this is why many bodybuilders feel much less confident if they take time away from the gym, because they feel as though they're "shrinking". For them, losing muscle mass is tantamount to losing their personal significance. So, in order to maintain their sense of worth, their training becomes obsessive, driven by the fear of losing what they've worked so hard to achieve. It's a losing battle!

So, skills and abilities just are what they are. They in no way point towards anything more than that. It's also important to realise that developing *behavioural confidence* in any area of endeavour is actually remarkably simple, given that you are prepared to invest the time necessary to develop the skill you wish to gain confidence and mastery in. I'm not saying that it's *easy*; I'm saying that it's *simple*. The *process* never changes; and there is no secret to the process at all.

The process is this: if it's your desire to become so capable and efficient at doing something that you feel totally confident in the enactment of that particular activity, then simply spend large amounts of time doing that thing. Apply your focus and attention to learning everything you can about that skill. Completely immerse yourself in everything related to it. Enliven your hunger to learn. Find good teachers and mentors who will guide you along your journey as well. Constantly read books and literature on the subject. Learn and study from those that already possess the level of expertise you want to achieve for yourself. Spend every day working, studying, practising, researching and developing. Repetition is the mother of skill; so repeat, repeat and repeat! Do these things and your proficiency in the area of your choosing will have no choice but to strengthen and grow – and, if you allow nothing to stand in the way of your steady and incremental development, you will achieve mastery.

Eventually, all of the many elements that comprise the skill will integrate into your muscle memory, and become so deeply and habitually ingrained that they become totally effortless for you. All of the cognitive processes that the skill necessitates will form brand new neural pathways in your brain; neural connections which will become stronger and stronger through time, requiring less and less conscious attention. And with this mastery comes confidence –*behavioural confidence*. It doesn't matter whether what you want to become confident at is public speaking, clay pigeon shooting, vascular surgery, mountain climbing or motorbike racing – the same foundational rules of attention, repetition, precision focus and continued study apply. You cannot invest thousands and thousands of hours learning a skill and not become more confident as a result. When you're willing to invest the time, energy and attention, the confidence is guaranteed.

So, an individual's *behavioural confidence* will always be strongest in the areas on which he focuses the majority of his time, energy and attention upon. The only reason that a person feels confident about doing corporate accountancy work, for example, and not confident about cooking a six course Chinese meal, is because he's spent 15 years of his life engaged in corporate accounting work and no time in the cooking and preparation of Chinese food. And, of course, it stands to reason that if he had invested that same 15 years learning to cook Chinese food (instead of accounting) we know that he'd be an exceptional Chinese cook, capable of producing irresistible and delicious oriental dishes!

There's no mystery to what needs to be done to have confidence in doing things. If you want a broader chest, commit yourself to 50 press-ups each and every day, and you'll soon have a broader chest. Simple! You'll also be very confident about doing press-ups! If you want to be confident speaking about the intricacies of English literature, then immerse yourself in the works of great writers – enter the literary domain of William Shakespeare and James Joyce and Charles Dickens and D.H. Lawrence and John Keats and Oscar Wilde and every other writer's work you feel drawn to – and study their writings for three hours a day, every single day. Do this, and, without question, you will be exceptionally confident in the sphere of English literature. If you want to be a confident poker player, then play poker every day for ten years – I guarantee you'll have tremendous confidence in the game! You see, there's really no secret! It's an easy formula to follow, and it applies to all things. It's simply a question of where you decide to focus your energy and attention.

This distinction is so evident and commonsensical it almost doesn't bear mentioning. Yet, many people still often confuse the notion of *behavioural confidence* (that which is about behaviours and capabilities) with *integral confidence*. Simply put – they are *not* the same.

Further, the reason I'm clarifying these differences so precisely is because it's important for you to know what this book is about, and what it is not about. This book is not about *doing*; it isn't about how to acquire and master new skills. Instead, this book is fundamentally about the nature of your *being*. It is about the relationship you have to yourself, and to the world that contains you. It's about what's required for you to have unshakable faith in who you are, and to be able to operate in the world from the foundation of this pervasive awareness. And *this* is the inner confidence – the abiding sense of integral power – that I refer to as *integral confidence.*

INTEGRAL CONFIDENCE

Integral confidence is unconditional inner certainty. *Integral confidence* is about feeling secure, solid and settled within yourself – and feeling a significant sense of worth – *regardless* of what's going on around you, and regardless of what you happen to be able to do, or not be able to do. It is the most authentic form of confidence. In fact, it's the only *true* confidence there is.

This kind of unwavering self-assurance draws from the deepest place within you. It relies on nothing other than the sustained awareness of who you are at your core, in the most vital and essential way. It is not dependent upon anything outside of you in order for you to feel secure. It operates at an entirely different level. It isn't reliant upon the things you can do well, or the personal "achievements" you have accumulated. It has nothing to do with how many promotions you've been given in the past four years, or how many condominiums you own. It's a quality of consciousness, and a way of *being*, that goes beyond all of these things. It's the knowing that you are *already* an extraordinary and divine individual, without you having or needing to do anything. It's the fundamental knowing that there's nothing missing inside of you, and that there's *nothing* you "need" for you to be complete.

This, of course, does not mean that you shouldn't attain *behavioural confidence* through developing the various skills and competencies of your choosing – you most definitely should! (A healthy balance is achieved by having both *integral confidence* and *behavioural confidence* in place; not just one or the other.) It doesn't mean that you shouldn't embrace your passions. It doesn't mean that you shouldn't work tenaciously towards attaining your own personal vision. It doesn't mean that you should stop taking positive action. It simply means that feeling the sense of deep interior assurance I'm speaking of isn't dependent upon these things, because *integral confidence* remains present and unshakable, regardless of these factors. It means that feeling whole and complete – and of great worth – is a result of that which is unchanging.

WHO WE ARE ALWAYS COMES BEFORE WHAT WE DO

Integral confidence isn't about what you *do*; it's about who you *are*. It's far and above any of your behaviours. It's far and above the possessions that you own. It's about the gift of your being.

It stands to reason that you can't *always* be confident about what you're *doing*, purely because there will always be particular things that you don't know how to do. So if your sense of confidence derives *only* from the level of your capabilities, as soon as you're faced with something you're unable to do well – and you believe that your feelings of security are dependent upon this – your confidence plummets. But if you operate in the world in such a way that your true worth and certainty as an individual is independent of what you can or cannot do in any given moment, independent of what you have or do not have, and independent of all other factors that exist outside of you, you are then able to enter into any situation and *still* feel inwardly secure. This is because the aspect of you that is changeless operates as your guiding interior strength – and *this* is what *integral confidence* really is.

Remember: what you do isn't who you are; who you are is infinitely much more than the actions that you engage in. And while it's definitely true that you cannot help but bring your own uniqueness to the things you do – in the sense that your distinctive human expression becomes discernable through your activities – the things you do are *still* not who you are. The activities themselves serve as a medium through which you express your individual nature. So you might not be certain about doing particular things, but when you have certainty in the truth of you, it allows you to take on whatever you desire – even those things that are totally unfamiliar. It allows you to face up to new challenges with sureness and ease, knowing that you have the potential to master anything you choose to undertake. It allows you to bring your *integral confidence* – the source of your true inner strength – into whatever it is that you're doing. Like this, even though you don't yet know how to do something, you function with such certainty that the way you approach learning new skills and behaviours becomes so much more effortless, and so much more pleasurable, because you're bringing the potency of your authentic nature into your very actions!

When you *do* extraordinary things – when you accomplish goals, develop high expertise, break through personal challenges and limitations and you feel that pleasurable surge of feelings throughout your body – you are essentially reminding yourself of your inherent power. You are reminding yourself of the dynamic potential that you already possess. You are reminding yourself that you are worthy and capable and gifted. You are reminding yourself of your own interior truth. But when you arrive at the level of awareness in which you know that *this power never leaves you* – regardless of what you do or do not do – you begin to realise that you don't actually have to "do" anything in order to feel this way. You can just settle into yourself (wherever you happen to be) and feel that potency resonating within the depth of you, knowing it to be your truth.

Integral confidence, then, is the awareness we experience when we connect with our unconditional sense of power. It's knowing that we already contain unique and astounding potential. It's knowing that there is nothing missing inside of us. It's the internal realisation that we are enough – just as we are. And when we fully embody and express this, we feel what it's like to be the way we were designed to be.

> The only way we can experience true inner power is to connect to what is changeless.

Genuine confidence is *unconditional*, not conditional. It is unconditional because it does not rely upon anything external in order for a sense of security to be present. If our confidence is dependent on factors that remain outside of us, it will never remain stable, because those extrinsic factors we believe must be there for us to feel secure can never remain permanent – they are always subject to change. The things around us are always in a perpetual state of fluctuation; ever evolving and ever changing.

There is no doubt or question that we live in a world of perpetual change. This, of course, is not unusual. It's never unusual. In fact, the idea that things never stay the same is one of the few "guarantees" we can count on. It's not possible for change in our environment *not* to happen. It's an inevitability of the world. There is change taking place all around us, and change doesn't stop for anyone. Heraclitus, the Greek philosopher, summed this up rather nicely with his often cited statement, "The only constant is change."

Our living conditions are subject to change and uncertainty in countless, immeasurable ways. Very often, the things that "appear" to be secure turn out not to be secure at all. Finances are always subject to change. Nothing in the domain of monetary standing is ever *totally* secure. Millionaires become bankrupt virtually overnight – it happens more than you think. Sometimes even banks (those places that make us believe that our money is "secure") can't even keep up! Tax regulations change. Interest rates change. Governmental rules change. International laws change. People that we love unexpectedly die. Friends come into our lives, and friends vanish from our lives. People that we trust let us down. Fires destroy buildings. We make plans, only to discover that something totally unanticipated stops us from fulfilling the plans we've made. Property changes hands. People move to different countries. Important packages don't show up in the mail on time. Managers lose crucial information. People unexpectedly get fired from their job. Computers crash, cars break down and flights are delayed! In New York City, one September afternoon, the Twin Towers were once there – then they were gone. These are all examples of the unpredictable, ever-changing state of the world. Most everything around us is subject to change at any moment. We have no idea what's going to happen next, and there's simply no way that we can predict or control it all!

In 1963, Harry Weinburg, an American professor, was delivering a class to his students about the nature of fallacies, and the tendencies of humans to make assumptions about what they believe to be true. Weinburg was speaking about the idea of "certainty" and drawing attention to the fact that the things we think are certain actually contain much less certainty than we think they do.

As an example, he asked his students who the president of the United States was. Needless to mention, all of the students pointed out that John F. Kennedy was the President. They also pointed out the ridiculousness of the question. After all, who else could it have been? Of course it was Kennedy! Wasn't it perfectly obvious who was holding office at that time? What was this professor trying to prove?

Weinburg then invited the class to consider the fallacy in the statement, "John F. Kennedy is President of the United States", because no one had actually checked before entering the classroom that Kennedy was still in power. But many of the students still doubted Weinburg's concept. The lesson shortly ended and the students left.

After leaving that classroom, what everyone in that room, on that particular November day, soon discovered was this: during the time of that very class, John F. Kennedy had been shot and killed, and Lyndon B. Johnson had taken the oath as President of the United States! Kennedy had literally been put to death during the very hour of that class. The date was November 22nd, 1963 – a day America will never forget. It was taken entirely for granted that Kennedy was still president. His assassination was an entirely unexpected and shocking happening. Yet, it was an instantaneous change that became the prevalent talk of the world! And such is the nature of things – things are endlessly changing!

So what does this mean for us? How does the fact that things are either always changing, or subject to change, play into how we need to operate in order to have real certainty in who we are?

Think, again, about the term "self-confidence". What it *really* means is actually contained inside of it – in the very words themselves. Yet, people miss this entirely. People miss the obviousness of it. But the true meaning is right there. It's as clear as day. It's as apparent as it can possibly be! The word has two parts: "self" and "confidence". "Self-confidence" is therefore *confidence* that comes from the *self*. In other words, it's a sense of certainty that is cultivated from inside of *you* – not from outside of you! After all, if it were about feeling confident due to the things that you owned, it would be called "possession-confidence". If it were about feeling confident due to other people's opinions about you, it would be called "opinion-confidence". And if it were about feeling confident as a result of your physical appearance, it would be called "appearance-confidence". But it isn't. So, clearly, "you" are the significant factor.

Let's consider an example: if a man's primary source of confidence is derived from his involvement with his career – if he believes that his job is the only real support for his self-worth – what happens when he suddenly discovers that he's just been laid off? Instantaneously, his sense of personal security languishes and collapses. The very factor that facilitated his feelings of confidence disappears in a single moment. It's like someone sawing off all four legs of a dining table – there is no longer any way for the table to still be able to remain standing. This is because a "job" is a factor that is subject to change, regardless of how "secure" it *appears* to be.

If a man's source of confidence comes from his ability to "prove himself" to others, as soon as other people are no longer impressed with or interested in what he does, his self-confidence diminishes as a result, and he has no control over when or how this might happen.

If a woman allows her source of confidence to derive exclusively from her physical appearance: her body, her hair and the condition of her skin (which is undoubtedly the case for many young and highly attractive females) – and from the compliments and the adoration she receives from others about her youthful beauty – she sets herself up for an inevitable crash of her perceived sense of value and worthiness. Physical beauty is another factor which is always subject to change. There is no escape from this. The potent and alluring attractiveness of youth does not last – for anyone! So as this woman begins to age through time, and as her skin begins to wrinkle – and when the compliments she was so used to receiving become less and less frequent – she is no longer able to accumulate enough exterior validation from the people around her to sustain the same level of self-assurance she once had.

Consider another example: if a woman enters into a relationship with a man, and allows that man to be the reservoir of her self-confidence, as soon as the relationship comes to an end, so too does the illusion of security she once felt. Once again, an intimate relationship is a factor that is subject to change. This doesn't mean that it can't be special, and it doesn't mean that it can't be deeply meaningful. To be in a relationship and to experience true connection with another person can be totally joyous and wondrous. It's one of the most powerful experiences: to share a deep connection and intimacy with another human. But, in spite of this, the status of any relationship is *still* always subject to change, even when it appears to be permanent. And we know this to be true, because almost all of us have been in relationships which at the time we believed, so indisputably, would last *forever* – and they didn't!

What's more, an important aspect of being in a contented and healthy relationship is the ability to remain true and connected to your *own* independent power, whilst also being able to share and enjoy the interdependence that such a unity entails. But when the idea of the relationship itself becomes the principal support structure that holds your feelings of security in place, as soon as it goes away, so too does your sense of confidence.

Obviously, this is a strategy for sustained confidence that is incongruous and unsound. Yet, there are countless people who live their lives this way. There are so many people that eagerly cling on to the factors that are subject to change and allow those to function as the principal determinants of how they feel about themselves. And, of course, it's clear and observable that solid and authentic confidence is not cultivated this way. It simply can't be!

> True self-confidence is the ability to move along the ever-changing journey of your life – through a wide and expansive range of experiences – and to hold the very foundation of who you are solid and intact, regardless of the changes that take place around you.

OUR CHANGELESS POWER

Existing inside of a world abounding with perpetual change, the only way we can genuinely feel a sense of authentic self-assurance is to connect with the essence of us that never changes – our vital inner strength. The only way to be fearless is to realise that true security is cultivated from inside of us, and from our connection to the power that brought us into being.

In all of my work – and within all of the ways that I consider what it means to live and breathe with conviction, certainty and inner strength – this idea of staying connected to the changeless aspect of who we are rests at the heart of the message I convey. It really underpins and encompasses everything that I speak about. *This* is how I see the spirit of confidence to truly be: solid, unshakable and changeless – because the deepest aspect of us *is* nothing less than solid, unshakable and changeless.

So now that I have expanded upon my specific definition of what confidence really is, there is one last consideration to address before moving forward. And that is to touch briefly upon the notion of "self-esteem".

WHAT ABOUT SELF-ESTEEM?

People often ask me about "self-esteem", and whether there is a difference between self-esteem and self-confidence, and in what way they are related. Obviously, this is largely a semantic consideration. More so, it's not often that I use the term "self-esteem" at all. This is because I believe that the term "self-confidence" is far more expansive and, in fact, subsumes the meaning of "self-esteem".

In terms of specifically defining what "self-esteem" is – since the verb "esteem" means "to value" or "to hold in high regard" – self-esteem literally refers to your capacity to value yourself (the capability for *you* to "esteem" *you*). It means to hold yourself in high regard; to honour and love the person that you are. "Self-esteem", as a description, is very often used in close association with the notion of "self-confidence"; in fact, these two terms are regularly used interchangeably.

So, since, by definition, "self-esteem" is about holding yourself in high regard (operating from self-love and self-acceptance) and since you know that the term "confidence" is about having "certainty" and "faith" in yourself – your certainty in the power, possibility and potential present within you – it stands to reason that it would not be possible for you to have true sustaining faith and certainty in you without also holding yourself in high regard and expressing compassionate love for who you are as well. In order to truly value who you are as a unique individual in the world, requires the *certainty* in yourself to be able to do that. A self faith that is wholesome and complete *includes* the capacity to esteem yourself, to love yourself, to fully accept yourself. That's why, when you have genuine faith in the very spirit of your existence, you automatically have love and deep appreciation for the essence of you, because part of this faith comprises the capacity to love and accept yourself unconditionally.

So the notion of confidence, in the way that I define and express it, naturally includes the capacity to *both* "esteem" ourselves *and* to function from an awareness of deep faith and certainty. They are interconnected. It's a description that speaks to the acknowledgement and understanding of the strength within us that carries us forward. It's a way of referring to how we are when we feel the fullness and power of our very presence; the essential potency of our place in the universe. And this is why I favour the term "confidence" – it's a far more encompassing description of what it means to show up to life with a sustaining sense of inner power, and the understanding of our completeness.

So remember that whenever I use the term "confidence" (or "self-confidence"), I'm using it in such a way that the quality of self-love (self-esteem), is a capacity that is assumed and inherent in the definition itself. Put simply, it is a full and extensive description.

FOUNDATIONAL INNER SECURITY

Ultimately, in the most fundamental way, having real confidence is about coming home to your own truth. It's the interior assurance you have when you realise that you need *nothing* in order to feel whole and worthy and complete. It's about having an unyielding sense of belonging to the universe that contains you, and of which you are an integral part. It's the abiding awareness of your unconditional divinity; your eternal preciousness. It's the knowing that all that makes you strong – and all that you need to feel grounded and secure – is *already* within you, and has been ever since the moment of your creation. It's the absolute embracement of that vital force that's inextricably woven into the foundation of your very essence.

This is the core of it all. *This* is true security. *This* is true confidence.

"*To stand boldly in the world – fully embracing every aspect of who you are, without excuse and without apology – is the greatest expression of power you can generate, and one that enriches your life in ways that are astounding.*"

–Julian James

CHAPTER THREE
Confidence: Your Natural State!

"It's not who you are that holds you back, it's who you think you're not."

–Author Unknown

We have all had that sense – that inner awareness – which resounds as an echo of something much deeper, something much more expansive. It's the pervasive knowing that, at the very centre of who we are, there's a force that is incredibly potent, powerful and divine. And we realise, ultimately, that we are inseparable from this. And in the midst of this wakefulness, we come to know the truth of ourselves.

What would happen if you began to consider the entire notion of what it means for you to be far more confident – powerfully confident – from a totally new perspective? What would happen if you de-programmed yourself from all of the layers of conditioning – all of the lies and the distortions which have been imposed upon you – that have served to keep you from being fearless in the world? What would happen if you stopped believing what *wasn't* true about you? What then?

It's typical for most people to ask themselves the question, "How can I *get* more confidence?" And although this isn't necessarily a bad question to pose, it overlooks an integral distinction that is crucial and fundamental to us all. This is because the question leads us outside of ourselves, instead of *inside* ourselves. It misses the inherent significance that we *already* contain, and, in its place, sends us on a search to find something that we've been led to believe we don't already embody as our deepest truth.

Rarely are we told that we are already so much more than we believe we are. Rarely are we told that we are truly extraordinary creatures. Rarely are we told of the incredible potential that is present inside of us. Unfortunately, it's far more common to look around and receive messages from our environment that tell us that we are incomplete, undeserving and in need of "fixing" in one way or another. That's why true personal confidence is cultivated out of the decision to not accept what doesn't strengthen us; to reject anything that stands in the way of us living from a firm ground of resourcefulness, solidity and composure. And once we realise that we possess the power to control what information to take in, and what information to disregard, our perceptual filters become alert and attuned to see and allow only that which fortifies us. This, by itself, is exceptionally powerful.

And so, I want you to embrace a *new* question. I want you to begin from a standpoint that shifts your awareness towards what is already true of you. So, right now, ask yourself: *What do I have to let go of so that I am present to much more of the confidence I already contain?*

Notice that this question isn't focused on what you need to acquire from outside of you; it speaks, instead, to what you need to eliminate, clear away and move beyond, so that what's inherent *within* you can become the dominant positive force of your very being in the world. This question, when you explore it to the extent that it exposes what's really going on, will ultimately remind you that any ideas you hold about yourself that are limiting and disempowering have been imposed upon you. They are nothing more than external ideas you have inherited, through osmosis and by the messages and influences which bombard your awareness – and almost all of them without your consent! These messages are not there for your best interests. They are ultimately put in place to control you. But realise that they are not real – they are not accurate descriptions of who you are – because you are greater and far beyond these ideas could ever be.

RETURNING TO YOUR NATURAL STATE

"To be whole. To be complete. Wildness reminds us what it means to be human, what we are connected to rather than what we are separate from."

–Terry Tempest Williams

One weekday afternoon I was relaxing back in a comfortable chair at the downstairs seating area of the large *Starbucks* on London's Tottenham Court Road. I've always enjoyed the environment of these coffee shops. There's just something about that distinctive aroma of fresh coffee which is pleasing to the senses. There's also something very appealing about spending time in these types of environments, where lots of individuals come and go, and meetings and interactions are taking place between people from all walks of life. It allows you to soak in the eclectic flavour of cosmopolitan London.

I had just completed a session with one of my personal mentoring clients, and I decided to enjoy another fresh apple juice before getting up to leave. It was rather busy at the shop on this particular day. I noticed a mother with her young daughter. They came into the sitting area and sat down by a table near the bottom of the stairs. I couldn't help but to have my attention instantly drawn towards them. This lady's daughter was no more than two years old and was perhaps one of the most adorable young girls I'd ever seen. She glowed with a warmth and energy that was delightful in every way. Her mother was observably gleaming with pride for her young daughter. It was clear why.

This adorable child had been elegantly adorned in a charming yellow outfit with a tiny matching yellow hat, and, of course, matching yellow shoes! And, this little girl didn't just have my attention; she had very quickly begun to capture the attention of most of the other people that were there as well! In fact, she had created an audience for herself – an audience of adoring fans! The people seated nearby – and even from afar – couldn't help but to be drawn in by her natural exuberance; her primal energy. Just by being who she was, in the most authentic way, she exuded a special magic that was captivating.

Whenever a new customer came into the seating area, she immediately ran right up to them, looked them in the eyes with a smile that would soften even the most hardened of people, and greeted them with an impassioned and heartfelt "hello!" And she repeated this delighted introduction again and again, running over to offer her personal greeting to the next person and then to the next and the next. Every time she met someone new, it was just as charming as cheerful as the previous – each customer getting their very own personal welcome. It was a joy to watch as she made her way around the coffee shop, meeting as many fresh faces as she could. And all the while, her mother watched in obvious adoration of her special child. This young starlet didn't miss anyone out. For her, it was so natural to do this. It was clearly coming from the place within her that was genuine and affectionate and from the desire to make a connection with others. She would even occasionally approach a person she'd already greeted, and greet them a second time, with just as much delightfulness and lovability as the first!

I couldn't help but to be totally enchanted by this child. She reminded me, once again, of what it's like to truly be in the world in the way we were brought into the world to be. We didn't arrive here to shrink and withdraw into ourselves. We didn't arrive here to be timid or anxious or ashamed. We didn't arrive here to hide ourselves away from others. We didn't arrive here to neglect the boundless possibilities that are open to us in abundance. We were brought here to celebrate the gift of who we are and to *be* who we are in the fullest possible way.

Self-confidence, like any muscle in your body, is something you can build upon and strengthen, given the correct approach. But at a far more essential level, confidence isn't something you really have to "get", in the sense that most people think about it – it is a *way of being* that you have to *reconnect* with, and then keep stable and pervasive as the essential way that you move through the world. That's why, in those moments when you feel truly confident and unstoppable, there is an aliveness about you which is unmistakable, even formidable. And it's because, when you're like this, you connect with who you are at your core. When you're like this, you remind yourself of who you really are: a powerful, unique and wondrous human being.

FUNDAMENTAL CONFIDENCE

"I was always looking outside myself for strength and confidence, but it comes from within. It is there all the time."

–ANNA FREUD

Being who you are is about returning to your *natural state* – your vital essence – and ignoring those elements in your environment that try to pull you away from this. We've all known what it's like to live with a natural relatedness with the world, because we've all been babies. And when we were infants, we were absolutely like this. We accepted ourselves unconditionally. We totally embodied the flow of our inherent and distinctive energy. We had no choice other than to just be ourselves – in this way – because, at that time, we hadn't yet learnt the necessary skills to pretend to be any other way. (The posturing and pretence of inauthenticity is something that's learnt later on, as we're erroneously taught that we need to be like *others.*) So there was no other option for us – we just had to be who we were. And, because of this, our pure confidence exuded from within us.

Have you ever noticed that unmistakable sparkle in a baby's eyes? Babies are so much more willing to explore their environment and the people around them – to do more, to see more, to enjoy more. The reason that infants seem so effortless in this way is because they haven't yet learned that it's "not okay" to be like this, which is the message that comes out of the conditioning we're subjected to from our environment. Babies haven't yet been present to all of the acculturation within our consumer-driven culture that contains messages which serve to inhibit and constrain us. Babies notice the totality of the possibilities that are open to them, whilst adults have learned through time – from the constant exposure to these messages of limitation – to cut themselves off from this awareness. Babies don't feel the social and interpersonal restrictions that most adults feel. That's because these restrictions are nothing more than *beliefs* that have been forced upon us with regard to how to operate. In short, they have been inculcated into us through years and years of venomous conditioning. Most people blindly accept these ideas without a single thought for themselves about where they're coming from, and why. But *you* don't have to accept them. The power will always be yours to make that choice; and it's a choice that changes everything!

When you were a baby, the adults around you were totally intrigued by you. They were absolutely enamoured with your energy. You compelled them with your essential and charismatic spirit! They looked into your eyes and felt that intuitive impulse that just made them smile. And, in those moments, you reminded them of what they were missing in themselves – that effortless way of being, which is *naturally* attractive, *naturally* confident and *naturally* vibrant.

When we were babies, we didn't worry about whether or not we had enough confidence. We didn't feel embarrassed or ashamed about how we appeared to other people – we were too busy enjoying ourselves! We embodied the joyful expression of being alive. We didn't worry about feeling accepted; that idea didn't even enter into our minds. We lived our lives unselfconsciously and with a joyfulness and carefreeness that drew others to us. We didn't feel nervous or anxious about interacting with other people. We didn't feel the need to funnel down half a bottle of red wine before we felt comfortable meeting someone new. We didn't need the approval of others in order for us to feel good. In fact, people wanted to be around *us* because the way we were made *them* feel good. We just flourished with a flow of vital energy that was fresh and bright and alive, and was compelling and irresistible. People wanted to be near us so that they could soak up this magical essence that we emanated. Confidence was our instinctual way of being. We weren't afraid to make new friends; we weren't afraid to try new activities and we didn't get nervous about entering into unknown territory. We were natural explorers. We marvelled at life. We adored and were fascinated by the world. We didn't view the world through the lens of fear – we viewed the world through the lens of intrigue, fascination and adventure. When we encountered something new, we saw it as something to explore, something to learn, something to discover.

And this essential nature is *still* the truth of who we are. It is *still* the truth of *you*. Confidence is *still* your natural state. This is the blueprint that you came into the world with. This is the way you were designed to be: confident, fearless and fully embracing of the gift of life. And when you are like this, you are living from your truth.

According to studies, babies laugh between three and five hundred times every day, and adults laugh only up to 20 times a day – if at all! This really puts things into perspective, doesn't it? The good news is that, every once in a while, you meet an adult who has "slipped through the net" – a person who has not allowed himself to be throttled and suffocated by the poisonous outside programming designed to limit and restrain us. This kind of rare individual stays connected to their inherent strength. It's a joy to be around people like this. They remind us of the power we all contain. And there's nothing I'd like more than for this to be the way that *you* engage the world – to be the kind of individual that won't allow yourself to surrender and weaken to the cultural messages that tell you that you should "be like everyone else", put your head down and disappear into the vast expanse of *sameness* and *conformity*. I want you to be the person who is remembered for embracing your deepest truth, and never letting go of who you are.

Holding onto your uniqueness, in the most fundamental way, is the greatest endeavour of your life: to be fully who you are, without excuse or compromise, and to embrace the world with nothing less than the interior strength that is your birth-given state. There will never be another *you* – ever! You are an expression of total uniqueness. So do not allow even a second to pass in which you're not operating from your deepest truth. You are here to flourish.

Unfortunately, there will always be people whose intention it is to pull you away from who you are. And this is why part of what it means to be truly confident is to refuse to allow what goes on around you to shape what goes on within you. In fact, as you develop and internalise these ideas so that they integrate into the dominant way that you navigate through the experiences of your life, you will begin to *shape the world around you by shaping the world within you!*

People are not broken, nor are they helpless – they have simply invested into broken and helpless beliefs about themselves. So, in many ways, a large part of capturing the spirit of authentic confidence has to do with rediscovering this primal sense of fascination and awe about people, about yourself and about the world that contains you. It's about shaking off all of the limiting toxic ideas that you have previously taken on as being the underlying truths of your life, and seeing the *falseness* in them. Once you do this, the false ideas no longer hold any power over you – you can begin to laugh at them the same way that you would laugh at images in a comic book. They become weak, powerless and insubstantial. They then disappear so that your real truth can emerge.

CONFIDENCE RESIDES AT YOUR VERY CORE

You do not need more confidence. What you actually need is to connect to the awareness of your true essence, which is both immeasurably fearless and immeasurably confident.

Imagine a diamond that's totally shrouded in dirt and mud, and has been left that way for years and years. In this state, you cannot "see" the diamond – all you can see is the opaque layer that surrounds it and covers it up. The *gleam* – the *sparkle* – is out of sight. But when you clean and clear away the grime, the diamond begins to reveal its truest form. The beauty of it is once again able to fully flourish, because that's what has always been there. The magnificence of it has been present the entire time – it is just that it hadn't previously been allowed to be brought to the surface; to glisten and shine.

Remember that confidence is your natural state. Remember that confidence will be yours in abundance when you clear away the "mud" that tries to restrict and constrain you. Remember that confidence is the potent energy you exude when you operate in the way you were brought into the world to be.

There is no question that the moments of our lives will frequently be arbitrary and unpredictable. They will surprise us without notice. They will challenge us at the most unexpected times. And this adventure of discovery, and of growth, is the most magical experience we can have. It represents our unique and incomparable adventure. And inside of it all, we can connect to the core of that unyielding power that never retreats, never withdraws and never diminishes. It's the awareness of the eternal force that underlies everything. And when we look closely enough – when we peer into the depth of this resolute and resounding force – we feel its greatness reflecting itself back to us. And the ultimate realisation comes in the moment when we widen our awareness, and know this power as who we are.

"*You can either choose to believe that your life is empty and meaningless, or you can choose to believe that your life has great value and great significance. This single decision will affect the very foundation of how you embrace the world around you.*"

–Julian James

CHAPTER FOUR

Operating from a Solid Foundation

"When we establish within our thought a non-resistance to the Power which is greater than we are, we are at the same time accepting within ourselves a stability that is the stability of the Universe. We find ourselves secure, for we know that we are Part of That which causes change but is never affected by any of the changes."

–Ernest Holmes

Some years ago I was entertaining a group of business people in the private room of a hotel in West London. I had been hired to perform for around 150 guests – employees of a large accounting cooperation – who had all congregated for an evening of cordial social exchange, fine food and mystery entertainment.

After the end of my presentation, I gathered my belongings together, said goodbye to the lady that had booked me for the function and headed into the hotel lobby where I called for a taxi. While I waited, I sat and reclined on to one of four large green studded leather sofas that were arranged in a square formation next to the reception desk. My intention was to use the time to ruminate and reflect upon the show: a pleasurable practice of relaxation and contemplation that I enjoy after every one of my performances. It's something I look forward to. It's a conceptual ritual that allows me to consider things from multiple perspectives, as I focus on the outcome of the event. It allows me to make decisions about what to change within my presentations, what to keep the same, and what to add into the mix the next time around in order to generate even greater impact and audience enjoyment. It's my way of ensuring that I'm moving along a trajectory of continual improvement, and remaining open to ideas and inspiration along the journey.

During these few moments of pondering, my internal attentiveness was suddenly distracted by the call of my name from across the other side of the hotel lobby. As I looked over, a man dressed in a beige suit with long well-groomed silvery hair was signalling for my attention. He swiftly paced over towards the sofa and introduced himself to me. He told me his name was Adam, and that he'd like to talk with me for a few moments. I could tell there was something he'd been waiting patiently to ask me about, and he'd now finally got his chance to do so. Adam sat down beside me with a countenance that bespoke extended anticipation.

I quickly learnt that he did indeed have a question for me, but it wasn't the question I had expected!

As a *mystery entertainer*, I've become somewhat accustomed to expect what I refer to as the "typical question" from those who come to see me perform and take part in the experiences that I present. The "typical question", of course, is the one I'm most often asked, and it's the one that shows up in a variety of forms such as, "How exactly did you do that?" "What's your secret?" "Can you teach me how I can do things like that too?" But, despite its many faces, it's principally the *same* question posed in different ways: it's essentially the expression of a desire to discover more about an art form that is fundamentally arcane and mysterious. Most people are fascinated by the inexplicable, and that's part of the joy of offering people the experience of *magic* and *mystery* – it opens up their senses to a world of possibility that transcends the limitations of rationality. Not only is it intrinsically captivating, it engages people on an emotional level. And, because of the tendency for people to want to discover more, it's reasonable to come to expect this kind of enquiry.

However, on this occasion, with Adam sitting next to me on the green leather sofa, my immediate assumption about what he'd planned to ask me was totally mistaken. He hadn't planned on asking me the "typical question" at all. In fact, it quickly came to pass that what he actually wanted to talk about was something quite different. It transpired to be a question which triggered within me a quality of reflection that was, in many ways, far deeper and far more integral. It was a question that spoke to something that rests at the very heart of it all. It was, if you will, a glimpse inside of the magic *behind* the magic – the secret *behind* the secret.

With a vocal tonality that was earnest yet impulsive, he said, "Tell me something ... how are you able to become so comfortable performing on a stage for so many people that you can just relax and interact with the audience, have the freedom to be spontaneous, and know that things will go the way you want them to go?"

His question carried a significance that I rarely encounter. It was something that connected to the truth of my entire conviction about what matters most. It was a question that pointed not to what was going on externally, but, instead, to what was going on for me *internally*. It was about what had to be present in order for all of the other things that were present to be the way that they were. And this is a distinction that lies at the core of what this book is really about – that's where the real power resides.

The things that you *do* (whatever they happen to be) can only ultimately be carried out and derived from the foundation of who you *are*. And being able to show up in the world with a sense of grounded inner strength, and the capacity to relate and interact with others in a way that is both impactful and sustainable, comes from embracing this essential way of being and making it the very ground from which you operate. It's about coming to know, in the most intimate way, the changeless power that resides at your core, and allowing *that* to remain the pervasive force in all that you express.

> What's on the outside only has true and lasting impact when it's being driven and directed by an authentic power that resides on the inside.

Most people, when it comes to the idea of being confident – and the desire to be *more* confident – want to learn *behaviours*, "techniques" and "magic words" to cause them to feel this way. Such methodologies – those popularised within particular domains of the *self-improvement industry* – have often been made to *appear* to be the overnight "one-stop-solution" to attaining enduring self-confidence. Ultimately, though, they are not. With this said, there are many related approaches, when employed preferentially, that can have their place, and certainly hold great value. But do not be fooled or inveigled by their ostensibly facile nature. There are no shortcuts. There are no "magic pills". There are no "quick fixes".

One of my own corporate coaching programmes entails working with managers and executives who want to have more impact in delivering their messages to others. This programme includes the training of certain "presentation skills" and styles of delivery that are designed to heighten interest, capture attention and communicate more influentially. Given my background, this is a specialist area of attention within the work that I do. There are also other skills – derived from theatrical disciplines and schools of performance art – which have their place, too, in allowing people to strengthen particular areas of communicative competence. And many of these I am well versed in, and some of which I teach and train as well. However, in spite of the value in all of these things, it is imperative to always ultimately come home to where our power truly resides; to not lose sight of what it means to be *authentically* and *powerfully* confident in the world: the truth that resilient self-confidence of the most essential kind is about something far deeper, far more fundamental and far more integral to an individual than simply learning a menu of "things to do" or "things to say".

Those people who are led to believe that learning certain persuasive "magic words" will allow them to attain true personal satisfaction are always left feeling that something integral is missing at a deeper level. Unfortunately, there is an abundance of "self-improvement" seminars – offering "life-skills" in *communication, influence, persuasion, seduction* and *sales* (to mention just a few) – which offer such a restricted, surface-level approach. Many (but not all) of these "trainings" claim that the "secret" is to be found exclusively in the *language* and the *behaviour* – inside of the words and the actions themselves. They claim that if a person learns exactly "what to do", "what to say" and exactly "when to say it", then everything else will somehow fit into place. Yet the result is that participants leave such trainings with a nice list of "magic phrases" and "special formulas", but without the substantial and fundamental awareness of how to operate from a way of being that is unconditionally stable and strong. There is little or no focus on authentic personal expression. And without the presence of this essential foundation, these supposed "magical techniques" actually hold very little power.

There is tremendous value in having the capacity to use language elegantly and with precision. This is unquestionable. However, on their own, without solid grounding, memorised "phraseologies", "presentation skills", "performance skills" and other modes and manifestations of prescripted communication – however "clever" or "interesting" – are nothing more than surface-level behaviours. They are merely a set of learnt skills and language constructs. They are secondary. And despite the lies you have been told, in *effective* communication of any kind, the central and predominant factor is *not* the words and behaviours themselves. Rather, it's about where those words and behaviours are coming from. Without the right energy behind them, they hold very limited power. At their basic level, they're just noises and movements. What's important is what exists *behind* the words and behaviours. Powerful communication is about what brings those words and behaviours to life. And, of course, what's behind the communication is the *essential being of the individual.*

At the deepest part of us, we know this to be true. Examples of this in action are abundant. A man can approach a woman he's romantically interested in and attempt to be "linguistically clever". He can try to charm the female with what he believes to be alluring and seductive communication. But if his personal energy is not strong – if he's operating from a weak foundation – she will *feel* this and be repelled by it. She will sense his incongruence, and his words will carry little weight! It simply won't matter to her what he says at all, because anything he does say will be negated and nullified by the discordance he's projecting. Yet, a man who is deeply and authentically confident – who has control of his energy and is operating from a source of integral strength – can approach the very same woman and actually say very little, but because his energy is grounded and congruent, he will emanate a totally different resonance. As a result of this, she'll literally *feel* the distinctiveness of his presence, and will recognise him to be authentic.

Potent and authentic human expression is felt intuitively by others. It is discerned even from great distance. When a person is grounded within himself in such a way that his true personal command forms the very solidity from which he connects with others, when he speaks, his words literally become permeated with the essence of his being. Everything that he says – all of the words that flow from his lips – become extensions of that same essential energy of certainty and conviction. *This* is power in communication. And *this* kind of dynamic engagement is something that cannot be faked by way of peripheral "technique" – it has to emerge from an individual's *true* source, which is only possible when that person has a deep inherent awareness of who they are.

This entire idea is vital. I cannot emphasise this explicitly enough, because it brings us back to what is at the core of it all: the relationship and connection we have to ourselves and to our awareness of the power that encompasses us. It shapes and moulds everything that is expressed *by* and *through* us. Literally, how we're *being* in the world forms the undercurrent for everything else.

The awareness of who a person fundamentally knows himself to be – at the most primal level – pervades everything that they do. When we connect to that power inside of us that allows us to align with and operate from our greatness – our innate strength – then all that we do, and how we show up in the world, has no choice but to flow from this greatness!

"The greatest truth must be recognition that in every man, in every child is the potential for greatness."

–Robert F. Kennedy

Adam explained to me that he had just returned from a retreat in South America, where he had spent several weeks learning how to quieten his mind and find his centre. He told me that what I had spoken about resonated with his experience in South America because he came to the realisation, during his trip, that what causes a person to become powerful on the outside is about finding that locus of power on the inside. And when he returned to his work in England, he was able to integrate these principles into how he lived his life.

He went on to explain that this shift in awareness changed everything for him; even his ability to have more satisfying and restful sleep. It also led to an enhancement in the quality of the relationships he had to those people that meant the most to him. He told me he'd also recently began learning to play the piano – something he had had a passion for since he was a child, but was somehow never able to find himself committing to. There was a glow about Adam. I could see that he'd really come to know himself in a way that was profound. His words touched me distinctively and viscerally. Something inside of what he was saying deeply resonated with me.

As we began to deepen our discussion of these ideas, my taxi arrived, and I left promptly. I only wished that Adam and I could have talked for much longer, as we rested on that green sofa at the hotel, sharing our thoughts and experiences. There was a rapport between us that was instantaneous, and which required no effort at all on either part. Our affinity just organically flowed out of our delight in speaking about the things that had great meaning for us.

I never met Adam again. I probably never will. But I will always remember what our brief discussion enlivened in me, and what it enlivened in him as well. It's a fond and cherished memory of a fleeting encounter that let me know that we can draw so much more from all of our encounters with others. So often we *miss* the "magic" contained inside of what appear to be mundane situations. But, when we open ourselves to great possibilities, great possibilities find a way of opening up to us. And it's in these moments – these moments of effortless connection and heightened awareness – that we can far more easily see the greatness in ourselves.

CULTIVATING A STRONG FOUNDATION

"Greatness is a measure of one's spirit, not a result of one's rank in human affairs."

–Sherman Finesilver

There was a certain lady that I'd meet from time to time at my local gym. What was different about Susan is that she'd always take to time to engage in conversation with me and the other people who would turn up. She was the kind of person who wasn't fearful of opening herself to others, and sharing her energy and her ideas. This made her different. It made her shine, which is why I enjoyed being around her.

Susan was married to a Cypriot man, and, knowing that I was half Cypriot, she'd tell me, on many occasions, about her husband's ongoing project to build a brand new house in Cyprus. They'd planned on eventually emigrating there, with their newly-born son, to be closer to family. It was an undertaking they had been working on for over five years, and was, piece by piece, slowing coming together. Susan's husband had always wanted to commission and work with a team of architects to design a house which was entirely of his own creation. All of his collected personal wealth, including a great deal of Susan's life savings as well, had been allocated to the funding of this dream. They had put their heart and soul into this endeavour.

At the gym one evening, I saw Susan. By this time, I hadn't seen her for over a year. During her noticeable absence, I naturally assumed she was already in Cyprus, living out the reality she had worked so hard to create with her husband. However, the moment she walked through the door, I just knew something was wrong. As soon as our eyes connected, she sauntered over towards me and told me the bad news.

It seemed that the design and building of the house wasn't quite as straightforward as they'd assumed it was going to be. Since the last time we'd seen each other, Susan had been back and forwards to Cyprus several times. These journeys were necessary to meet with the various contractors involved with the building project. Although the planning permission for their new home had been fully granted and the building of the property had been well underway for many months, a serious structural problem had only recently come to light.

They were informed that a major structural error to the house had been detected. It was something that set the completion of the building back by many months, and also one that necessitated a further injection of cash if it was ever to be corrected. Quite simply, the foundational structure for their new home had not been properly set in place on the area of land they'd purchased. The house had not been built upon a groundwork that was entirely solid. Instead, there were positions of great instability within the foundation, which were only discovered after much of the property had already been erected. These errors had begun to cause significant misalignment problems within the brickwork, mainly in the form of large cracks in two of the walls. Part of the flooring had also begun to buckle and come away. This put stress on other areas of the building, including much of the plumbing work, which had ruptured in several places. There was no question that things were very bad. The foundation was not secure; it was not strong. These errors could not be ignored. It was a serious issue, and Susan worried for the future of their new home.

THE COMPONENTS OF INNER STRENGTH

By this time, I hope you're beginning to see that the real secret to deep and lasting confidence isn't connected to what goes on outside of you, but to what goes on *inside* of you – your very foundation. It's about aligning yourself with that deep inner solidity; that changeless and unconditional power which is the essential truth of your being. When you establish your connection to this foundation – when you resolutely stand within the strength of your birth-given fortitude – what takes place on the outside of you will have no choice but to be charged and ignited by the internal power you generate from within. And this becomes the *foundation* from which you operate – a foundation that is fully grounded and unshakable and strong; not weak, uncertain and unstable.

This is why trying to approach the development of your own self-assurance by placing the majority of your attention on exterior factors will never ultimately be sustainable. In the same way that a house can never be stable if it is built upon unstable foundations, if you try to build "confident words" and "confidence behaviours" upon a foundation of weakness, the weakness and instability will affect the words and the behaviours that you're enacting. They will be filtered through a position of weakness. They will collapse. While it's true that learning particular language structures and behaviours is useful and effective when employed within particular contexts and environments, it is *truer* that what will allow them to have real impact is the solidity of the groundwork upon which those behaviours are expressed.

In communicating with others, when you try to force words through fear, the words become coloured by the fear. When you try to force behaviours through doubt, those behaviours become coloured by the doubt. But when you operate from the place inside of you that is *free of doubt* and *free of fear*, your words and behaviours become effortless and striking and yield powerful influence. There will be a distinct exquisiteness in the way that you interact with others. This distinction is at the core of powerful communication, yet it's one that's missed by those people looking for "quick-fix solutions". And, as I've already stated, there are none!

> Real confidence is the expression of authentic inner strength, not the manifestation of the "appearance" of strength.

If you have a piece of furniture – a dining chair for example – and the wood that comprises it is completely rotten, you can paint the chair to *appear* as though it's not rotten. You can adorn it and dress it up with all kinds of fine fabrics and trimming, and you can finish it using the most expensive quality paints and varnishes. You can even try to convince yourself that its structure is solid and firm. It might *look* pretty. It may even *appear* to be solid. But guess what? The wood underneath it is *still* rotten! It is *still* weak! What's more, before long, someone's going to sit in the chair and the chair's going to break and collapse, because its very internal structure is unsustainable.

Do you see that learning peripheral "techniques" will ultimately be rendered futile if a strong foundation is not in place? Relying on superficial elements might work for a short time; it may even "fool" some people, but it won't fool *you*, because you'll know what you're trying to compensate for. It's an approach that is totally unsound. That's why this book is *not* about trying to leverage the configuration of pretence. There's already an abundance of that kind of information available to you, should you choose that path. The instant "magic pill" approach is very seductive, and very alluring. However, underneath its fanciful exterior, nothing lasting and enduring is present.

This book is about cultivating your *foundation*. It's about connecting you to the centre of yourself – to your very source of power! Whilst most information will encourage you to work *outwardly* – to generate the "appearance" of confidence – this book (and ultimately everything that I stand for) is about working *inwardly*, where true strength resides. It's about the fundamental internal work that puts in place a personal foundation which comprises the very stable ground that supports all that you do. It's about generating a sense of personal clarity and directedness that is real and authentic and intimately connected to *who you are* – so much so that even the idea of falsehood becomes foolish and unnecessary. This is because real power emerges from within you when you let go of those things you've placed in the way of you actually being this way; pervasively and unshakably.

The amazing part in all of this is that when you commit yourself to this authentic journey of expression – one which flows out of the solid foundation of your inextricable personal truth – you'll become aware of yourself *naturally* behaving more confidently, in all of the circumstances of your life. After all, an orange tree can *only* produce oranges, because that's the foundation that these fruits originate from: an orange tree. A tomato plant can *only* produce tomatoes, because that's the innate make up of it – that is what it is, at its roots. And, in the same way, operating from *your* foundation of strength will naturally produce positive and confident actions in you, because that's at *your* roots as well. You'll begin to notice, and become delighted, that how you function – the very things that you do – have no choice but to be aligned with that very same strength that exists at your centre.

There is a creative force at the centre of your being which is beyond fear, beyond doubt, beyond the physical. It is a dynamic power that is absolutely certain, absolutely strong and absolutely unyielding. When you hold yourself internally from the enduring essence of this power, you will emanate a remarkable and distinctive energy. It's an energy that will be recognised by others as genuine presence. You will feel its resonance inside of your body as an enveloping interior force – an unwavering sensation of solidity, clarity and composure. And when you make this the foundation from which you operate in the world – regardless of the things that take place around you – you will feel it as the way you were designed to be all along. You will know it as your innate and essential truth.

> "*When you connect to the certainty within you, you withstand the uncertainty around you.*"
>
> –Julian James

CHAPTER FIVE
Your Golden Birthright

"The ultimate creative act is to express what is most authentic and individual about you."

–Eileen Clegg

I want you to imagine this scenario: You are at home, and it's late morning. You hear the sound of the postman doing his daily round, and the loud clunk of your letterbox as a pile of letters drops on to your doormat. You rush over to investigate the mail of the day. Amongst the various envelopes, one letter in particular stands out to you. It's so different and so distinctive, and so unlike anything that you're used to seeing, you cannot help but to be totally intrigued by it.

It is a shiny golden envelope; expensive and luxurious to the touch. It has *your* name boldly inscribed upon it. By the sheer feel of it, you know it's from someone eminent and well respected. It has a style and prominence all of its own. You instinctively know that this is very different; that this is something *unique* and *special*. And so, sparing not a second further, you tear it open, anxious and thrilled to discover what's inside!

Inside is a personal and exclusive invitation. You have been granted an invitation to a "special event". But not just *any* event – the greatest and most extravagant event of them all!

As you eagerly read all of the information, you learn that millions attempt to be part of this exciting affair each and every day, and millions are declined and refused entry. Yet, *you* are one of the few that have been called upon to experience this golden opportunity. Just the thought of it sends rushes of excitement throughout your body. It is *you* that's been called upon. Something truly incredible awaits you. You can literally feel it in your bones!

THE INVITATION OF A LIFETIME!

Now let me ask you this question: If you did receive such an invitation – if you really were called upon to attend an event of such high calibre – would you refuse and neglect your invitation and pass up the opportunity to relish in all of the surprises and experiences that awaited you? Or would you fully and graciously embrace your gift and honour your invitation for all that it had to offer?

Well of course, you'd show up at the event! Absolutely nothing would stop you! You would arrive with full intention, and you'd make the most of every single moment. You'd be truly honoured to have been invited. You would feel special to be part of it all. You'd enjoy your exclusive invitation to the absolute fullest. And you wouldn't be troubled as to whether or not you should be there, *because you'd know that you had been invited!*

Why is it, then, when we have been given the greatest invitation of them all – an invitation into the world; an invitation to love, to share and to fully embrace every moment of our lives; an invitation to live out the fullest expression of who we are – that so many of us still don't feel worthy enough to be here? Why do so many people feel as though they're "not enough"? Why is it that so many humans are still walking around with their heads down, hesitant and terrified to embrace the gift they've been bestowed? Why is it that so many decline all that has been offered to them, and, instead, settle for the indignity of feeling inferior? Why is it that so many people feel as though they are simply not enough? Why is it that so many of us still don't see – *really see* – the profundity of our very creation, and accept the invitation of our lives in a way that makes us feel inwardly complete and fully alive? Why is it that so many of us simply feel unable to stand fearlessly in the world with a sense of *total entitlement, total confidence* and *total self-assurance* – the way that we were naturally brought into the world to be?

So many people, when faced with opportunities or tasks or challenges, say to themselves, "Who am I to do this? What right do I have to be in this position?" They overthrow themselves with doubt and self-limitation. They feel undeserving. They deny themselves their own innate significance. They distance themselves from what's most true of them: their inherent belonging to the universe. But if they only realised who they were at the deepest level – if they truly connected to that essential power that has been present within them all along – such questions or doubts wouldn't even arise. They would simply move effortlessly forwards, without fear or hesitation. And then, the question that they'd be asking themselves would become a different question altogether. It would become the question they should have been asking themselves the entire time: "Who am I *not* to do this?"

> By virtue of your very existence, you have been given the greatest invitation in the world! You have been granted the invitation to tread the soil of your own individual path and to fully express and celebrate your uniqueness!

"To have that sense of one's intrinsic worth ... is potentially to have everything."

–Joan Didion

A large portion of the socially constructed environment around you (the undeniable and ruthless influence of the media, and of cultural pressures and organised groups) tries to trick you into believing that in order for you to feel like "someone" – in order for you to be a valuable individual who can be loved and appreciated by others – you must first satisfy a level of necessary criteria that you've been told that you should comply with. These are lies and distortions. They are manufactured concepts that have no fundamental grounding. They are designed to keep you a slave to the contrived systems that attempt to convince you that the only way you can feel good about yourself is to accept the ideas that have been imposed upon you. They are designed to make you believe that you have to wait for permission from something outside of you before you're "allowed" to feel like a worthy person. They try to tell you that you'll only be significant when – and only when – they say you are, according to their "classifications", "standards" and "definitions". This is acculturation of the most insidious kind.

Realising your true inner strength requires you to see these lies for what they are – to refuse to give agreement to them – and to come to rest inside of the truth of yourself. What's outside of you isn't who you are. What's outside of you has no power to determine your intrinsic value as a human being, unless you decide to allow it to. Infinite worthiness has been yours since the moment of your conception. Your very emergence into this world is confirmation of this. Nothing will ever change this. It's the fundamental essence of your being.

> Everything that is present in the universe is connected to the very power that created it, and you have no choice but to also be connected to this same extraordinary power.

"You begin on the road to your own glory when you begin on the road to your own truth."

–Neale Donald Walsch

In the moments that you feel a sense of unworthiness – at those times when you feel disconsolate and dispirited – remember that these feelings only arise as a result of a *belief* that you temporarily hold, which isn't true. Realise that, just because you happen to hold a particular self-reflective belief, doesn't mean that this belief is universally and empirically true. It just means you're holding on to an idea that doesn't serve you, and never will, because it's not a reflection of who you really are. Beliefs are not fixed entities. Beliefs are pliable and malleable and can change. But *who you are never changes.*

Your entire human constitution is one that is united with total victory. Even at the most primal biological level, you are a victorious winner – and this is a truth that is indisputable. Before the moment of your conception, there was one single egg cell, having been released from the ovary of the female, which required a single sperm in order to initiate the awe-inspiring development of a human being. But although there was only one egg, there were around two hundred and fifty million sperm, all racing in the competition to fertilise it, like an enormous conglomeration of eager energy-fuelled athletes vying for the honour of the "golden trophy". Each one of these individual sperm held the potential for the creation of a human life. But out of all of the sperm that flowed along the lining of the uterus and up into the fallopian tube, only *one* stood the chance of being able to successfully penetrate the membrane of the egg wall and fuse with the egg itself – one single sperm amongst two hundred and fifty million – and that was *you!* So, knowing that you're literally the "winner" of the greatest biological race known to man – far more triumphant than any athletic one hundred metre race, or any Olympian long jump into a sand pit – how could you feel anything less that totally confident, totally accepting and totally embracing of the full embodiment of your very existence!

You did not create yourself. You were created by a source of power that is greater that you; yet it is an infinite force that you are intimately connected to. You need nothing more in order to be fully at ease and at rest with yourself – embodying your inborn significance – other than to live your life without losing sight of the realisation of this given power. And if you embrace only this, you will attain a level of consciousness that most others will never even come close to attaining.

You are *already* "enough". You have been graciously welcomed into the world. Your place here is not up for question. It is not something you need to work or strive for. It isn't something that needs validation or approval from others. It isn't a deadline to meet, or a distant target to hit – it is your given privilege! It's a priceless gift that has been given to *you* unconditionally. Your existence needs no explaining, nor does it need permission or acceptance from anything external to you. It is already yours! You have been created from a source that is powerful beyond measure. You don't need reasons that exist outside of you in order for you to feel complete; the reasons *within* you are all you'll ever need.

For as long as you feel that you need to obtain things, get approval, chase "achievements" or change yourself in order for you to feel secure, it will never *ever* be enough. It will always serve to reinforce the sense of lacking that these endeavours were intended to resolve.

And so, in order for you to be truly confident in the world – in a way that is solid and unshakable – you need only fully accept and embrace your essential truth: the truth that you are whole and complete and precious, just as you are. Recognise *this* as the foundation of your personal honour and inner strength. Live every day through the power of this knowing – holding this truth at the very core of you – and you will know what it feels to be authentically confident in the most pervasive way. A true feeling of belonging will be present for you. It will resonate through you in waves of abundance.

YOU HAVE AN UNEQUIVOCAL "RIGHT TO BE"!

Why should you *ever* question your significance? Why should you ever question your value? Why should you ever question your worthiness?

Everything in existence shares the very same creative force, and *you* are an integral part of this creative energy. The power that created the Sun is the very same power that brought *you* into being. The power that created Jupiter and Venus and Mercury – and *all* of the other planets – is the very same power that created *you*. The power that created the billions of stars that form the unthinkable expanse of the solar system – and the billions and billions of galaxies that extend beyond it into intergalactic space – is also the same power that bestowed *you* the gift of life. The water with which you cleanse your body and the air that you draw into your lungs – the vital elements that nourish and sustain you – have all been produced by the same universal intelligence that shaped and formed the total uniqueness of *you*. You are perfect because the very essence of the spirit within you operates as a pattern of perfection. Your emergence into the world is part of the same unimaginable force that created all of this, and *you* are intimately and inseparably connected to it. So don't ever think that you are ever anything less than a divine creation of wonderment and magnificence. Don't ever think that you could ever be small or unworthy or insignificant.

Let there be no question or doubt in your mind: if you are reading these words right now, then you have been granted a rare and exceptional gift – an extraordinary invitation. You have been invited into the ultimate experience. You *deserve* to be here in every conceivable way. You have an indisputable "right to be" simply by virtue of the fact that you are extant and alive! You do *not* need to "earn" this right – it is already yours. Nothing else is necessary for you to feel and be significant in the world. You have full entitlement to express your true nature as fully and completely as you can. Your significance is inextricably connected to your inherent nature. You do not need external validation from anything or anyone. There is no one you have to answer to. There is no one to whom you need to explain yourself. You are *already* vital and whole and complete, just as you are. Your "right to be" is unconditional.

The reason that works of art such as the *Mona Lisa*, or Vincent van Gogh's *Sunflowers*, are described as being "priceless" is because they are totally unique and astonishing creations. People have attempted to forge and copy these canvases of artistic expression, but they ultimately fail, because the *original* will always stand undisputed. There is, after all, only *one* true and original source. There can only be *one*. And if you only realised just how astonishing and totally unique *you* are, you would know that you, also, were priceless. And through this awareness, you'd instantly reconnect with that effortless confidence that resides at your core.

Realise that your sense of certainty and entitlement comes not from what you own, or who you know, of even what you do – it is yours because you have been given the gift of life. You have been given the extraordinary invitation to bring your uniqueness into the world and to celebrate the full expression of who you are. What you are capable of is astonishing. You have been imbued with the seed of unlimited potential and possibility. You are a divine and priceless being.

This is the greatest gift of them all – *the* greatest invitation – and it is rightfully yours. It is your golden birthright!

> “*You have an unconditional birth-given right to be in this world. Know that this right is your ultimate privilege. Know that this is the authentic source of your inner strength.*”
>
> –JULIAN JAMES

CHAPTER SIX
Embracing the Full Bloom of Human Experience

"Most people die before they are fully born."

–Erich Fromm

I can remember meeting with a friend, a number of years ago, at a local restaurant. He had just returned from a weekend "motivational seminar" – the type of seminar that is promoted as being able to "change your life" in three days flat! And over the course of our time together, as we ate and drank and shared thoughts and stories about what we'd been doing since we were last together, he was expressing his obvious exhilaration and enthusiasm about what he'd experienced at this weekend programme. In fact, his level of enthusiasm seemed almost excessive, and, somehow, not entirely sincere. At the time, it was difficult for me to place my finger on exactly what it was that caused me to notice this in him. There was just something about the way he was conveying himself that seemed somewhat contrived and not fully authentic.

The seminar he'd attended was a popular event in which many hundreds of participants had gathered together in a large stadium and were exposed to "tools" and "techniques" designed to help transform their lives. This type of experience typically involves loud music, the chanting of mantras, gratuitous hand clapping and jumping up and down. Such events are sometimes referred to as "large group awareness trainings", and there are many of them.

Now, as a person directly involved within the domain of personal transformation, I naturally value all experiences that serve to move people in the direction of becoming more empowered, more confident and more inspired to realise their desires and fulfill their true passions. After all, what could be a more worthwhile endeavour than facilitating a person to be the very best that he can be? In this regard, I honour and encourage *any* programme or technology that is designed toward effective personal growth – that is, as long as it is generated and delivered from the position of encouraging humans to be *authentically themselves*. This does not include the battery of progressive indoctrination procedures which ultimately serves to homogenise people.

THE FUTILITY OF INAUTHENTIC EXPRESSION

There seems to be an idea that is prevalent within certain (but certainly not all) "self-improvement" movements, seminars and trainings, that encourages people to believe that they should be "happy" *all* of the time. It's the idea, and presumption, that whatever's happening in our lives – regardless of what it is that we may be experiencing from moment to moment – we should be happy and elated and smiling *all of the time!* And that even if smiling and appearing "happy" before others isn't how we're genuinely feeling on the inside, where it really counts, we should try as hard as we can to *appear* to be seen that way anyway! That's right – happy, happy, happy – all of the time!

Imagine a huge room crammed with people fashioning fixed and false grins, spanning from ear to ear – like 600 robots, all huddled together – and you'll begin to envisage the lunacy I'm speaking of. This is the "shiny happy faces" syndrome! It's the result of people hearing messages of "positivity" and then distorting their beliefs about what it means to live this way. If you were to ever enter into some of these environments, you'd be able to recognise this almost instantly: lots of people milling around each other, with artificial smiles on their faces, *pretending* to be so very happy!

This type of zombie-like response from seminar participants may not always be the intention of the seminar leaders at all of these various programmes. But, unfortunately, and in many cases, such a response is very typical. Due to the nature of my work, I've personally attended countless such events, both as an attendee and also as a facilitator. And I've always been able to spot these people instantly. They are typically the individuals who attend the same events again and again and again – the "seminar junkies"! It actually became a humorous game for me to play by myself – to glance around the room and spot the "happy zombies"!

This type of behaviour is a misrepresentation and a misunderstanding of the "positive thinking" movement that began to surface at the latter part of the nineteenth century. In certain circles, this ideology seems to have been taken completely out of context, distorted and made to be something that it was never intended to be – at least by most! And somewhere in the process, we've somehow been conditioned to believe that we should be almost ashamed to feel sadness or despair, for example, and that only some emotions are "acceptable" – but not all of them. This is part of the onset of the cultural indoctrination that blinds so many people to the truth of our fundamental human essence – *that we are emotional beings!*

EMBRACING THE ENTIRE SPECTRUM OF HUMAN EMOTION!

The truth, of course, is that when we encounter people who are trying desperately hard to *appear* so very happy before others (because that's what they've been led to believe they "should" be doing) they are, in fact, denying and resisting the very organic and expansive range of human emotion that is the essence of their nature. And such behaviour is all based upon the erroneous belief that, somehow, any emotion other than being happy is "bad" and to be avoided at all costs.

In no way am I devaluing the idea of experiencing the joyful expression of happiness, as long as it's genuinely felt and expressed. Needless to say, to be truly fulfilled and content is a way of being which is not to be disparaged. I truly believe that the most settled and inwardly satisfied people in our culture are those who are able to operate from a state of well-balanced positivity the majority of the time: to see the good in others, to share, to contribute, to love, to forgive, to embrace and explore the magic of the world, and fully treasure the gift of being alive. And so, to be happy, in *this* sense, is natural and organic, and warms the spirit in a special way.

What I do not support is the idea of being *inauthentic* through the denial and resistance of all of the other emotions that we experience from moment to moment. What I'm emphasising then, is the idea that *any* expression of emotion is perfect and complete, as long as it's genuinely experienced, and not forced through the expectations of others, or impelled through group pressure. This is an integral distinction that seems to have been lost.

To be open to experiencing the full spectrum of our human emotions is what it means to live *authentically* in the world. In this way we are, in fact, our most human. As emotional creatures, to be nothing less than fully human is to function in the manner that we were designed to function. Once we really begin to become accustomed to this truth, the pressure to conform to how we think we should be drops away. And then what's left is the pure and authentic expression of who we are. This, alone, contains inside of it great power.

TRUE CONFIDENCE BEGINS FROM AUTHENTIC PERSONAL EXPRESSION

We think that our moments of *vulnerability* should not be observed by others. We've learnt to feel awkward and uncomfortable about this innate human aspect of ourselves, even though it's something, as humans, we all share. So we place our vulnerability into hiding, not realising that there's

> We have been led into believing that to do what it is that's most natural for us to do – to simply express our humanity; to operate through our most primal and fundamental nature – is something we should obstruct, cover up and hide away.

absolutely no reason for us to do so. It's been instilled into us that being this way is not "okay". But this is just another cultural myth. If others were to behold our vulnerability, it would only remind them of their own vulnerability in the process. And the truth is that the capacity to be vulnerable before others is not a weakness, but actually a form of strength: it's an expression of the strength required to be comfortable enough to be this way, despite the condition or the situation.

We don't see that it's entirely possible for us to be open and vulnerable in the presence of others – and to do so from strength – without compromising who we are. Yet, from this foundation, a person can feel his feelings and, at the same time, remain grounded and strong. And the embodiment of genuine confidence comprises this very capacity: to move through the world authentically and to fully *own* and be present to whatever is true for us in any moment. It means to fully embrace the expression of our very humanity – which includes the entire bloom of our human emotional range – without resistance, without avoidance and without denial. It's about realising that the experiences we have from moment to moment are not who we are; rather, they're simply the experiences that we're having. And this is what allows us to experience any emotional state from an underlying position of strength, because it's the strength which comes out of this very foundation of authenticity.

With these ideas in mind, I want you to begin considering the notion of *confidence* from an entirely different frame of reference. I want you to realise that to be truly self-confident actually *includes* the facility to be open enough to feel the full range of your emotions with honesty and truth, and seeing others as being imbued with the same universal human condition as yourself. This is far more authentic than expending energy in trying to hide or obstruct the manifestation of what you truly feel, and trying to present yourself in such a way that you appear to be discontented from what makes you human. It's not possible for you to be separate from this, so do not resist it.

To embrace this quality of openness is to experience a level of integrity that will fortify you. And since the notion of confidence embodies the concept of *certainty* (the certainty you have in yourself) you can extend this certainty in yourself to also being connected to the certainty of the truth of *all* humanity – the certainty that we are all, at the most fundamental level, one and the same. Because even though we are all totally unique – even though each of us brings a diverse array of characteristics and abilities and gifts to the world – we are also bound together by a *connectedness* that is undeniable and irrevocable. And when we live through this knowledge, we remain aware of a truth that resides at the heart of our very essence.

The embodiment of this certainty affords us great personal command. It draws us right back to the primal power we *already* contain. It allows us to no longer identify ourselves with our experiences and our emotions, because our experiences are just that – our experiences. They have no power to affect the fundamental truth of who we are, because *who we are is much more than any experience we will ever have.*

> We are not our emotions. We will always be far greater than the emotions we experience.

When we are not held back by our own resistance, we open ourselves up and connect to this power I'm speaking of. This is the spirit of real confidence: to be present to what's occurring – regardless of what's occurring – and maintain faith in the permanence of our vital power. This means that we're able to hold the truth of ourselves fully stable, despite the external circumstances and situations that would cause other people to lose composure. This is because the source of our true confidence is not external – it is internal. It's not dependent upon exterior factors. It doesn't rely on other people either. It doesn't need anything from the outside in order for us to feel complete, because *we are already complete.* In this way, our sense of who we are is absolutely whole, because it comes from the aspect of us that is changeless.

In order for us to connect to this power requires, first, that we give up the desire to resist how we think things should unfold: our environment, what others do around us, what others say about us and any external factor over which we have no control. We will never be able to fully control what happens around us, because what happens around us is always dependant upon much more than what we, alone, are able to direct. What we can *always* control, however, is the decision to remain completely true to who we are and to hold our integral strength intact. As a result, we can feel free to feel any emotion in its totality, without losing touch with what keeps us internally centred.

This means that when we cry, for instance – even though we're emoting in a way that most people would associate with "weakness" – we can actually shed tears from a position of strength. It's the strength that comes out of the realisation that to fully *own* our crying is part of our primordial human experience, and that to resist this is to resist ourselves in the process. It's the complete engagement to the idea that the full and uncompromised expression of our humanity is what brings the very aliveness into the experience of who we are. And anything that emerges from this primal foundation cannot be anything other than true and authentic and connected to wholeness.

> Solid self-confidence contains the capacity to welcome any emotion, and regard it as an opportunity to discover more of who we are in the process of experiencing it.

So, if crying is your natural and true mode of expression at any particular time – and to sob and shed your tears is what's most effortless for you in that moment – then cry with total abandon. Hold nothing back. Own your experience and know that it's perfect as it is, and doesn't and shouldn't need to be anything else. Fully live out every second of the experience. Embrace, and accept completely, your emotional expression. And, at the same time, realise that your crying isn't who you are – it's simply the manifestation of an emotion you're experiencing, and that you will always be far greater than that emotion. Cry as fully and as compassionately as you desire. And as you do so, notice the awareness of strength that lies beneath the tears. It's the strength that comes from the wakefulness of the distinction between *you* and simply what you're experiencing. It's the strength that remains present in the knowledge that this moment shall pass, just like every other moment, and that your humanity – your very place in this world – is rooted in a power that is beyond measure.

Let this be the same for the full range of your emotions – all of them! Let there be no denial of what's genuine and present for you, as you feel through each and every one. Feeling them doesn't mean you have to act on them, it just means staying present to them. And know that they simply are what they are – an array of visceral sensations inside of your body. They do not need to mean any more than that. This absence of resistance frees you completely. As long as you remain entirely authentic to the essence of your emotional flow, you will be ever present to the permanence of your integral power.

THE NATURE AND MAGIC OF "FLOW"

Take a moment to consider how things *flow*. Think about nature. There is a profound sense of flow through the course of nature, of which we're an inextricable part. Water, like everything else, flows along its own trajectory. To flow is its very essence. There is no force or effort required for it to be this way. It just *is* as it is, being that way completely.

And, just like water, there is flow in and through ourselves as well. Thoughts and ideas and feelings are constantly flowing within us. This is an innate component of being human.

But what happens when we resist this natural flow? Have you ever tried to block a stream of water? What happens? The water doesn't go away. It can't just stop existing. Instead, it builds up! Suddenly, there's great *pressure*. And, until the blockage is released, the pressure continues to build because the water's natural flow has been impeded. Flow is organic and uninhibited. It points to the effortlessness of *letting go* – not letting go of ourselves, but letting go of the resistance we hold that prevents us from being completely ourselves. Flow is about authentically experiencing the stream of our emotions, without giving them permission to define who we are.

Why do you think that flowing water is always cleaner than water that settles and lies still? It's because water that keeps flowing is oxygenated and fresh. Like this, it's not possible for it to stagnate. Water that's been lying in a pond stagnates and becomes stale. It has no flow; no direction. But water that flows is pure and revitalising, because it's not tainted with the sourness of stagnation and the resistance that's created when flow isn't present. People who live in the open, and drink from outside sources, know to always drink moving water as it's so much more nourishing for their bodies. And so, too, is there nourishment present in the welcoming of the natural flow that takes place inside of us.

Countless research has corroborated the fact that deeply impeded and restricted emotions are directly responsible for extremely high levels of negative stress within the body which, in turn, leads to a range of physical illnesses. As stress levels heighten, blood pressure increases and the hormone balance of the body is compromised. There is, for example, an increased presence of the stress hormone cortisol, which, for small periods, is essential, because it plays a primary role in the functioning of the sympathetic nervous system. But prolonged cortisol secretion results in significant physiological changes, many of which are detrimental in the long term, as the immune system is directly suppressed. And when the immune system cannot function at its optimum, the body is far more vulnerable to ailments such as chronic ulcers, impaired cognitive performance, depression, obesity, sleeping disorders, asthma, digestive problems and skin conditions such as eczema. It also precipitates the onset of potentially fatal physiological responses, including heart attack and stroke. This is why embracing the authentic flow of our emotions is a far more essential and vital component in sustaining good health than most people realise.

Nothing about what you experience is unsought unless you begin to resist it. Just like the nature of water, when we block the organic course of our feelings, we, too, begin to feel blocked. And this leads to personal stagnation. The resistance we impose upon ourselves stops us from being clear and open and in natural flow, as we should be.

> True power can never exist amidst resistance. When you let go of internal resistance, you reconnect to the source of your internal strength.

To try to resist your tears – to hold them back and pretend to be any other way – is an act of *inauthenticity*. By resisting, you're actually giving power to what you're restraining. You see, you can still shed tears, and hold onto who you are. You can still experience sadness and function from a foundation of strength. You can still feel worry and despair, and stay connected to your fundamental truth. After all, *no one ever told you that you have to give up who you are in the process.*

Resistance to your emotions diminishes your vital power. Denying and restraining what's true of you in the unfolding moment drains you. It stifles your unique and effortless expression. What you resist persists. And whenever you're in a state of such resistance, it's impossible for you to remain authentic and fully present because you begin placing your attention upon the things that block your natural flow, instead of upon the things that resonate with your integral energy. If you hold on to this resistance, instead of releasing it, it impedes how you are when you're powerfully engaged with life. You become disempowered and disconnected.

When you are full to the brim of unfelt or unreleased emotion, you are not in control – instead, your emotions are controlling you. But when you allow yourself to simply feel them from a foundational position of strength, the locus of control is *yours*, and under your direction.

Most people simply don't believe that it's desirable, or even possible, to let go of toxic resistance and embrace their essential truth. They spend most of their lives running away from the feelings they're having, rather than choosing honesty, and tuning into what these feelings are actually signaling to them! They opt for the route of blocking out the very signals that are there to guide them into making the types of decisions that lead to insight and deep personal growth.

It's only too easy to swallow pills, get drunk or get high. These are nothing more than different approaches towards the same end: for people to numb themselves against the very emotions they're experiencing, because they don't know how to handle them! As a result, people who do this never really come to know themselves in an essential and intimate way. They're never able to reach a sense of internal stability that generates fullness and satisfaction, because the very components that are required for this to be cultivated are constantly being inhibited. And how can a person be truly confident if he continues to disdain the very signals that would otherwise serve to guide him into beginning to operate from this sense of integrity?

The emotions and feelings we experience, when approached and considered in the positive manner I've been describing, serve as personal *guides*. When we faithfully open to them, they literally operate as guiding signals that offer us insightful self-knowledge, and let us know where we should be directing our attention at any moment. They point us towards making crucial choices about what to be doing. And it's truly remarkable, when we attune to these innate indications, what can happen for us. What emerges can often be magical and exciting. But we have to remain in a state of openness. Our emotions can only serve us in this way if we first release the resistance we're enforcing.

"Whatever the present moment contains, accept it as if you had chosen it."

–Eckhart Tolle

So commit to staying connected with your truest human expression. Those people who sustain this level of compassionate wholeness – whilst maintaining the grounded awareness of their internal strength – emanate a confidence that others envy and desire. But the same capacity is also within you. It is within us all. You need only make the choice to honour this commitment to yourself. When you do, you'll feel its resonant power permeating every aspect of your life.

THE INDOCTRINATED RESTRAINT OF EMOTION

Quite simply, anything that serves to inhibit the primal emotional expression of an individual is a movement towards dehumanisation.

In so many ways, the illusions and distortions that pour out of mass cultural conditioning teach us that it's not okay to authentically feel what we're feeling. When we were infants, we received overwhelming signals from the environment that taught us to inhibit ourselves in this manner. As very young children – since we hadn't yet developed the capacity for autonomous decision-making, or had the wherewithal to decide which external information to pay attention to and which information to disregard – we simply looked around us and *accepted* the messages and instructions we were exposed to. We saw it as "ultimate truth", because out ability to reason and to challenge existing prevalent ideologies was very limited. And by the time this faculty developed, much conditioning had already taken place.

In large part, we are present to a collective belief system which is rooted in the idea that, at many times, it's "not right" to feel what we're feeling and to be fully present to such feelings. We learn, both from the explicit direction of others, and also from more subtle implication, that it's better to just "hold it all in". And, as you know, this *suppression* does little to cultivate or sustain our humanity. Actually, it's one of society's attempts to take our humanity away from us!

One of my personal mentoring clients once conveyed something to me, which really exemplified this kind of indoctrinated emotional restraint. It was something that took place whilst he was visiting a friend's home.

His friend, a manager for an architectural firm, lived with his wife and their young daughter. As a Christmas present, the couple had bought their five-year-old daughter a 600-piece jigsaw puzzle. It was a giant "special edition" puzzle, which featured all of the characters from her favourite cartoon. This was something she'd wanted and had been excited about for a long time.

And so, ever since that Christmas, she'd been working on completing the puzzle, slowly, a little at a time, piece by piece. She had set up a large wooden board in her bedroom – big enough to accommodate the full size of the finished puzzle – and she spent time, each night, gradually piecing it all together. It was a source of tremendous excitement for her. She talked about it every day at school. All of her friends were aware of her endeavour to complete it. She'd enthusiastically tell them, each morning, how many more pieces she had placed the night before, and how many pieces were left to go. To this young girl, completing her jigsaw puzzle was something more that just a trivial pastime – to her, it represented the commitment to herself to achieve something commendable.

Now, on the particular evening in question – the night that my client was present at the house – it was late January. The young girl was upstairs in her room. By this time, since several weeks had passed, the puzzle was almost finished. And, with only a few pieces left to fit, she was almost there! At this point, she was perhaps minutes away from completion – the culmination of what'd been an exciting journey of laudable personal commitment towards reaching her goal. She was thrilled about the prospect of finally finishing the puzzle that night and enjoying the contentment of knowing she'd had no help, and had done it all on her own.

Shortly after, the moment came! She placed the last puzzle piece into the only remaining space on the board, and screamed with delight! It was done! Mission complete! Her scream of sheer exhilaration could be heard from the downstairs living room! And her parents, upon hearing their daughter, immediately sat up to attention.

Surging from head to toe with childlike cheerfulness, she ran all the way down the stairs and into the living room, exclaiming, "Mum ... Dad ... I've finished the puzzle ... I've done it, I've done it, I've done it!" She joyously leaped up and down. She danced with jubilation, throwing her hands into the air. She brought an instant dynamic energy into the room. It would have been difficult to see a child more gleeful than her. She was replete with inspiration; abounding with joy!

But what do you think her mother and father did at this very moment? Did they respond to their daughter tenderly and lovingly, embracing her deserved accomplishment? Did they step into her excitement with her so that they, too, could celebrate her success? Did they appreciate that what their daughter had done was deserving of acknowledgment and praise? Did they really see to the core of what was going on for this young girl at a fundamental emotional level? No – they didn't!

Instead of being warmed and enthused by her infectious zeal, they immediately "hushed" her to silence. Instead of celebrating *with* her, they made her wrong. Her father commandingly pointed his finger, dictating, "Shhh! Quiet down! Stop getting yourself so excited!"

They saw their daughter's delight as nothing more than an unwelcome interruption to their evening of television. They had entirely missed the *real message* in what was happening. They had totally missed how much this moment really meant to their daughter. There was no mention of her accomplishment at all – only a condescending instruction for her to "calm down" – which, essentially, was a stipulation to stop expressing the authentic and instinctive emotions she was experiencing in that moment. Her parents were far more interested in getting back to their television as quickly as possible!

And so, in a very patent manner, the accumulation of all the excitement, all the anticipation, all the nights and days of joyful expectation for this young child, were, in the moment of her parents' depreciatory rebuttal, marginalised and reduced. They had instantly disdained their daughter's genuine human expression. They had taken her heart-centred accomplishment and trivialised it. And, for a five-year-old girl, such an experience is painful and impactful – far more impactful than most adults care to fully appreciate, because moments that seem almost insignificant to adults are crucial contributory factors in the development of young children. Such occurrences send children unhealthy signals about how they are, and are not, "allowed" to function in the world. And, at this impressionable age, these experiences are not easily forgotten. These damaging effects are often carried through into adolescence, even adulthood.

With repeated exposure to many of these types of early happenings – in which children learn, through imposition, that they cannot express themselves fully and without fear – it's no real surprise that we grow to learn that to be open and authentic isn't "acceptable" to the world at large. We learn to "bottle it all up" and develop mechanisms with which to do so.

Do you see how important it is to *allow* our natural flow of emotion so that it is fully present, without having to put measures in place to change it? We are living within a culture which has established an expectation that works against allowing this natural and organic flow. But this is just an idea which has been *made up* – quite literally *made up* – like so many other "rules" that we believe so resolutely to be "true".

How people respond to laughter is another example of this same pattern. When you were at school, and laughed during class time, the teacher made sure he put a stop to your good feelings immediately! In school, laughing at the "wrong time" is associated with "bad behaviour". Children are made to believe that it is "wrong". And yet, to laugh is perhaps one of the most wholesome, healing and nourishing things we can do. When we laugh, a flood of natural and healing neurochemicals are released into the system. Our blood pressure is reduced, circulation is enhanced, stress hormones are lowered and we naturally feel calmer and more at ease. That's quite an attractive prospect for such a simple activity, don't you think? So why would there be any reason for us to laugh less, or be told to stop laughing? Doesn't it stand to reason that we should be laughing more? There even exists a branch of yoga referred to as *Laughter Yoga*, which employs group laughter exercises for the amplification of health and wellbeing in a way that is holistic and very rewarding. The benefits of the simple act of laughing are extraordinary indeed.

The act of crying is also something that people respond to in ways that are contrary to the inherent natural flow of human expression. Have you ever noticed that some individuals become nervous and uncomfortable around a person who is crying? It's almost as if they don't know what to do, or how to handle being around someone in this state. And I think that all of us have had the experience of crying as a young child, and had an adult place their arm around us, telling us, "Come on ... stop that ... don't cry!", not to mention the ubiquitous statement, "Big boys don't cry!" Again, it's no wonder that people grow to not want to be seen crying, or even to not want to cry at all – ever – because they've been conditioned to believe that it's a "bad emotion" which needs to be avoided at all costs!

We also forget that crying is not exclusively limited to the expression of sadness or despair. We don't just cry in times of great loss, we shed tears in moments of heightened delight and elation as well. We cry at weddings, we cry at graduations and we cry in response to being told incredible news. Again, these emotions are to be fully embraced – they are all integral components of the experiences of our lives. They must be fully lived out!

Have you ever woken from your sleep with a totally numb hand – entirely devoid of feeling or sensation – because you didn't realise you'd been lying on it all night? In the same way that you would have no feeling in your hand if the essential blood-flow through the veins that lead to it had been cut off, the kind of toxic interference present in the examples I've shared with you also cuts us off from the primary emotional experiences that are part of our human make-up. This is why reminding ourselves of our fundamental nature, in an ongoing way, is a treasured and valuable gift.

THE SIGNIFICANCE OF AUTHENTIC EXPRESSION

So, in light of these distinctions, you can breathe newly empowered awareness into how you express and how you emote. Feel the freedom in doing so. And remember that when you choose non-resistance, you're not letting go of yourself – you're not letting go of what makes you strong – you're just letting go of the resistance. And, as you know, doing so only serves to make you stronger.

If you are angry, then be authentically angry. Feel it in every cell of you. Function from the knowledge that there is a place for your anger, and that it need not be suppressed or disregarded. It's also important to know that feeling angry doesn't necessitate *acting* on your anger. Most people don't realise that they can just *be* with their anger, without having to *do* anything. Just because you feel the emotion of anger in relation to a particular person doesn't mean you have to grab their throat and strangle them. What's more, acting on your anger actually stops you from having the experience of being angry, because the behaviour that flows out of it typically makes you "feel better" (momentarily, at least): it removes the possibility for you to just feel angry without doing anything other than simply being present to the emotion.

> Authentically feeling your feelings doesn't mean you have to "do" anything at all. It simply means that you have the capacity to fully feel those sensations in your body, without tightening against them.

Similarly, just because you feel attracted to someone doesn't mean that you have to – or even should – pursue them romantically. You don't have to suppress the feeling, but you don't have to act on it either. Likewise, just because you feel the emotion of sadness doesn't mean that you have to place yourself in isolation, away from all other people. Pure emotion can simply be felt, experienced and moved beyond – all the time knowing there's a deeper aspect of who you are which is greater than *any* emotion you can experience. Feeling emotions is part of what it means to be human. Choosing to *act* on those emotions is a decision that you make. It is always your responsibility.

There is always a place for joy. If you are joyful, then express your joy without reservation. Live it out with everything that you have. Dance and swirl and delight in your experience, if that's what you feel like doing! But don't ever think that you have to be joyful *all* of the time, like the motivational "seminar junkies"! Don't think that "perpetual joy" is a requirement for your life, because that's a restrictive belief. Just stay aware that being joyful is simply *one* of many other emotions you're capable of experiencing.

> Whatever emotion you happen to be experiencing, simply give yourself permission to own it, without identifying with it. Realise that it's something you're experiencing – but it isn't *you!*

To have total diversity in your emotions is completely necessary for you to operate in a way that is full and enriching. Your moments of despondency are just as necessary as your moments of pleasure. Your moments of despair are just as necessary and essential as your moments of connection and love. Your moments of pain are just as necessary as your moments of joy. They must *all* be in place. They are all part of the entire colourful tapestry of your life. An incredible piano concerto features a full and expansive range of notes – not just the same one or two notes being played over and over again. Every single moment counts. And the *spaces* are important too. There must be spaces in-between the notes of a piano concerto in order for there to be music that flows and that captures the hearts of those who listen. Without these spaces – the moments of "nothing" – there would be no music! Those seemingly meaningless "nothings" are just as integral to the creation of the beauty of the music as the very notes themselves.

If every moment of your life was replete with total joy and ease, you actually wouldn't know that what you were experiencing was joy. A fish that lives in the ocean doesn't known that it's wet, because it has never known what it means to be dry. And so, it's the very existence of the dichotomies in our lives – the elation and the melancholy, the happiness and the worry, the sweet and the sour – that serves to shape and mould our experiences into what they are, and give them perspective. To accept and embrace this organic ebb and flow as pure inevitability frees up tremendous energy inside of us to do things and to make connections with possibilities that wouldn't otherwise be present.

It's these very dichotomies that bring richness and texture into our lives. After all, if there was never any darkness – if there was only light – it wouldn't be possible for us to see the beauty of the stars.

> One of the secrets of living confidently is about learning to embrace *every* emotion without thinking that it needs to be different from the way that it is!

I truly do believe that one of the greatest realisations we can make as human beings is to arrive at the position of appreciating that all of the emotions we feel are not really separate from each other. They are all ultimately connected; just as humans are all ultimately connected. They are not present to be labelled as "good" or "bad", but, instead, to draw us back to the truth that they are all integral to the totality of the ongoing adventure of our lives. They are just as fully connected as east is to west, or as winter is to summer. They are just as dynamically related to each other as inhalation is to exhalation, and as morning is to evening. They are just as primary and necessary for the uninhibited expression of our being in the same way that a compass must have opposing poles in order to function as a universal guidance system. One cannot exist without the other. Why do you think it's possible for humans to cry with sadness one day, and cry with joy the next? It's because the mode of expression we refer to as "crying" is connected to an expansive range of experience, not just to that of upset or despair. From this consideration, no experience that we have is a "bad" experience, or even a "good" experience – *it just is what it is!*

When we function from this wakefulness, *this is when we are our most human* – when we accept completely the full expression of our humanity, regardless of what's going on around us or whom we're with. And this is what it's like to be completely open to whatever shows up – and yet fully confident – because there is simply no resistance to the organic unfoldment of what's occurring. We realise that whatever's occurring is unable to strip us of the essence of our fundamental strength, because that aspect of who we are is changeless.

Remember: *you are not a victim of your feelings*. You only become a victim of your feelings when you identify with them. And, regardless of whatever feelings you're experiencing, what carries you through any of these moments is the realisation that you are so much more than the sensations inside of your body, and always will be!

> Real strength exists in owning your emotions, instead of allowing your emotions to own you.

You own your emotions as soon as you realise that you are always greater than they are. Owning your emotions is about feeling through them fully and completely, whilst maintaining connection to your deeper strength. It's about knowing that your solid foundation never changes. And you can also allow your confidence to be consolidated by the knowledge that the emotions you experience are the very same emotions that all others humans on this planet are vulnerable to as well. Don't ever believe that you are alone in this way. We are all emotional creatures. Our vulnerability is part of what makes us human, and we're all being pushed and pulled by the very same forces of the universe that contains us.

When you come to know that your emotions are not who you are – but simply sensations that you're experiencing in your body – it changes the very relationship you have with yourself. You function from a higher standpoint. You become the observer of your emotions, instead of a victim of them. You command a pervasive state of awareness that exists *over* and *above* all of your emotional experiences. This is a powerful position to operate from. It means that you're ready for anything. It means that, whatever you're experiencing, you can experience it fully; at the same time knowing there's a deeper place within you that is greater. And this stable core – this essential foundation – exists independent of what's happening. And through the potency of this, you no longer fear or have anxiety about what feelings you're going to experience, because you know you're strong enough to endure anything that comes along. Instead of reacting, and creating dissonance inside of you, you maintain your inner reserve. You simply notice. You notice from a place of heightened and empowered consciousness, without the exhausting struggle of resistance.

There is also tremendous value and deep personal comfort in remembering that *all* of your emotions and experiences are part of a much wider and far more expansive journey than only what's observable in the immediate moment. There is contentment to be found in becoming aware that all of the emotions that run through you are all serving to lay the foundation for events in your life which are yet to come – events you couldn't possibly know about. Even your moments of suffering and anguish and despair are preparing and strengthening you for those very times ahead.

> When you connect to the certainly within you, you withstand the uncertainty around you.

Real confidence means looking at whatever's taking place, and how you're emotionally responding to it, and seeing the deeper truth that's behind it all – the powerful essence of you. Real confidence is about choosing to ride the unpredictable wave of life without ever losing sight of the connection you have to your unconditional source of strength, no matter how challenging or strenuous things become. It's about being able to have a conversation with another person – being unashamedly open about yourself – and allowing them to appreciate the sincerity in your voice and your behaviours as you speak. It's about not being ashamed of saying, "Actually, things are very difficult for me at the moment" – if that's what you're truly experiencing – and being completely comfortable expressing that, without guilt. True confidence is about letting go of the need to convince others that you are "perfect" and infallible. It's about being willing to openly share your humanity with people because you know it's the *same* humanity that's at the heart of all of us.

There is so much interior strength to be found in the authenticity of being this way. When you operate out of this openness and authentic expression, you never lose your power. It generates connections between people that are incredible. People around you instinctively respond to you more positively, because they feel the deep resonance of your truth. There is no posturing or pretence. They sense your personal integrity, and it inspires them to be more of who they are.

Living this way, even up until the moment in which you are about to draw your very last breath, you'll be breathing certainty into the knowledge that you were able to simply be present to every one of the experiences of your life – all the sorrow, all the joy, all the pain, all the suffering, all the longing, all the delight, all the desire, all the surprise, all the grieving, all the loss, all the passion, all the love, all the laughter – and you'll realise that *every* one of those moments contributed to the vibrancy and the richness of your life. Every one of them!

This is part of what it really means to be *confident* in the world: to openly welcome and embrace *all* of the moments of your life, and to be able to do so without letting go of who you are! In living through the potency of this awareness, you will be imbued with the very interior resources that fortify you to face great challenges, and move beyond them each and every time.

"When your confidence is based on what's outside of you, your sense of security will always be tentative and unstable, because what's outside of you is always subject to change. But when your confidence is based on what's inside of you, you generate an internal stability that is permanent and unwavering, because the truth of who you are never changes."

–Julian James

CHAPTER SEVEN
Give Up the Need for Everyone to Like You

"The highest level of consciousness is one in which we give up the need for the approval of others."

–Abraham Maslow

If there's something you can decide to do immediately to move powerfully in the direction of living your life from a position of integrity and strength – as opposed to being at the mercy of exterior influences – it is this: *completely let go of the desire for everyone to like you!*

This seems to be such a simple notion, yet it's something most of us find very difficult to accept. We don't want to be disliked by others. We would much rather walk into a room and know that everyone is going to instinctively like us, understand us and appreciate us. We want unanimous acceptance. And, when we don't get it, we feel there's something "wrong". We seem to be so against the idea that there are simply going to be certain people who, for whatever reason, won't resonate with who we are, or value the qualities that make us unique. But this is not a reasonable desire or expectation to hold, neither is it an expedient one!

Here's the truth: not everyone that you meet is going to like you! It's the sharp taste of reality! There will always be those that won't like you, no matter what you do! Put this candidly, it seems somewhat draconian. Yet it's true for us all. And when you meet someone who responds to you this way, you don't need to question it, you don't need to find out why, you don't need to respond with hostility and you don't need to try to "resolve" anything. All that you need is to accept that this person's viewpoint represents part of the unfolding of his or her journey, in that moment. As such, the best way to acknowledge it is from a place of compassion, not resentment. You simply have to recognise that their response to you is as much a reflection of *them* as it's a reflection of you. You must regard it as just a pinpoint on their individual path to coming to understand their relationship to the world – and to others – through the perceptual filters that they use to make sense of things.

What others think of you shouldn't be what's most important to you. What's most important to you should be what *you* think of you!

The need for approval is nothing more than a manifestation of fear. It's the fear that others won't think highly of you, or accept you in some way.

Therefore, to begin to access a way of being fearless in the world requires you to give up the need for the approval of others.

> It's an inevitability of life that you're going to encounter people who won't like you! Becoming *comfortable* with this truth affords you tremendous personal freedom.

I used to know a woman who was so afraid of the idea of other people not liking her that she bent over backwards – trying to please *all* people, *all* of the time – just so she could be "liked" by them! She literally did everything she could to get on the "right side" of her peer group and co-workers, regardless of the consequence.

The result, however, was that – through her neurotic fixation towards being accepted by all of the people in her environment – many of them lost their trust in her. This was because she tried so hard to accommodate and oblige *everyone*, she relinquished her connection to her most valuable quality: her personal honour. She did things and said things that appeared totally out of character, as her behaviour began to operate out of a sycophantic and ingratiating position. She allowed her congruence to seep away. Her impassioned desire to be liked started to erode her character. She spent far too much time and effort making sure that everyone around her responded to her in a favourable way. As a result, her entire energy shifted. It actually became very unpleasant to be around this woman. She exuded the stink of desperation.

It is impossible for a person to hold onto their honour and integrity as a human being when they have made it their priority to put other's opinions of them *before* their own.

> Never compromise your integrity in order to ingratiate yourself with another person.

We've all had the experience of encountering a certain person who has clearly had a *negative response* to us, from the very first moment. This might not happen very often, but, from time to time, this primal response is bound to occur – and it takes place in spite of our best intentions. No one is totally exempt from this potentiality. This kind of occurrence takes place between people in offices and nightclubs and restaurants and aeroplanes and every other environment you can imagine. And it can happen (and very frequently does) even *before* we get to speak to the person or interact with them in any way. This is because our personal energy transcends the realm of language. People just become aware of our presence, and their response to us occurs entirely instinctively and intuitively. It occurs *preconsciously*. This means that it takes place *before* they are able to rationalise it for themselves in a cognitive way.

This is attributed to the fact that we are *energetic* beings. Our personal energy is the discernable quality of resonance that we radiate from within ourselves. We both exude energy and are able to sense the subtle vibratory energies that emit from those around us. These energies affect how we feel about certain people and how we respond to them. And when we hear people talking about "good vibes" and "bad vibes", this is precisely what they're referring to – the intuitive feelings they "pick up" from people. The term "vibe" (used colloquially) is simply the abbreviated form of the word "vibration".

There is nothing enigmatic about the notion of human energetic vibrations. It's a very primitive and primal characteristic that's inbuilt into the instinctual way humans interact. Energy is highly discernable by us. (It's also, of course, a dominant trait of the animal kingdom.) We sense and become aware of people's energy all of the time, in different environments. We all know what it feels like to be around people who send off "positive" vibrations, and we also know what it feels like to be around people who project "negative" vibrations. There are just certain people that, through their very energy, make it enjoyable and effortless for us to be with them. And, at the other end of the spectrum, there are certain kinds of people who make it less desirable to be around because their personal energy is dissonant and discordant with our own energy.

We can sense threatening and hostile energy from people. We also recognise the energy some people exude which makes us unable to trust them. People also commonly report instances in which they spend a few hours with a particular person, and feel totally "drained" as a result. These are all examples of how the energetic vibrations of those around us are integral to how we respond to our fellow humans. People's energy can also have a negative impact on our own, unless we know how to manage and control our internal resources such that we remain unaffected.

Our "vibrations" are connected to our emotional states. As our emotional states change – based on the events that take place in our lives, and how we choose to respond to those events – our vibratory energies also change. Our vibes create a particular "atmosphere" or "resonance" around us.

If you return home from a funeral, your energy is likely to be a certain way. But when you spend a whole hour in a yoga class, and you're feeling a sense of balance and euphoria, your energy is very different. If you have a corrosive and bitter argument with your partner, you emanate a negative vibration. The energy of the disputation permeates you. It seeps into everything you do, until you compose yourself, realign and come back to your centre. But if you go to see a spectacular Broadway show – the kind that enlivens your spirit and your senses – your energy also becomes enlivened.

Our energies shift and change according to a multitude of factors. And even though this is true, it's also true that most people have a baseline vibration, which is the energetic vibration they emit the majority of the time. It's their default energy. This is their predominant vibration, which is recognised by others, and specifically associated with them. Just think of someone you know very well. What do they project the majority of the time? How do they show up to the world? That's their default energy.

So, in light of this knowledge, it makes sense that not all energies, from all people, are going to be congenial *all* of the time. This is very normal; even expected. Therefore, when we notice unfavourable responses from others – in relation to *us* – their responses can often actually have *nothing* to do with us at all. Instead, their responses serve as a reflection of who *they* are. So if a person with a weak and unstable energy (someone with very limited self-confidence) encounters someone who exudes a resounding energy of strength, confidence and composure (whose vibration is much greater than the other person's) the other individual can feel overwhelmed by this, and have an instantaneous "negative" response. He may feel perturbed and disconcerted. And this isn't because there is anything "wrong" with the energy of the more confident individual. It's actually because the more confident person reminds him of what he isn't able to express for himself. He reminds him of his inability to remain stable and composed.

Marianne Williamson – the remarkably talented and renowned spiritual writer – touched upon this idea when she wrote: "There is nothing enlightened about shrinking so that other people won't feel insecure around you."

This is why it doesn't make sense to be constantly looking around us, hoping not to offend anyone or to make anyone feel uncomfortable. Ultimately, this is something that is out of our control, because we never know what's going on for other people. We never know what may, or may not, trigger such responses in others, because these "triggers" are inevitably different for everyone. And so, as long as we hold good intentions for ourselves, and for all humans, we should remember that what's of far more importance is to stay true to the expression of our inherent uniqueness – to be who we are completely. Being *this* way, we're more capable of inspiring those around us to find connection to their own unique gifts. And we don't need to make any "extra effort" in order to do this – we need only be who we are, and express ourselves without shame or reservation.

THE INTERPLAY OF PERSONAL ENERGY

The "dance" and interplay of the different energies that emanate from people are fascinating to observe. And, as I've already mentioned, it is unreasonable to expect *all* people to agreeably connect *all* of the time, within *all* social and professional contexts. Life just doesn't work that way.

Imagine a private dinner party. Numerous guests attend, but many of them have never met before. In circumstances such as these, it's not uncommon for a certain member, sat around the same table, to not like the "vibe" of another guest. And, for the most part, none of this is explicit. It takes place on a level that is predominantly unspoken, and is felt *energetically* by those concerned. It manifests viscerally in the body as a set of instinctual signals that, if translated into words, might be interpreted into something like, "I'm not sure about her ... there's just something about her I don't like!" This is as primal as it comes. The person is unable to put this exactly into words. It's just a "feeling" that they get. It's energy!

The same kind of discordance can also transpire when a brand new employee enters into a working environment for the very first time. This is especially true when all of the other workers have already been there for several years, and therefore have their "hierarchical positions" – the explicit, and sometimes more implicit, status positions within the group – well established. The sudden introduction of someone "new" threatens the positions that these people hold (both professionally *and* socially), and can therefore incite aversion, and, in some cases, direct confrontation. There is a tendency for many people to simply not like the introduction of a "new player" into the working nest. It alters the energy in the room. They would much rather stay with what is *familiar* to them, because there's comfort in familiarity.

And there are countless other examples of this same initial negative response that is generated and discerned through the many layers of our often subtle communicative channels. It happens in business meetings, at the local supermarket, at the bank, on the street, at weddings – anywhere that people are present! It might not be "fair" – it might not seem "right" on some occasions – but the truth is that it happens. That's just the nature of human beings. As much as we can and should grow to embrace and accept all kinds of individuals, it is *still* inevitable that "clashes" between people will occasionally take place. And when they do, the worst thing we can do is to react with resistance.

"Lean too much on the approval of people, and it becomes a bed of thorns."

–Tehyi Hsieh

Regardless of how or why these "clashes" happen, there is no virtue in allowing them to disconcert us. They don't even need to be anyone's "fault", because looking for blame rarely reconciles such encounters anyway. Sometimes we find out why a person feels this way, and other times we don't. But we don't even need to know why. We are all on different paths. We've all been present to different life experiences. We all hold different beliefs about people, and about the world.

As I've already mentioned, people can often make up their mind about you before they get to know who you really are. And this can be based on something as minimal and exterior as the type of clothing you choose to wear, or the way that you speak, or even a certain mannerism that forms part of how you communicate. And if a person has grown to associate a particular mannerism, or a particular style of speaking, with someone that they don't like, they will instinctively make that decision about *you,* as well, when they recognise that similar feature in how you express yourself. In many cases, that person won't even know why he feels as though he doesn't like you. The association will be so deeply rooted at a subconscious level, he won't know the reason. He'll just have an innate visceral response generated by the triggering of those negative associations. From this perspective, he can't be blamed for things that are taking place outside of his conscious awareness, especially if he doesn't have the knowledge or resources to gain deeper understanding. So the best we can offer is our compassion, even if such consideration isn't being returned. And it's possible to have compassion without weakness, which is the kind of compassion I'm speaking of – compassion which emerges from a position of strength.

I remember being invited to a summer barbecue party in the heat of July. Various people were sitting at different positions in and around the garden – drinking, eating and talking. When I arrived, I immediately sensed great dissension between two particular female guests, who'd already been there for some time. Everyone else could sense this. The "resistant energy" permeated the air. These two women had never met each other before this day, yet the coming together of their energies generated a "resistance" that was impossible to ignore. In fact, in this case, intervention by the host of the party soon became necessary before their disharmony escalated towards a physical scuffle.

It's so interesting that two human beings – with no prior knowledge of each other – can come together within the same environment and just not "connect" in that moment. This is never the most preferable outcome, when it happens. But, when it does happen, we just have to accept the inevitability of it. We just have to accept that the way people arrive at their own feelings about others – and about *us* – is almost totally out of our control. It's an inescapable component of the ongoing experience of living in a world of tremendous diversity. This doesn't mean we shouldn't operate with kindness and consideration. We should always commit to our *own* good intention towards our fellow man. As long as we operate from honest compassion – regardless of how others react and respond – we can rest in the contentment of a principled standpoint.

Ultimately, we are all on the same side anyway. Despite whatever takes place between people, we are all part of the same ongoing human experience. We all share the same fundamental humanity – *all* of us. And when we can regard others – even those people who express dislike towards us – from a place of compassion, instead of retaliation, it frees us to be more of who we are. It allows us to move forward in the direction of our lives with a sense of ease, instead of becoming consumed with things that ultimately bring us no value or gratification.

SEEING WHAT'S BEHIND THE COMMUNICATION

"I'd rather be hated for who I am, than loved for who I am not."
–Kurt Cobain

Once you give up wanting every person you meet to approve of you – when you truly let this go – you will raise and fortify your energy. You will emanate a refreshed and empowered personal vibration. Your sheer energy will cause the people that are not aligned with your deepest values to retreat. But, at the same time, you will instinctively draw new people to you – people you'll effortlessly resonate with. You'll connect with these people instantly and establish valuable lasting friendships and relationships. You won't have to "work" at this – it'll happen all by itself. Your very way of being will take care of everything. By being totally true to who you are, and to the values you hold – in a completely uncompromised way – you'll bring into your life the people who will support and nourish you the most, and who'll naturally create the space for you to inspire them as well!

Countless times, I have seen examples of this in my own life. Once I let go of a person who is no longer aligned with my personal energy and direction, this opens the space for brand new possibilities. I then find myself unexpectedly meeting people who just "click" with me. It's magical! But you have to clear the space for this to occur. You really wouldn't believe some of the unusual situations in which I've met new people, who have become very good friends! But every time this has happened, I've always been fully centred within myself. I've always been fully connected to my truth.

> The moment you allow your own worth to be based on how someone else feels about you is the moment you give up your power to them, and assign them permission to control how you feel.

The embracement of this way of operating is totally liberating. Literally, when you commit to this quality of authenticity – completely letting go of the need to win the approval of any particular individual – *you will be free*. It lifts the burdensome weight that bears down on you when you are too invested in the thoughts of others. Because of this, you'll feel a pleasurable lightness in your body. You will emanate the essence of self-directed truth. No longer will you feel the pressure to diminish who you are for anything, or anyone. You'll just be who you are – fully expressing the gift of your uniqueness – and fully expressing what you stand for in the world. It will always be far more essential to stay true to who you are, and remain congruent with your values, than to compromise and devalue yourself in the attempt to gain the admiration, respect, attention or agreement from someone else. Living like this, absolute confidence will have no choice but to be present for you in abundance.

PEOPLE'S FEELINGS TOWARDS OTHERS ARE ALWAYS SUBJECT TO CHANGE

Can you think of someone who you initially didn't enjoy being around, but with whom you eventually became very good friends? As peculiar as it *seems*, things can very often turn around 180 degrees! It's an outcome that happens more than you think. People, who, at first, don't "connect" with each other, can, over time (or sometimes very quickly) begin to see things within the other person that they grow to appreciate and respect. On occasions, the people that initially don't "gel" with us can even eventually become some of our closest and most loyal companions. It's happened to me many times.

This is also attributed to the fact that, as we evolve and grow, our tendencies, needs and values change. We are drawn towards *new* people, and away from the kinds of people we used to spend time with. This is all part of the "dance" of human interaction. There's nothing really "wrong" or "right" with any of it – it just *is* what it is. It's all a component of our journey. And the more we begin to accept this – once we really become comfortable with the possibility of *any* outcome – the less we feel "bad" when we discover that someone doesn't like us, or share our sense of humour, or see the world the same way we do, because we see the inevitability of it. We realise that this person is simply on his own path, the same way that we are on ours. If there's a "bad connection", it doesn't always mean it will stay that way. And even if it does, this serves as further learning for us as well. Either way is just perfect.

The nature of how humans operate, interact with and perceive one another is fascinating. We are highly sentient beings. There are so many subtle distinctions that comprise the way we communicate. We correspond with others through what we say, but also what we don't say. We send signals to our fellow humans through how we move and shift our bodies, even via the tiniest of mannerisms and expressions. The qualities inside of our vocal tonality, as we use language, also have powerful effect. There are millions of pieces of data emanating from us, all of which are sending signals to those we come into contact with.

Being aware of the subtleties woven within the fabric of how humans interact is an important factor to appreciate. This relates to all of the ideas I've been expressing here, because there are limitless "reasons" and "rationalisations" people will arrive at in trying to convey why they don't like certain other people: "He's too serious"; "She's not serious enough"; "He's too intense"; "She just makes me feel uneasy"; "I don't trust the way she looks at me"; "I don't like his voice"; "She moves too slowly"'; "He smiles too much"; "She doesn't give enough in a conversation"; "He puts me on edge" ... and on and on it goes!

"I cannot give you the formula for success but I can give you the formula for failure, which is: Try to please everybody."

–Herbert Bayard Swope

Regardless of your age, regardless of your ethnicity, regardless of the values and the qualities that you possess, just accept the fact that you are *still* going to encounter people who aren't going to like you, or respond to you positively.

Some people will mention that they like us because of a particular personal characteristic, whilst others won't enjoy being around us for the *very same* reason! I remember someone telling me, at a networking event I was performing at, that they felt uneasy around me because I seemed very "mysterious" to them. Yet, on the very same evening, I met a lady who told me, "Julian, you're not like most other guys. You're different and mysterious, and I really like that about you!" So do you see how trying to control people's responses to us is a hopeless endeavour? There are just far too many factors present to be able to modulate them in order to be liked by all people – even if you wanted to! There is absolutely no virtue in even attempting to appeal to the differences and expectations of *every* person that you meet in the desire to ensure they like you. Don't even try! Just let go – let it *all* go! Instead, commit to being who *you* are authentically, because being your authentic self will always be your most valuable quality. It's what makes you, *you!* People will recognise this authenticity in you, and know it to be nothing less. And the few individuals who don't resonate with you will have their own reasons, and sometimes they won't even know why. It really doesn't matter.

WHO YOU TRULY ARE DOES NOT INCLUDE OTHER PEOPLE'S THOUGHTS ABOUT YOU

Too many people are infatuated with the idea of having a "good reputation". Yet the term is misleading. The term "good reputation" implies a collective consciousness about an individual. But such a thing isn't possible. It's not possible for there to be only *one* reputation. There can only be *many* reputations, according to the individuals doing the "reputing".

Why do you think feature films receive such varied and disparate reviews? Why are film reviews never consistent with each other? Why do you think that the *same* film can receive absolute praise and commendation from one source, and be criticised by another? It's because the different reviews have come from *different* people, with *different* tendencies and *different* ideas about what constitutes a great film! This seems almost too obvious to even need to mention, but it's astonishing how people just don't see the simplicity in this. Having one singular and pervasive reputation is not possible. It's only possible to have multiple reputations from multiple sources.

So, as you move along the journey of your life, realise that you will always have *both* "great reputations" and "terrible reputations", and all other kinds of reputations as well – all at the same time. And also realise that none of these are "true"! They're just the interpretations of other people. And the reason these interpretations cannot be "true" is that real truth is constant, and never changes. There are very few "real truths" in this sense. The law of gravity is an example of real truth. We can test it, and receive immediate feedback from our environment that consolidates our knowledge of this universal pattern! (Just let go of your pen and watch what happens to it.) We know that, for as long as we are on planet Earth, the law of gravity will always apply – it will always be true. There is no condition in which this law doesn't apply. It's a law that is constant.

In the same way, *you* are the only constant. But what can't be constant, and what you can't control, are the beliefs and ideas people make up *about* you. And when you really understand that these are just *meanings* that they've constructed – and not "universal truths" – any concern you have about them drops away. And then, once again, all that's left is the space for you to simply be who you are!

If a person claims that they feel "uncomfortable" around you, you have to realise that such a response is predominantly a reflection of *them*, not a reflection of *you*. After all, consider what would have to be going on inside of that person that would allow them to feel that way around you? What would they have to be lacking for them not to be able to remain internally stable whilst in your presence? In a similar way, you've also probably come across people who say that they find certain people "intimidating". Again, this kind of behaviour is more a reflection of *their* own inability to maintain composure than it is of anyone else's ability to "cause" them to feel that way. If someone feels nervous around you, this is evidence that they haven't developed the capacity to maintain control of their own internal responses. It's proof that they lack equanimity. They have allowed themselves to become destabilised by another person. It's therefore about *them*, not you.

> There is no such thing as an "intimidating person" – there are only people who *allow* themselves to be intimidated!

If you walk into a post office, and the server behind the counter isn't friendly towards you (but has been seen to be friendly to the other customers) just remember that these kinds of responses and reactions take place *everywhere*, with all sorts of people – not just with you! If there's a particular person you work with who makes it clear that they don't enjoy working with you or being around you – and your job demands that you have to interact with them on a consistent basis – this may pose a challenge. But, from a more empowered perspective, it presents you with an *opportunity* to strengthen your character and deepen your core confidence.

If you're at a social gathering and you make the effort to engage someone in conversation – and it's clear that this person isn't interested in speaking with you – just accept that this is what's happening, even though it may not seem to be particularly pleasant. You have no idea what this person has been through. Perhaps they have just lost their mother, or maybe their job has been placed into jeopardy, and they're in deep thought about their financial future. Don't become angry, just accept it, embrace it, and move on. And, all the while, in your thoughts, wish this person the very best for their life – and *mean* it! Send them good thoughts. Wish for them great health, prosperity and contentment. Sincerely wish them well. When you do this, you operate with centredness. It feels wonderful to be this internally free. It's far better than allowing your awareness to become preoccupied with unhelpful clusters of ideations and projections about the other person that really don't serve you in any way at all.

> *"To be one's self, and unafraid whether right or wrong, is more admirable than the easy cowardice of surrender to conformity."*
>
> –Irving Wallace

Just remember that these types of encounters are all part of the unavoidable nature of being human and co-existing within a colossal pool of billions of other humans. Not *all* humans are going to connect *all* of the time. Don't expect everyone to support you. Don't expect that everyone will be "on your side". And, at the same time, don't become addicted to the people that *do* support you. Just notice that there is a balance. Become comfortable with either outcome. As long as you hold good intentions for people – and act from sincerity, strength and purpose – you're doing the right thing. No one can fault an authentic, well-intentioned person.

We should always be well-intentioned towards others, because we are all ultimately sharing the same experience. But trying to "force" things to be a "certain way" will be rendered futile. All we can do is operate from our own sense of integrity, because these are the elements that we *can* control. Then, from this position, we can just allow whatever happens to unfold in its own way. This includes allowing others to have their own negative responses – even if those responses happen to be to us!

There are around seven billion people on the face of the planet. Seven billion! Consider the immensity of that! There are so many people in the world that you couldn't possible hope to meet even a tiny fraction of that number through the course of your lifetime. So why would it even bother you that a certain individual doesn't like or approve of you when there's a glorious and enormous ocean of rewarding human connections awaiting your exploration?

When your source of confidence is connected to that which is changeless – that divine essence within you that is unconditional, ever faithful and ever present – it *isn't possible* for another person to make you feel "small" or unworthy, because they have no control over that changeless essence within you, which can never be taken away!

Ultimately, being a confident person – having unshakable confidence – encompasses the awareness that standing solidly in your truth sets the foundation for engaging with others authentically. When you can be this way, you'll no longer be affected when a person doesn't approve of who you are. You'll be able to recognise the predictability in it, whilst also realising that their response to *you* is more about *them*, even if they think it's about you. And when all of this is observed through compassionate eyes, you can simply view it as just another singular moment along your journey, as you move through the world, being who you are unconditionally.

"*You are whole and perfect and complete, just as you are. If you should ever feel anything less than this, what's missing isn't your state of completeness – what's missing is your awareness of your completeness in that moment. And you can shift your awareness in an instant.*"

–Julian James

CHAPTER EIGHT

Finding Comfort Inside of Discomfort

"Step into discomfort and get comfortable with it!"

–JULIAN JAMES

The picture above is a photograph that was taken during a particularly frosty afternoon, in the month of December. Not long before this moment was captured, it had been lightly snowing. And so, for me, this was the perfect moment to venture down to my local *London Underground* station with my yoga mat. I took off my shirt and assumed some *al fresco* yoga positions, right in front of the station entrance! Meanwhile, people were entering and leaving the station. I did this in the name of *outrageous fun*, because that's the kind of sense of humour I have! But there's more to this, as you will discover!

You really should have seen some of the reactions of the people who passed by as I sat there, bathing in yogic bliss! (You can see the gazes of bewilderment from two people in the photo; but I can tell you that there were many more besides.) This was a very entertaining experience; much more entertaining for *me* than for anyone else! And that's exactly part of my motivation for doing such a thing.

I really do find it regrettable as to how awfully *serious* we've become as a culture. Most of us seem to be hurtling about at lightning speed, desperate to please the "boss". Most of us don't take a moment to stop, be still and breathe; because everything's so "important" and "serious". Yet, what we've missed is the fact that – when all is said and done – life actually isn't really that serious at all. Life is *precious* and *special* – yes – but it's not so intensely serious. One of my favourite authors, Bertrand Russell, said that, "One of the symptoms of an approaching nervous breakdown is the belief that one's work is terribly important."

When we bring intense seriousness to life, we miss the magic of it all. When we think that it's all so important, we get in our own way. We lose sight of the specialness inside of us. When we become so embroiled in this pandemic state of weighty importance, we disconnect from that place within us that is effortless, centred and at rest.

Needless to mention, the responses from the passers by at the station, as I engaged in my yogic pleasure, were nothing more than extremely predictable. It seems that this society finds it increasingly difficult to just let go once in a while, loosen up and lighten up. We have become so enmeshed in the "busyness" of life that we've forgotten how to see that it's all just made up anyway! We've forgotten how to stand aside from the chaos, breathe, and reconnect with our truth. But when we take the time to do this – when we give ourselves this gift of standing apart from the chaotic frenzy of our constructed culture – we rest into a pleasing state of equilibrium. When we are like this, we are living from our deepest essence.

THE CONSTRAINTS OF CULTURAL EXPECTATION

I sometimes think of the way society is structured as being like a very tight, overworked muscle: there's little room for movement, there is restriction, and there is pain and discomfort. But when that same muscle is mobilised, stretched, relaxed and massaged – not only does it feel wonderful – it opens up possibilities that, before, weren't possible at all.

For me, choosing to engage in what many would perceive as outlandish behaviours – such as my "experimental yoga" (and other fun activities) – is, besides being great fun, really about *stretching* the mould of what's *typical* and *expected.* It's my way of lightly poking fun at the fact that most of us are asleep. Most of us have fallen under the spell of the illusions of societal construction – the cultural fiction that engulfs us – all of the stipulations imposed upon us about *how* we should be, and even *who* we should be in the world. Therefore, by implication, our culture defines for us (and without our expressed permission) what it *means* to be human. But the truth is that this definition is *made up*, and does not bespeak universal truth.

That's why I see a great deal more inside of this single photograph than just a little eccentric amusement. In many ways, it stands as a metaphor for the importance of breaking through and reaching beyond these illusions, and embracing who we really are, instead of trying to be who others would prefer us to be. In the midst of this high-flying, fast moving world, it's a way of alluding to the fact that our society is, for the most part, bound and enslaved by these illusions. These fabricated distortions have been designed to keep us to be a certain way – the way that is *expected of us*. What's more, society tries to make us feel uncomfortable if we even dare do anything outside of the realm of what we've been told is "normal".

But are the people that have made a true and lasting impact in the world the types of people that stood safely at the sidelines of life and merely did what was "ordinary", "normal" and "expected" of them? Or did they step outside of the realm of "standards" and "expectations", fully embrace the totality of their uniqueness, and make a new stand?

The ideas imposed upon us only *appear* to be real because we have accepted them as real. Our strategy of knowing how to operate and behave is derived from our observations of others. Most people ignore their own sense of true inner direction. Instead, people look *outside* of themselves for that which can only truly be derived from inside of them. They look to others as a guide and a benchmark of "how to be", and then simply mirror what they observe through the behaviours of their fellow human beings. As a result, they become like sheep inside of the same pen – all doing what the other sheep are doing, with no one daring to step beyond the small confined space of the "conventional". Staying restricted in this way, humans miss the very *magic* inside of them – their unique individual expression! And part of the secret of reaching our deepest truth is in deciding to leave the sheep behind and escape from the pen!

Doing so, though, is not always a "comfortable" endeavour, as it inevitably includes the resistance imparted from those people who don't want us to reach our inspired individuality, because they'd rather that we stayed confined and restricted. That way, they're not forced into the position of having to evaluate themselves, and discovering that the reason they want to keep us "in the pen" is because they fear what it will reveal about *them* in the process.

Those who know me personally – my closest friends, my family, colleagues and associates – are more than aware of my *outlandish* sense of humour. They know I'm the kind of person who doesn't settle for the mundane or the "ordinary". They know that I enjoy "moving the bar"! And, to me, not settling for the mundane and the ordinary should be everyone's priority. Why? Because we are not mundane and ordinary creatures. We are divine and extraordinary beings! So why should you or I settle for anything less than our birth-given divinity? Why should we be quashed and repressed by those who want nothing more than for us to just be the same as all other people, so that we can be more easily controlled? Common behaviours generate common results.

Why should you compromise who you are based on the expectations of other people, or because of a set of false rules that have been put in place in order to control you? Here's the truth: you can either fall victim to these illusions and settle into the state of homogeneity (the state of being the same as others), or you can raise your personal standard and fully commit to being the fullest expression of *yourself*, embracing your gift of incomparable uniqueness. Which do you think will ultimately enrich you and fulfill you at a deep and lasting level?

BALANCE, ALIGNMENT AND TRANSCENDENCE

Yoga is fascinating to me. I discovered the form at a period in my life in which I was experiencing significant muscular imbalances. I was searching for a way to address these, and bring my body back into alignment. I was looking for something that would keep my body aligned, and allow my physical functioning to become more effortless and free from tension. Yoga, in addition to a number of other somatic disciplines – such as the incredible work of Thomas Hanna and Moshe Feldenkrais – gave me many of the answers I needed.

When you first move your body into many of the yoga positions (the *asanas*), they can be *uncomfortable*; even *extremely* uncomfortable. They force you to engage your physical structure in ways that you have probably never before experienced. You notice, for example, that particular muscles are tight and need to be lengthened. You notice, also, that other muscles are weak and required strengthening. You also notice asymmetries, which, over time, can be brought into balance. And the progressive integration of yoga discipline allows you not only to bring your musculature into alignment, but also to develop a much greater awareness of your body. It underscores the systemic relationship between the areas of your body, and how they function as a unified and cohesive organisation.

It emphasises the mind-body relationship. It also brings your attention to the regulation and conscious control of your breath. And commanding conscious control of your breathing patterns is, in itself, an incredible and transformational skill set.

If you were to ever approach someone immediately after they'd been practising yoga for an hour, and asked them to describe how they were feeling, the terms "wonderful", "glowing", "ecstatic" and other such adjectives, would typically comprise how they spoke about their experience. However, even though yoga (and other related somatic disciplines) facilitates and engenders sensations of incredible pleasure, the very same practice can also be very *uncomfortable.*

Especially at the initial stages of learning, when you are acclimatising yourself to the various positions and movements, there can be, and often is, great discomfort. But when you breathe and relax *into* the discomfort – when you breathe relaxation *into* the tightness of the muscles, and *into* those areas of your body that are highly contracted, the tightness begins to loosen and soften. Everything seems to open up and come to rest. And over time, what was once extremely uncomfortable becomes an enormously pleasurable and desirable sensation. It feels wonderful. Powerful neurochemicals pervade your body and these stimulate the desire to experience it more and more. And all of this speaks to the *magic* of "embracing discomfort", and finding comfort inside of it!

STEPPING INTO DISCOMFORT

Regardless of who we are, there can be lots of things that make us feel a sense of unpleasantness. For some of us, it's speaking to certain people on the phone. For others, it's leading a group activity or getting up to dance when people that we don't know are watching us. Some people feel uncomfortable learning new skills. Some people feel uncomfortable simply asking for what they want. Others feel uncomfortable in the presence of particular co-workers, or around members of the opposite sex.

In spite of what these specific behaviours or circumstances happen to be, there is a way to organise yourself internally such that, regardless of what's going on, or what you're doing, you are able to experience the awareness of feeling discomfort from a totally new frame of consideration. I sometimes call this being "comfortably uncomfortable".

We all have a threshold of comfort. It's different for each of us. It is also different for us within different situations and environments. A military soldier, for example, might be totally comfortable within situations of great threat and violence. He might be completely at ease amidst all of the aspects of warfare: guns firing, grenades exploding, the sounds of screaming men and the ever present threat of death. He might be totally unaffected by the duty of carrying dead bodies to the sideline. But the very same man can feel anxious and uneasy when he notices a woman he feels attracted to at a party. He can stumble over his words, go "red in the face", and exhibit signs of embarrassment and timidity.

And so, in thinking about the situations that make *you* uneasy and uncomfortable, what would happen if you actually found a way to be comfortable being uncomfortable? What would happen if you breathed and settled *into* the discomfort so that whatever you did, you knew you could relax into doing it, even if it was something you'd never done before? How would things be different for you if you operated *this* way? What would you be able to do more of? What fantastic experiences would you be able to have?

"To dare is to lose one's footing momentarily. Not to dare is to lose oneself."

–Soren Kierkegaard

I'll always remember the time that I suffered from blisters on my feet – blisters that lasted almost an entire week. My mother had purchased for me a new pair of school shoes to replace an old pair that had worn out. One morning, I sat down and forced my feet into this stubborn and inflexible pair of black leather lace-ups, straight from the box. To say they were uncomfortable would be a modest understatement. There was no softness or flexibility to these shoes at all. The leather uppers were tough and stiff. They felt like they'd been crafted from hardened steel! And as soon as I tightened the laces and stood up, I just knew that my innocent little feet were guaranteed a large dose of unpleasantness for the day to come!

I trotted off to school, trying in vain to ignore the top part of the shoes, which constantly and unforgivingly rubbed against the outside area of my ankles. By early afternoon both of my ankles were red and sore to the touch. My walking was awkward and unavoidably affected by the bulbous blisters that had quickly formed under each of my big toes. Even though I couldn't actually see the blisters at this point, I could feel that strangeness of sensing those unusual bags of fluid that squelched beneath me every step I took.

When I arrived home, I threw the shoes off my feet and carefully peeled away my socks. I prodded the blisters with my finger. They were unbearably sore and tender. I'd never had blisters before. This was my first exposure to them.

When I griped and complained about the blisters to my mother, she smiled, assuring me, through the tonality of calming maternal wisdom, "Just keep wearing those shoes, Julian; they'll soon wear in!" She was right. After just a few days, the shoes did wear in. The leather softened, and the shoes moulded and adapted to accommodate the specific shape of my feet. The discomfort disappeared very quickly. It was only then that I actually noticed what a smart and good looking pair of shoes they really were.

Wearing those shoes brought me stability and comfort for many months. In fact, when they eventually wore out, and it was time to replace them, I was almost sorry to see them go. Yet, now I had an understanding that the next pair of shoes might indeed be uncomfortable for a short while, but the discomfort would be fleeting and transitory, and my *experience* of that discomfort would *not* be the same!

What are your "shoes of discomfort"?

We've all had the experience of doing something that we felt ill at ease with and uncomfortable doing. We all know what it's like to feel a sense of tension and anxiety building up inside of us when we're faced with unfamiliar situations.

In the same way that there was great discomfort for me in stepping into those new leather shoes, what are the "shoes" – those things you know you really want to integrate into your life – that you've been putting off stepping into? What are the experiences you really want to be having, and know will ultimately serve you, but have avoided and held yourself back from, because it's more "comfortable" to stay exactly where you are?

If you are not experiencing the feeling of discomfort often enough in your life, you can be sure that you're not fully growing. You may be making small incremental changes, but significant growth requires us to step boldly into what makes us uncomfortable, and to do so frequently and with intention. So, if you don't experience discomfort regularly enough, you've more than likely found out where you feel "safe". You have more than likely decided to keep behind this illusory "safety-boundary" of your own construction. You've more than likely conditioned yourself to automatically avoid all circumstances that might move you too far beyond what you're currently accustomed to. But to stay within these confines is to deprive yourself of deep personal fulfilment, magic and discovery!

> Every time you experience discomfort, instead of allowing it to cause you to become uneasy, use it as an indicator that lets you know you're growing. Allow it to make you feel good that you've discovered a new threshold to transcend. Realise that staying with the discomfort until it passes will strengthen your capacity to endure future encounters with ever increasing degrees of confidence.

The great sadness is that most people will literally die not having experienced even a tiny fraction of what is truly possible for them, simply because stepping outside of what they feel is comfortable seems like "too much". And yet, the alternative is nothing more than a life of compromise – a life stripped of the very vital essence that makes life exciting and boundless, and the adventure it can be for all of us!

So give yourself the gift of transcending your experience: *step into discomfort and get comfortable with it!*

"Life begins at the end of your comfort zone."

–NEALE DONALD WALSCH

Below is a simple exercise. Follow the exercise all the way through. Don't just passively read the words, actually engage yourself and perform the exercise as I describe it to you:

EXERCISE: CHANGING YOUR LANDSCAPE OF COMFORT

1. Stop for a moment and fold your arms. Simply fold your arms in front of your chest the way you normally would.
2. Now look down at your arms and notice the specific way that you have folded them. Is your left arm over your right arm? Or is it right over left? Just notice how you have folded them.
3. Now *swap* the position of your arms. Put your arms into the *opposite* orientation to the way that you normally fold them. You will probably notice that this feels uncomfortable to you.
4. Hold this position for 10 seconds.
5. Now fold and unfold your arms 5 more times, each time putting them into the *new* position, and holding it for 10 seconds.
6. Now pause, and just notice how the new position feels after having completed this exercise.

> When you give yourself permission to become comfortable being uncomfortable, you open the pathway for unstoppable power and unlimited possibility!

What did you notice or discover about how your arms felt in the *new* position? At first it probably felt strange or uncomfortable, didn't it? However, did it feel as uncomfortable after you'd reached the end of the exercise? Or did you begin to generate a sense of familiarity and even *comfort* from the new position of your arms? Experiences like this teach us that, given the right input and intention, our entire system can adjust, adapt and re-learn incredibly quickly.

You probably discovered that the new position of your arms felt increasingly comfortable, even to the point of it feeling *familiar*. And this is a wonderful realisation to arrive at. It lets you know – experientially – that you can very quickly dissipate discomfort, and replace it with comfort. And all it takes is for you to make the decision.

What's also fascinating is that, before I drew your attention to this exercise, and to the specific way that you crossed your arms, you probably had no idea as to which way you habitually folded them. Yet, in the past, every time you've crossed your arms, you've crossed them exactly the same way. And you didn't even need to think about doing this. It was as if your arms just knew where to go, all by themselves, and they went there! This is referred to as an *unconscious behavioural pattern*, because it doesn't require any conscious awareness on your part to put your arms into their positions. Your body has performed the action so many times that the pattern becomes a deeply habituated process. And you have thousands of other unconscious inveterate behaviours.

EXPERIENTIAL INTEGRATION

Since you have patterns of behaviour that operate automatically and subconsciously, it means that many of the ways you respond to the stimuli in your environment are outside of your intentional control. However, there is a very specific method of managing your responses to the world around you so that you can function with tremendous power. You can actually employ the process of intentional habituation to move *towards* the experiences that are unfamiliar to you – automatically – as effortlessly and unconsciously as folding your arms. This means that when you are faced with a challenge or a situation that makes you uneasy, instead of making excuses to withdraw, your entire mind-body system is instinctively compelled to move *into* the experience, instead of away from it.

To do this – to deeply integrate this new way of responding – requires that you first make the shift consciously and with great intention. In the beginning, it will require a heightened awareness of the things that are taking place around you, combined with a large dose of willingness and tenacity to effectuate your desired outcome (in spite of how unpleasant it initially feels). Then, after many iterations of the process, your system will eventually come to learn the *new* response, which will then become your default behaviour. Ultimately, it will actually feel pleasurable and exhilarating for you to step into discomfort. You'll actually *enjoy* doing things that, before, made you extremely uneasy!

Scientific research substantiates the precept of *brain plasticity*. This refers to the fact that the brain structure is not fixed in form. Instead, it's an organ that is able to literally re-wire itself very quickly and very efficiently. The brain is capable of establishing brand new patterns, sequences and combinations of neural-firing (the way that neurons interact with other neurons).

This means that patterns of thought and action, repeated in an intentional and consistent way, create circuits which are referred to as *neuro-signatures*. These neuro-signatures are a specific integration of interconnected brains cells that carry the structure of a particular habit, feeling or behavioural response. And because our brains are extremely malleable – in that they are open to adapt and respond according to the direct feedback sequences that we process into them – we can, without difficulty, create more desirable habits and automatic behaviours through the repetition of specific and deliberately intended thoughts and actions. And as a result of every sequence of repetition, these neural pathways strengthen, and they continue to strengthen with every iteration. Eventually, the desired habits override and *replace* the old (less desirable) ways of functioning so that they become the dominant and automatic default responses (a process referred to as *neural pruning*).

Having a basic understanding of this process allows you to realise that you have at your command great power, great choice and great flexibility. The possibilities for your life are astonishing and exciting. Knowing how your brain learns and re-learns – and how you can replace one response with a totally new response – means you can feel comfortable stepping into uncomfortable situations, more and more of the time. It means you can choose how, when and where you wish to feel at ease. By doing so, you are literally installing into yourself a way of operating that goes far beyond what most people would even conceive of being possible for them. To do this is not just powerful – it is transformational beyond your imagination!

What's more, you will also be able to hold inside of your awareness the fact that, after the experience is done and is behind you, you'll have refreshed and solidified your confidence in that moment! You'll feel a sense of deep satisfaction knowing that you came through, and arrived at the other side of the event. You will feel uplifted that you didn't retreat. There will be a growing sense of personal freedom. Your neural connections will become thicker and stronger, making things even easier for you in future situations. You will delight in the knowledge that your very approach to living this way will serve to cultivate great comfort, integral strength and deep self-assurance.

DISCOMFORT INTO CONFIDENCE

> Waiting on the other side of doing the very thing that you know makes you uncomfortable will always be a refreshed sense of confidence. This is because you reinforce your capacity to go beyond what is familiar to you, and the very act of this strengthens and fortifies you in the most powerful way.

Another internal strategy that you can add to the entire way you approach entering uncomfortable situations is to go to the feeling of comfort *first*, and then act! After all, if you know that you're going to feel that wonderful sense of accomplishment and heightened integral confidence *after* the fact, then why wait until afterwards? Why not go there first? Why not bypass the discomfort and just go directly to how you'll know you'll be feeling after the experience?

I want you to really consider this concept, because it's something truly amazing! It will literally change the way you move through the world: If you know that after going through an experience you're going to feel wonderful and empowered, then you can go to that sense of feeling wonderful and empowered *before* you do whatever it is you're going to do! And you can do this because you have enough past experiences to draw from – of feeling empowered *after* the completed event – that let you know that this is how you're going to be feeling. And since you already know this, you can have certainty in how you'll be feeling. And you can therefore use this certainty to function as a sensorial bridge between the moment before the event and how you know you'll be feeling after it, such that how you'll be feeling after it becomes how you're now feeling before it!

This will become progressively easier for you – and increasingly satisfying – every time you run the process. This is about you taking control over your internal neurological responses – the mapping of your brain's neural network – which lead to this internal state. Eventually, the feeling of controlled comfort you experience will become so *familiar* to you that it will be available for you whenever you choose it to be. Your way of cognising what's going on around you, and your entire visceral response to what takes place, will shift to a new level of effectiveness and capability. And you will reach a point in which you'll hardly have to give this process any conscious thought or attention at all. It will happen automatically.

You don't increase your confidence by doing things you've always done. You increase your confidence by doing the things you've *never* done, continuously expanding your ongoing range of experiences. By following this principle – including everything I've taken you through thus far – you become far less amenable to the sensations of anxiousness and perturbation. Your inner reserve strengthens and solidifies. Like this, you feel unstoppable!

EVERLASTING TRANSFORMATION

Did you know that if you take a metal spring and stretch it beyond a certain point, it can never fully retract to its natural resting position? This is because every spring has a "threshold point" – the point at which, when exceeded, the spring literally changes form. So if you stretch a spring beyond its threshold, you alter the nature and behaviour of the spring – permanently! It literally cannot function in the same way again. The spring becomes lengthened and extended, and it *stays* that way. It cannot ever be shortened and returned to how it was. This is good news!

What I've been sharing with you here, relates directly to this very concept of the spring, because it's ultimately about transcendence. It's about "stretching" your parameters of comfort so much, so far and so wide, that you simply cannot go back to operating the way you previously operated! Your entire ongoing experience of the world is widened, enhanced and enlivened. You totally break through your former boundaries; and you do this so completely, and so expansively, that things cannot possibly return to how they were before. You rouse the lion of your audacious spirit. And when you commit to never stop treading this path of adventure and exploration, life can only become more and more fulfilling. Like this, it has no other choice! This is the *magic* of transcending your threshold experiences, because, waiting for you on the other side, will always be gifts and rewards in all manner of designs. When you live life *this* way, opportunities reach out to you through avenues that you simply cannot fathom. You will be surprised and delighted again and again.

So decide – right now – to make some personal decisions that will have a lasting effect on the rest of your life. Ask yourself what you've been holding off, up until now, that you know will make the most profound difference for you if you take immediate action. Find those "thresholds of comfort", and go beyond them! Go way beyond them! Step into the discomfort, and revel in it! And whatever these personal experiences happen to be for you, apply all of the distinctions I've been describing. Move powerfully in the direction of making these changes in how your respond, and let nothing stop you!

If, at the moment, you feel uncomfortable about the idea of going out on your own, or eating out on your own (without the "safety" of being with a companion) – and you know that this tendency is something that holds you back in many ways – then make immediate reservations for a "table for one" at your favourite restaurant! Make sure to put on your best clothes, and perhaps a splash of that lovely fragrance you save only for special occasions. And when you arrive at the restaurant, let nothing get in the way of you having the most exquisite and enjoyable meal. Order some champagne, or your favourite cocktail! Have a real party – all on your own – and care less what others think or say! Come to truly and honestly appreciate your own company, and realise that you're having dinner with a special and remarkable individual – yourself! Find yourself feeling more and more at ease being out in a public restaurant, and sitting at a table that is just for *you*. Enjoy every moment of the experience. And if anyone asks you why you're dining by yourself, you can tell them that you're celebrating the joy of being alive!

If you are uncomfortable speaking to new people, then go out and don't come home until you've spoken to 50 new people! Speak to new people in line at the supermarket, speak to new people in the high street, start a conversation with the old lady in the park, ask the librarian how his day has been when you return your books to the library, speak to that police officer you've never seen smile, spend a few minutes of your time chatting to that boy at the end of the road who always plays with his football, speak to the person sitting next to you on the train ... embrace *every* opportunity you can to engage others in conversation! Express genuine interest in the people you encounter, and realise that you have a fundamental connection with every one of them that is inextricable. Revel in the freshness of each connection you establish with a different human being. Do it again and again and again. Do it so much that the discomfort you associate with communicating with people you don't yet know has no choice but to dissipate, and be replaced with self-conviction and assurance. Do it so much that any thoughts of hesitation or apprehension become drowned out by the overwhelming sensation of the new and enveloping comfort that begins to pervade your mind-body system.

There are many people who feel uncomfortable walking into shops and department stores, to look at products, because they think they'll be forced into making purchases they don't really want to make. They don't want to encounter those proverbial "pushy salespeople" that ask you what your size is, and impel you to "try things on". They don't want to walk around a store and have an attendant watch and burn their every move. And so, the result of this is that there are lots of people who won't even dare to step inside some shops; especially those that are privately run, like the high-end women's boutique that featured in the film *Pretty Woman,* with Julia Roberts. Instead, they prefer to stand outside and peer through the window. This way, they avoid the discomfort of being scrutinised.

If this is you – if you are amongst those who feel a sense of awkwardness upon entering a shop in the way that I've described – then it's time to blow this useless and unnecessary response out of the water! So find the most expensive clothes boutique in your area. Set your watch for twenty minutes and make the resolute decision to not leave the shop until twenty minutes has passed. It may seem like forever, but this personal challenge will offer you a transformational and enlightening experience you will never forget. It will have a powerful positive impact upon you.

Go into the shop and have a good browse around. Also, if you are the only person in there at the time, this is all the better. Be friendly. Look the owner or the sales assistant in the eyes and tell her (in the nicest possibly way) that you have absolutely no intention of buying *anything!* Tell her you like what you see and that you intend to have a good look around, but that you're not going to make any purchases at all – absolutely none! Walk around the store. Do not rush. Bide your time. Enjoy yourself. Feel free to pick clothes up and even try them on. If you notice anyone staring at you, give them a smile. Tell them that you're really enjoying looking at their items. Stay there until you feel the discomfort reach its pinnacle and then notice how it begins to subside as you release the desire to continue feeling that way. Realise that, regardless of however anyone else in the shop happens to be behaving, that those behaviours are about *them* and not about you. Relish the moment.

You will find that, even before your twenty minute target has elapsed, you'll feel much more at ease. Understand that the "pressure" or discomfort most people feel in this kind of situation is generated more by *them* than by anyone else. After all, feeling uncomfortable is a decision that *you* make, not one that is made by others, for you! No one can *give* you discomfort – that actually isn't possible. If you feel uncomfortable in a situation like this (or in any other situation) it's because you have allowed yourself to feel this way. But it's ultimately a choice, and one that is under your control.

One evening I was having a conversation with a Sikh friend of mine. We were talking about the various traditions and religions of the word. She was explaining to me that few people realise that the Sikh temple (referred to as the *Gurdwara*) actually welcomes, and is open to, *all* people – regardless of belief or background! She also went on to say that, in spite of the friendly and convivial nature of the Gurdwara, she only sees Sikh people at the temple – hardly anyone else shows up!

Needless to mention – upon hearing this – I immediately suggested that we go along together, to join in on the prayers and the rituals, and to enjoy the food and drink offered afterwards. The idea of doing this was yet another way for me to widen my realm of comfort, and to become comfortable doing something totally unfamiliar. I didn't see it as something to avoid; I saw it as an opportunity to grow. After all, how many people would really go out of their way to place themselves in an environment in which they were effectively the "odd one out" in the entire room? Well, on this occasion, that's exactly what I did! I stepped right into the experience! And how fun and interesting it was! What's more, the dhal (a delicious hot lentil dish) and the fresh hot rotis made a wonderful meal to end the visit before we left.

Whatever those areas of experience happen to be for you – those situations that make you feel awkward or embarrassed – identify exactly what they are. Then, one by one, step boldly *into* the discomfort of each of those experiences! Make this not just a temporary task or assignment; make this your way of living! Make it a total priority in the strengthening of your character, and the fortifying of your confidence. Search out opportunities to place yourself into the kind of environments that challenge you, and don't stop until you've moved beyond them. Move boldly forwards until all discomfort inside of you is banished and annihilated! Smash to pieces the limitations that hold you back, and just notice how your confidence explodes through the roof!

> The experiences that exist outside your realm of comfort are the very experiences that contain your greatest rewards.

I once used to be very uncomfortable making phone

calls to businesses and potential clients. I just didn't like doing it. There was something about the process of contacting people on the telephone, in relation to business matters, that made me feel apprehensive. I wasn't even sure why I felt this way about it. Nevertheless, I'd always find creative ways to shift my attention away from these tasks and on to other less rewarding undertakings. The result, however, was that I began to sabotage potential opportunities and my own capacity to have control over this area of my life.

One day I made myself a promise. I simply promised myself that I would spend an entire hour doing nothing but making all of the phone calls I'd been putting off. I assembled a list of the people I needed to contact, and begun making those calls. And in the very beginning – during those first few conversations – my discomfort was at a level that was very unpleasant. But I didn't resign. I didn't forgo the personal promise I had made to myself. I kept on making those calls, one after the other, each time crossing off names from the list as I worked my way through it. I proceeded onwards in spite of the discomfort I was experiencing. And it wasn't long before I noticed something remarkable taking place within me.

Much *before* reaching the conclusion of the hour I had allocated to being on the telephone, I felt a potent shift. This shift was unmistakably present both in my physiology, and also in my entire cognitive awareness about doing what I was doing. Not only did I feel much less uncomfortable about dialing the various numbers and speaking to the people who answered, there was a rush of aliveness about me that felt wonderful, even transcendent. The awkwardness I previously felt had become displaced. A brand new way of relating had taken form. I became aware that what I'd been uncomfortable about was in fact just a simple list of tasks – nothing more than that – and the awkwardness I felt in relation to making those calls was a result of what I had "made up" about doing that. But it just wasn't true!

So the discomfort I initially experienced dissolved very quickly, and in its place was a pervasive sense of personal veneration. Since that day I've never again felt the same feelings of awkwardness in relation to carrying out this part of my business activity. Now I can just move forwards and take action. Making business calls is effortless for me. There is no hesitation; there is no discomfort. There is only a forward moving momentum that takes me from the awareness of what needs to be done, directly into the action itself. And this is the kind of ease and effectiveness that can be attained, within any area of endeavour, once the initial false response to discomfort is overridden.

When you notice discomfort inside of your body, instead of allowing it to concern you, become excited. Recognise the discomfort as confirmation that you're standing at the cusp of taking your personal command to the next realm of expansion and growth. Remind yourself that the feeling of unease is not permanent, only temporary. Allow this knowing to fill you up with positive energy and enhance your drive to achieve more, and to go further.

At the time when I was very dedicated to weightlifting, I remember being in the gym and enjoying the feeling of the lactic acid building up inside of my muscles as I'd squeeze out the last few repetitions of the weight. It was uncomfortable – yes – but in a certain kind of way, I loved it; even craved it! I thought about how my muscles were growing and strengthening, and it made me smile on the inside. I connected the feeling of discomfort with imminent strength – and this transformed my entire experience of it. Every week, I'd go back for more. And, each time, I pushed myself further. I built a momentum that drove me powerfully forward. And, in the same way, when you encounter situations that make you uncomfortable, you must hold at the forefront of your consciousness the idea that embracing the situation – and staying fully present *in spite* of what you're feeling – is causing you to become stronger from the inside out!

RELAXING INTO DISCOMFORT

Change the meaning of what discomfort offers you. Every time you feel ill at ease in a particular circumstance and you step inside of the discomfort – focusing only on relaxing and breathing *into* it – the discomfort will fade and dissipate. Ultimately, it has no other choice, because the signals that you're sending to your system are communicating that "all is okay". And all *is* okay. And what will be left over is a feeling of empowered clarity, at the core of you, knowing you've once again transcended the limitations of your previous comfort threshold, without conceding or withdrawing. It reminds you that – in the end – there is really nothing to be anxious about, because any anxiety has been created by *you* about the situation; not by the situation itself.

The next time you feel as though you're out of your depth, instead of going into your typical anxious pattern of response, simply *breathe into the discomfort* (your breath is the extension of your life force energy). Allow the discomfort to soften; to loosen up. Notice what happens when you stop resisting and engage with the natural flow of your inner centredness. Bring stillness into the discomfort, with an intention to maintain the stillness, and you'll build the priceless capacity to manage what life throws at you from a sense of interior stability.

This is why learning to physically relax the system – at will – is one of the most valuable and rewarding capabilities you'll ever develop. To literally decide to relax your musculature – when *you* decide to do so – as opposed to being uncontrollably at the mercy of the situations and the people around you, is where true internal power resides.

What I'm speaking of is *active relaxation*, not *passive relaxation*. It's a relaxed alertness that allows you to stay centred and calm, whilst also being fully able to handle immediately whatever needs to be handled at any given moment.

WELCOMING DISCOMFORT CAUSES DISCOMFORT TO DISSOLVE!

Educating your mind-body system – through the progressive internal cultivation of a foundation of *relaxed stability* – will enhance what I've been speaking of in ways that are very significant. The skill and capacity to bring your musculature into a state of rest – at your own volition – allows you to be present within environments (that would have otherwise caused you to become tense and anxious) with total ease, and free from worry or concern. And this is because it's possible to reach a level in which your own capacity to stabilise and control the somatic responses within your body becomes *greater* than any markers in the environment designed or intended to undermine you, intimidate you or cause you stress.

Most people, however, are unable to do this. Most people are actually unable to maintain full control of the internal responses that take place through and within their own bodies. As a result, they become powerless victims of their environment. They enter into situations in which the context and content of the environment overrides their ability to remain grounded and centred. They become overwhelmed, overthrown and destabilised. They lose all composure. They allow the situation to control them, instead of *them* having the ability to manage their own interior resources – remaining purposeful and unaffected – despite what's taking place.

Part of the exciting work that I carry out in my *Extreme Confidence Breakthrough* elite mentoring programme, with my private clients, is the development and mastering of this very skill-set: the ability to intentionally bring the system to a state of internal rest, and to do so *regardless* of the events taking place within the environment. Operating from this essential and unwavering foundation, an individual has much more choice, much more control and is much less susceptible to external negative influences. Naturally, this is a vital capacity to have. If a person isn't able to control the emanation of their personal energy, it renders them incapable of efficiently dealing with potential mistreatment or threat. It makes them vulnerable to those people who will exploit this shortcoming and take advantage of it.

Within my mentoring programme, my clients get to directly experience the power of this for themselves, in *real time*. I actually take them into the very experiences and situations that cause them to feel unstable and ill at ease. And then – whilst I am standing right there besides them – I lead them into the experience of what it's like to be totally comfortable, totally fearless and in total control of their energy. So by the time we are finished, their old fearful way of responding isn't there any more. It has been replaced with a powerful internal command that they can bring into *any* future experience they wish!

Embodying this wisdom and skill ensures that you can function optimally and powerfully and with great intention. It begins by noticing what takes place for you – and within you – when you are internally at ease, grounded and directed; and then making this the pervasive foundational way that you move through the world.

TAKE YOURSELF TO YOUR EDGE, AND GO BEYOND IT!

"It is impossible to live without failing at something, unless you live so cautiously that you might as well not have lived at all."

–J. K. Rowling

I have already touched upon the concept of *neuroplasticity*; that making the "shifts" I've been speaking of literally impels your brain to forge new neural pathways. It's the innate tendency for the brain to adapt and expand – to literally change form – as a result of one's experience. This is crucial. It means that the range and diversity of experiences a person exposes themselves to is directly proportional to the amount of new neural connections that are made.

Taking this notion further still, what has also been substantiated is that "comfort-seeking behaviour" – the type of behaviour designed to stay only within limited personal parameters, avoiding experiences that are unfamiliar and potentially uncomfortable – actually *reduces* brain plasticity. It actually has a negative and disempowering effect upon us. As our brain plasticity diminishes, we become more and more fearful and less able to adapt to circumstances. Clearly, this is something we most certainly want to avoid.

Ross Ashby, a prominent pioneer within the field of *cybernetics* (the study of *complex systems* and the interrelated structures that function within those systems) expressed a precept which he termed the *Law of Requisite Variety*. This law essentially emphasises the idea that the element within any system which has the greatest degree of flexibility will always be the *controlling element*. Therefore – simply put – the greater amount of personal flexibility you're willing to engender, the more control you will have; both internally (for yourself) and interpersonally as well.

Comfort-seeking behaviour can therefore be thought of as "junk food" for your brain and nervous system; whereas intentionally exposing yourself to a huge spectrum of experiences is literally good and nourishing for you. It supports your ability to adapt within all situations and to ultimately feel more comfortable, composed and in control.

So there is a choice for you to make: you can either choose to nourish and fortify your mind-body system towards vigour, drive and dynamism; or you can choose to neglect it and allow your great potential to dwindle and diminish, making you far less capable of dealing with the hurdles life throws at you. The decision you make will unquestionably affect the very quality and satisfaction of your life. And it all rests upon how you decide to engage with the world!

Even Charles Darwin, author of the seminal work, *The Origin of Species*, through the codification of his knowledge and research, expounded the notion that the strongest and most potent individuals are those that are more able to *adapt* to their environment, compared to others individuals within the same species. This very "adaptability" encompasses the capacity to move into unknown territory, instead of only staying present to what is comfortable and familiar. It brings us right back to what I've been speaking about all along!

What I am leading you towards – through *all* of these concepts – is the facility to access and live from a much fuller and richer expression of yourself. It's about making the decision to break through those invisible boundaries that prevent you from being the fullest expression of *you*, so that you can step into where you've never been before and actually *enjoy* the sensation of unfamiliarity so much that you desire to experience it endlessly.

So, with all of these ideas in mind, the message cannot be clearer and more distinct: *step into discomfort*. Go out of your depth, and do it intentionally. Make this an integral pattern of your way of living. Step right into the experiences that make you uneasy. And don't only move into these experiences at the times when they happen to arise – seek them out! Actually go looking for them! Actually begin to look for these opportunities and begin to feel contented every time you do. Doing this is about taking total responsibility for your own development. It's about maintaining a higher standard for yourself.

After all, if you were sick and needed a particular type of medication, you'd go out to look for it, wouldn't you? And once you had found that medication, you would feel better because you'd know that you were close to seeing an end to your sickness. So, in the same way – since you know that moving into discomfort ultimately fortifies you – why wouldn't you go out to look for it?

And, as you do, hold the awareness of your connection to your core – your deep interior strength. Keep it stable and pervasive. And every time you fully embrace the luxury of an uncomfortable experience – and decide to find comfort within it, until you *do* – you will have stretched the "spring" of your current experience so far that it becomes impossible to go back! It is then that the "shift" takes place within you! It always does eventually; and it's a magical moment! Do this time after time, and you will feel that explosion of confidence inside. You will remind yourself, again and again, of the potency of your true internal resource. You'll feel the essence of it resonating within. You'll know that being and feeling *this* way was how you were truly designed to be. You will instinctively know it as your truth.

WELCOME AND INVITE DISCOMFORT INTO YOUR LIFE AND ENJOY THE MAGIC THAT SHOWS UP!

"There are only two ways to live your life. One is as though nothing is a miracle. The other is as though everything is a miracle."

–Albert Einstein

When you get a taste of how good this feels, it will be like a healthy drug! You'll want to taste it more and more. And each time that you do – every time you stretch your limits – you'll sense that essential connection to your authentic provenance of *confidence*. You will recognise the unyielding source of it, and it will settle you and bring you back to your centre. Like this, it is addictive!

Just remember, the next time you feel that sensation of discomfort in your body, I want you to smile! Smile on the outside – and smile on the inside – and come to know that what you're about to take on is going to ultimately strengthen you, in the most integral and authentic way. Realise that you're about to make internal changes at a fundamental, cellular level. This will cause that initial hesitation to turn into feelings of excitement and wellbeing, because you'll know that where you're leading has magic in store for you! And you can allow that smile to grow even more as you think about all of the new challenges you'll be able to take on and accomplish – effortlessly and powerfully – because you will have embraced something that most others will never do in their lifetimes!

Being this way – living from this state of openness and possibility – is the domain where deep personal growth and unbounded new experiences live and breathe. It's where fresh and exiting vistas open up to you! It's where discomfort becomes very comfortable! It's the place where energy and vitality are to be found in total abundance, and where every living moment becomes a gift and an opportunity to express your uniqueness unconditionally, as you celebrate your divine presence in the world.

"There is an extraordinary quality within you that only reveals itself when you become willing to be fully present to the magnificence of your existence, and to see yourself as nothing less than the manifestation of this absolute power.

When you allow this truth to be the very ground upon which you cultivate your unique expression in the world, you will discover an inner strength – an unshakeable force – that will be eternally present for you, and guide you fearlessly through the moments of your life."

–Julian James

CHAPTER NINE

Absolute Self-Acceptance: Being Totally You – Without Apology!

"To be nobody but yourself – in a world which is doing its best, night and day, to make you like everybody else – means to fight the hardest battle which any human being can fight, and never stop fighting."

–E.E. Cummings

There is an extraordinary quality within you that only reveals itself when you become willing to be fully present to the magnificence of your existence, and to see yourself as nothing less than the manifestation of this absolute power.

When you allow this truth to be the very ground upon which you cultivate your unique expression in the world, you will discover an inner strength – an unshakable force – that will be eternally present for you, and guide you fearlessly through the moments of your life.

There is a single shift of awareness that needs to occur within you in order for you to begin living from a foundation of dynamic solidity and strength. I'm speaking about the kind of potency you exude when you harness connection to your divine limitless expression – a way of being that is certain, fearless, and absolutely unique. But to reach this level of functioning requires that you first give something up. Most people will never – in their entire lifetimes – be prepared to make this commitment to themselves. This is because it requires great courage. But it is the most freeing personal promise you will ever make. It is the most valuable gift you will ever give to yourself. It is this: *give up who you think you need to be in order to please the world!*

This single standpoint – this singled embodied shift in consciousness – is the most transcendent paradigm you can live by. It is the fundamental core from which all else flows and comes forth. It is the wherewithal to be who you are completely – without hesitation, without compromise, and without apology.

You did not enter into this world to be like others; you came into this world to be *you*. We have all known people who don't want others to see them as they *truly* are. These people don't want to expose to the world their authentic individual expression. So they construct a totally different character – a false or “pseudo character” – and then convince others that this is who they are. And this apocryphal exhibition is fashioned out of the fear that they will not be accepted, because they believe that just being themselves isn’t “enough”. They believe there is something “lacking” in them. They believe that who they are isn’t worthy of people’s respect, admiration or recognition. So they layer something over who they are and present *that* to the world instead. It seems to contain less risk for them to do this. At least, this way, if people don’t accept them, they don’t feel quite as bad, because it is not really *them* being rejected – it’s the “character” or the “role” they are exhibiting.

> Authentic self-confidence is abundantly present within you when you commit to the total and absolute acceptance of who you are.

“Let the world know you as you are, not as you think you should be, because sooner or later, if you are posing, you will forget the pose, and then where are you?”

–Fanny Brice

In a culture that works so hard to try to define who we “should” be, instead of encouraging us to celebrate the rarity and splendour of our interior uniqueness, accepting ourselves unapologetically is something many have simply given up on (and that’s if they ever dared to begin living this way at all). And this is the greatest sadness. To relinquish the authentic expression of our true and essential nature in order to be considered “acceptable” – by those that tell us that we need to apologise for who we are – is to disdain the gift of our very existence, and to trade in the essence of our spirit for a homogenous substitute.

Yet, it’s easy to see why this tendency yields such predominance in modern culture. In a society abound with imposition, rigid expectancy and a set of “rules” and “standards” (both spoken and unspoken) – which emphasise the ostensible importance of “following the herd”, being compliant and only doing what is expected of us – joining the ranks of homogeny is presented as the only option.

For many, claiming their true self – embracing all of the elements that comprise their birth-given uniqueness – is actually a terrifying idea. The notion of operating in the world authentically and from this sense of unconditional acceptance is a prospect that brings with it the possibility of abandonment. That’s why there is a certain comfort to be found in retreating to the realm of *sameness* – being "just the same as others" and not daring to "rock the boat" or approach things differently – because it offers this illusion of safety.

It seems so much easier to conform to the beliefs and behaviours of the masses, and blend into an ocean of uninspiring similarity. Joining the "social collective" offers the ostensible elimination of the possibility of having to worry that others might not approve of something we do, something we speak about, or something that aligns with our deepest values. It appears to appease and satisfy the need we have to be accepted, and, at the same time, protects us from resistance. But, in spite of the "comfort" it seemingly brings, there is a price to pay for this illusory sense of security. In fact, it is the most devastating and dehumanising price we could ever bear the cost of: *the giving up of who we are!*

This form of devastating self-compromise is ubiquitous. It's the apologetic alternative to expressing, in every moment of our existence, our true and undeniable being; to fearlessly stepping into the world and celebrating everything about us that makes us who we are, making no excuses for doing so. Choosing to shrink and diminish – to literally fade into the multitude of uniformity, where we more or less become invisible, and what it is that makes us special is stripped and whittled away until all that is left is what we feel others will accept us for – is a ludicrous and disempowering way of living our lives. Yet, it seems to be a very popular option, because this is precisely how the majority of individuals choose to operate. They would rather stifle and repress the gift of their original human expression – and allow themselves to become homogenised – than to expose to the world their raw distinctive *edge* and stand firmly grounded in the absolute and unapologetic embodiment of this truth.

However, those who boldly face the world – fully open and fully expressive of their authentic essence – are not afraid of the words spoken about them by others. They realise that those words can never supersede or be greater than the value they hold for themselves. They simply aren't affected by the thoughts others have of them because what comes with the sheer awareness of their intrinsic power is the capacity to remain solid and unshakable amidst the inevitable incursion of exterior value judgments.

> Making the decision to no longer apologise for who you are – and to live this way in spite of all that you encounter – opens a source of confidence within you that is astounding.

"Thus to be independent of public opinion is the first formal condition of achieving anything great."

–Georg Wilhelm Friedrich Hegel

For as long as you spend the moments of your life wishing to be *different* than the way you are, you will always experience anxiety and disquiet. You will always continue to live in a perpetual state of disharmony. You will never truly be able to settle into the *truth of you* and feel fully at rest, fully at ease.

True self-confidence will be yours when you let go of the idea that you can only feel good about yourself once you've altered an aspect of you that you believe "isn't right" (or that others tell you they don't like), or once you've reached some predetermined point in your future – that point in time that you've convinced yourself will be the end to all of your concern and worry and foreboding. Confidence will be yours when you embrace what is true of you, in the here and now, and relax into simply being just as you are, letting go of the need to change a thing.

Understand that accepting yourself in an unconditional way doesn't mean that you can't or shouldn't invest your time in developing yourself as an individual. It doesn't mean that you shouldn't work on those areas in your life that you want to improve or move beyond. It doesn't mean that you shouldn't progress towards strengthening your body and your mind and your creative capacities. (Naturally, all of these things are essential to your growth and evolution.) It simply means, *in this very moment* – in spite of what's going on around you, in spite of what you have or do not have, in spite of what you can do or cannot do, in spite of who is with you or who is not with you – simply making the choice to fully accept yourself, just as you are! It's about deciding to come to love your core essential being without reservation, fully and completely. It's about realising that you are greater and infinitely more powerful than the features and details of your external appearance. It's about settling into that place within you that allows you to simply come to rest – to be still – knowing that you are *enough*, and always have been.

When you begin to embrace this quality of expression, you operate from a wakefulness that refreshes the depth of you. Your spirit becomes enlivened. You draw from a strong and robust channel of power. You begin to experience authentic compassionate love for yourself. As a result, you have no choice but to be more lovable and attractive to others. The people you come into contact with feel the distinctive presence that you emanate. They instinctively feel drawn to you because you remind them of what it's like to be internally free. You begin to resonate with the joy in staying present to the magnificence of your essential nature.

When you are like this – when you live and breathe through nothing less than your divine personal liberty – the frantic desperation to make yourself different (to change yourself, to mask your individuality, to hide yourself away from the world) dissolves, dwindles and dissipates. There is release, relaxation and internal rest. You feel an unmistakable wave of contentment that saturates you from the inside. And this sense of contentedness needs nothing from the outside in order for it to be so, because it's a pleasurable and encompassing sensation that is beyond condition and beyond restriction. It draws from your very foundation, where true power resides. It fortifies you with the strength to let go of all the ideas of how you think you need to be – and have been told you need to be – and, instead, allows you to return to your ultimate truth: that you are powerful beyond measure.

> You are whole and perfect and complete, just as you are. If you should ever feel anything less than this, what's missing isn't your state of completeness – what's missing is your awareness of your completeness in that moment. And you can shift your awareness in an instant.

Absolute self-acceptance means that wherever you happen to be in your life – whatever stage you are at along your path, and regardless of what's happening around you – you are able to connect to the formless and changeless aspect of you, and sustain this quality of awareness in a pervasive way. And yet it seems so demanding, in the midst of our modern world, to do this. We are bombarded with messages and signals that tell us we're not allowed to feel good about who we are until we've accumulated the right amount of material goods, attained the right levels of knowledge and spent the right amount of time gaining "certifications" and "qualifications". It's been ruthlessly drummed into our heads that there's so much we have to do, and so much we have to get, before we can even stand a chance of feeling worthy and secure! We've been trained to look to others and say, "Please tell me you like me. Please tell me I'm special. Please tell me you approve of me, because that's the only way I can really feel good about who I am!" And this constant and chaotic rush to "keep up" stands in the way of us connecting with those things that truly matter: honouring our spirit, coming to rest in the here and now, welcoming all that we are and sustaining our sense of unity with the very creative force that brought us into being.

People who have deep self-confidence *own* who they are – they own everything that comprises the totality of their individual nature. They *own* the words that they speak. They *own* the subtle and explicit gestures present in the way they move and carry themselves. They *own* their place in the world. They *own* their power. And to be able to operate this way extends far beyond external factors. It surpasses the superficial details of our physical appearance. It transcends all of the capabilities that we have, and don't have. It's the freshness that emerges from having deep gratitude for the gift of our life, and choosing to celebrate that gift in every moment.

"Believing in our hearts that who we are is enough is the key to a more satisfying and balanced life."

–Ellen Sue Stern

What is it about you that makes you *you*? What are those things about you that are the most distinctive and unique? What are those special qualities only *you* possess?

Unfortunately, according to the "rules" of our consumer-capitalist society, unless these qualities of yours are in agreement with what the "authorities" tell you is "normal", it would be more advantageous for you to hide them away. This culture encourages you to mask your idiosyncrasies so that you can be more like "others". It presents you with plenty of "role models" and "exemplars" that demonstrate how you "should be", and then inveigles you into a comparative position. And, of course, if you're unable to "do" and "be" like these false ideals, the message imparted to you is that you're not good enough and need to change.

But as forceful and influential as these insidious messages are, it's important for you to know that the unique aspects of you do not need to change – ever! This is because they are gifts, not mistakes. It's important for you to realise – without question or compromise – that every detail that makes you what you are is something to be celebrated, not something to be ashamed of.

I remember the petite dark-haired girl at my high school. She had a very distinct way of laughing. Her laughter had a pitch and a rhythm to it that you would never forget. It was inimitable and unlike anything anyone had ever encountered. It attracted a great deal of attention. Even the teachers frequently mentioned the curious style of her laughter. In fact, her laugh was so "different" that she became renowned for it. Everyone was aware of "the girl with the funny laugh".

Unfortunately, though, it offered others a pretext with which to insult, ridicule and bully her. They would mock her individual self-expression by feeding back to her, through relentless histrionic exhibitions, exaggerated and embellished versions of the way that she laughed. And, in a manner that is typical of many young school students, this onslaught of merciless taunting was incessant and ruthless. It demonstrated no regard for her at all. These painful experiences caused this young girl tremendous distress and sorrow. Her schooling years were far from pleasant. They became a constant struggle. She was made to believe that there was something fundamentally wrong with her; that she was "weird" and "strange".

As a result of the perpetual mockery, the only way she was able to deal with what was happening – the only coping mechanism she could effectively employ – was to simply stop laughing altogether. This meant that whenever a situation arose in which she even came close to laughing, she'd immediately remind herself of what would happen if she did and so instantly impeded what was actually a totally natural and joyful human response by shutting herself down. She literally trained herself not to laugh at any time. She conditioned her system to restrain one of the most healing, effortless and powerful forms of human expression: the magic of laughter. After all, to be able to let go and just laugh – to express the fullness of the joy of releasing natural healing neurochemicals into the system – is one of the special gifts of life. But she had developed a way of stopping that from taking place. It affected her emotional state and general sense of well-being in ways that were incredibly disempowering. This would often bring her to tears. She suffered greatly because of it. I often saw her sitting in the same corner of the library during break time. She became more and more withdrawn. She wanted to be invisible.

Instead of realising that she had a gift – something no one else had – she learnt (mistakenly) that it wasn't okay to express herself in her own individual way. She learnt that because she wasn't like "the others", in this particular manner, her uniqueness was therefore "bad" and "unacceptable". Instead of realising this was part of what actually made her lovable, she wanted it to be different.

Looking back, I only wish there had been someone who could have told her that the way she laughed was perfect, just as it was. But no one ever did. I only wish someone had been there to help her see beyond the *illusion* that the only way to be accepted was to behave just like everyone else. But no one ever did. I only wish someone could have guided her towards a level of self-awareness in which she was able to fully love and to fully *own* every aspect of who she was. But no one ever did.

I have no idea where she is now, or what she is doing, but I somehow find myself thinking about her from time to time. I cast my mind back to those memories of school. I wonder how she is now living her life. My wish for her is that she has grown to accept *all* that she is – including every single one of her idiosyncratic gifts – and that she is able to feel comfortable and at ease simply being herself, free from the desire to be any other way. (And being *free*, in this way, is ultimately my wish for *all* people.)

Based on this recollection, what's interesting to me is that, throughout school, this young girl was presented with an array of persuasive suggestions that alluded to the idea that she wasn't "normal". And this, in itself, is a notion that invites much questioning, because in order to be considered "normal" (or not) we have to first decipher just exactly what this term means.

THE ILLUSION OF "NORMALITY"!

I have always been fascinated with the idea of what people consider to be "normal". We often hear others speak about people being either "normal" or "not normal". But how can the state of "normality" be accurately measured? What is the standard or the benchmark for doing so? Is there even a universal standard for "normality"?

What I have come to know is that there is in fact no universal standard for normality at all. How could there be? No defining basis for comparison exists. People are people; and the nature of humanity is that different people have different tendencies, different interests, different likes and dislikes, and different ways of approaching what they do. We look different, we have different ways of dressing, we speak differently, we move our bodies differently and we communicate in different ways. The only way there could ever truly be a generic state of normality in the world would be if everyone operated in *exactly* the same way. But then we wouldn't be human anymore – we'd be robots!

So if someone tells you that you don't seem "normal" to them, do not take offence at such a declaration. In fact, assume this to be one of the greatest compliments you could ever be granted! After all, if you've been described by another human as not being normal, all this person is really telling you is that he doesn't recognise you as fitting into the "majority" – the mass of individuals who are so afraid to be who they are that they have instead settled for behaving in the manner they've been conditioned to behave. And because you know that there really is no such thing as "normal" anyway (because there are only humans, who, by default, are *not* the same as one another) you can only interpret this kind of remark as a way of someone else confirming that you're not afraid to be who you are. This is good news, of course! It's evidence that you're on the right track!

"Insist on yourself; never imitate. Every great man is unique."
RALPH WALDO EMERSON

For a person such as this – through his lens of myopic perception – he has bought into the belief-system that all people have to fit into one singular category of constrained and inhibited human beings, or else there's something terribly wrong with them. For him, being "normal" is, essentially, about existing as a controlled and conditioned robot: this means that people must do exactly as they're told, behave as the masses do, eat only what others eat and think only what others think. They must also never ask questions, never dare to embrace what is unique about themselves, never say anything unexpected and never challenge authority. They must be willing to move through life happy to have their thoughts, behaviours and beliefs programmed and instilled into them from the outside. And – if they do all of these things – then, and only then, can they ever stand a chance of being considered "normal"! How's that for a meaningful, rewarding and fulfilling life?

Never strive to be "normal" – it takes you away from who you really are.

What a person like this *doesn't* see is that being a robot – and therefore denying our true nature – is as far from "normal" as we can get! What's "normal" about limiting and repressing our uniqueness so much so that we become homogenous zombies? Where's the personal freedom in that?

This is exactly what the film, *The Stepford Wives*, is entirely about. (I'm referring to the original 1975 motion picture, directed by Bryan Forbes. The re-make was somewhat of a parody and didn't capture the deeply unsettling essence of the original narrative.)

The film centres around a group of men, living in a small town called Stepford, who desire from their wives total and absolute subservience. They want the women to whom they are married to be predictable, obedient housewives, and to do exactly as they're told, exactly when they are told, and to not think for themselves in any way. They want the perfect cake-baking, shirt-ironing, floor-scrubbing, bed-making, house-bound slaves, complete with impeccable "Barbie doll" features. And so, these husbands subject their wives to a shocking and dehumanising process in which the women are literally replaced with robotic versions of themselves.

So what makes each and every one of these women individual, autonomous, attractive and special is stripped and stolen away from them; their identities substituted with a sophisticated series of computer programs that controls their every action and their every word. And, if you've ever seen the original film, you'll know just how sinister and chilling this is to experience; because to steal a person's true nature is the most devastating act of thievery that could ever be perpetrated. Yet, so many people allow those around them, and the larger societal structure in which they live, to do this very thing. And it's a horrifying idea!

So, the next time someone tells you that you're "not normal", thank them! And, after you've thanked them, feel good inside knowing that you've chosen not to become a *Stepford Wife*, because you've made the decision to hold on to who you are!

> Remember: there is nothing wrong with you. There's only something wrong with you if you decide to believe the robots that tell you there's something wrong with you!

Whenever I have dinner with my friend Peta Heskell – the original *Flirt Coach*, and author of the book by the same title – I can't help but to adore the way she eats. She is so carefree and authentic when she does. Peta is a very sentient and sensual lady. She engages the world in a highly sensorial way. When she orders a salad, for example, at a restaurant, she will eat the salad from the bowl with her fingers. In fact, when she orders *any* type of food, she eats it with her hands. Now, in Western civilisation, this is not something that is considered "normal" or "acceptable". But this "rule" is just another cultural stipulation that cannot really be supported by any viable or sustaining reason. After all, if it's good enough for the people in India, why can't we eat that way too? Why must westerners follow a different set of conventions? Part of this is due to the fact that we simply don't ask enough questions. More often than not we blindly "follow orders" and accept the "rules" as they are presented to us, without ever asking or considering why they are being imposed this way, as opposed to any other way.

Peta doesn't eat with her hands in order to generate attention or to be noticed by others. She isn't concerned with those things. She eats this way simply because it's the most pleasurable way for her to enjoy and savour her food. She makes no excuses for it. She just does what flows out of her naturally, and she's totally comfortable with doing so. In the eyes of the majority, she is "breaking the rules", but, to her, she's just being who she is.

Peta has actually recounted to me a number of stories regarding her "finger eating" adventures. She once told me about the time she was dining with a male friend, who'd taken her to a very expensive restaurant. Naturally, when the food arrived, she sat there at the table, eating with her fingers. Upon seeing this, her gentleman companion immediately exclaimed: "Stop that right now!" And when Peta asked him why he wanted her to stop, he continued, "Because it's just too sexy!"

On another occasion, a different gentleman invited Peta out for drinks and dinner. When he saw Peta eating with her hands, and being so uninhibited and at ease, he gazed at her directly in the eyes and declared, "You know, I could fall in love with a woman who eats like that!"

Peta realised, a long time ago, that she loved to eat with her fingers and that she didn't want to be with someone who disapproved of it. These two occasions really helped her understand that what her mother had taught her as a child – about "niceness" and "polite eating"– was plain nonsense. She realised that if she refused to make excuses for how she was, she'd inevitably and organically connect with the right man – a man who appreciated this aspect of her nature – and everything else that made her special. Needless to mention, Peta's husband also eats with his fingers!

When Peta expresses her true character – fully, completely, without apology and from self-love and total acceptance – her intrinsic confidence flourishes, because she's not trying to "conform" to any belief structure that's being imposed upon her. Instead, she just *is* who she is; and she fully owns all that she is. She knows that some people will be drawn to her, and others won't; and she's totally comfortable with either outcome. She has no attachment to external approval. She would rather stay authentic and have people not approve of her than to give herself up in order to win their acceptance. And the reason Peta has no interest in this sort of approval is because her sense of worthiness is *internally* referenced – it doesn't come from outside of her.

"When you're a beautiful person on the inside, there is nothing in the world that can change that about you. Jealousy is the result of one's lack of self-confidence, self-worth, and self-acceptance. The Lesson: If you can't accept yourself, then certainly no one else will."

–Sasha Azevedo

For me, this is what accepting yourself unconditionally is truly about. It's about recognising those things in you that are unique and distinctive, and being totally contented with them, delighting in them and being at one with them. It's about seeing these highly personal and highly individual traits, not as "weird" – but as gifts – because they are expressions that only *you* can bring to the world. It's about choosing to celebrate these things. And when you organise yourself integrally such that this is how you show up, it's a very powerful way to move through the world. It's also the most authentic way to be, because there's nothing about you that you're resisting. Everything is open, everything is flowing and everything emanates from you effortlessly.

> When you operate from others' expectations of you, you become contracted. But when you function from your natural inspiration, there is a compelling aliveness about you that is attractive and irresistible.

Yet most people want to hide away from even the possibility of being this free. Most people are literally terrified of the idea of being this open and engaged with life, because it's apparently not "normal". And, not to mention the ubiquitous internal question: "What will others think of me?" I truly do believe that it's not that such people don't want to be this way – because a deeper aspect of them yearns to be – it's that they're scared to even begin. They are scared because they choose to believe the "rules" of their environment over and above their own fundamental instincts. They have learnt, through years and years of incessant programming, to trust what's outside of them more that they trust those internal signals that come from their source of inner wisdom.

However, for those who are willing to live from this foundation of authenticity, what comes from choosing to be this way is the greatest confidence one can embody. It is the confidence of being nothing other than the full expression of *you*, in everything that you do and with every person whom you encounter. Nothing is more internally satisfying.

So this choice becomes a crucial one, and one that significantly impacts on every element of our lives. Either we decide upon the facile path of minimising ourselves to join the ostensible safeness of uniformity by restraining our uniqueness in the world – and ultimately becoming less than we can be as a result – or we fully embrace our uniqueness, rejoicing and exulting in all that we are, and relish all of the wonderful gifts that flow from the wellspring of fearless living.

What's more, because this way of being appears so magical and alluring to others, it can often incite jealousy and disdain. It's very typical for certain individuals to see a person being effortless in this manner and choose to condescend and mock them. And, in cases such as these, it's easy to see what's really going on. You see, it's the individuals who ridicule people like this that actually most want to be like them. They quietly yearn to have this level of carefreeness and self-acceptance. But, as they are operating out of fear – because they are unable to find a way to be like this – the only way they can handle the situation is to make the other person "wrong" for being so open and authentic. At least in this way, they can feel better that they enforced their "control" over that person. It serves to move their awareness away from the fact that they, too, would truly love to be as free as this for themselves.

> It is the people who decide to be nothing less than the full expression of themselves – and all that they stand for – who make the greatest impact in the world!

"Our entire life, with our fine moral code and our precious freedom, consists ultimately in accepting ourselves as we are."

–JEAN ANOUILH

A notable woman, who served as a pivotal catalyst in radically changing the attitudes and behaviours of the world, was Rosa Parks.

On a winter's day in 1955, in Alabama, Rosa Parks – a black lady of 42 years of age – said "no" when she was asked to give up her bus seat to a white passenger.

At that period in history, in many ways, black people were not considered equal. They were deemed undeserving and did not have equal privileges to people with white skin. But Rosa saw through the illusions of control and segregation that had kept so many black people enslaved by an unjust system of discrimination and unequal human rights. She saw the grave injustice inside of this imposition of ruthless prejudice. And so, she boldly and strongly decided to make a stand – not just for herself, but for black people all across America. She refused to recoil into submission and allow another person to devalue her and brand her as unworthy. She refused to allow another human being to take precedence over her because her skin was the "wrong colour". She refused to be made to feel unequal and insignificant. She allowed no one to take away the birth-given privilege of her fundamental human right to be in the world. Instead, she chose to embrace all that made her human and to recognise the inherent value of her life.

And as a result of this powerful and prevailing decision, Rosa Parks made a significant and unforgettable impact upon the world. Why?

Because she refused to let go of who she was! Many wouldn't have dared to even think about doing what Rosa did; but because she refused to allow anyone else to convince her that she was inferior, she helped to create a momentous shift in the way humans now relate to other humans. And we can have nothing but tremendous respect and admiration for a woman such as this – a woman who made a solid stand for herself, and for millions of others in the process.

Rosa Parks became known as the "mother of the freedom movement" – a hero and ambassador for the liberty of the world! And the strength required to make such an audacious stand is one that comes out of great faith and great self-acceptance – a means that is within all of us.

If we do not fully accept ourselves – and do so in a way that is wholesome and encompassing – we place ourselves into hazardous territory. We become ill at ease and unstable. We reach the false rationalisation that if we are unable to come to honestly accept who we are then our only remaining option is to instead find that acceptance through others. So we disregard and reject the wisdom in cultivating unconditional self-love, and go looking for other people to provide us with that acceptance so that we can feel secure. The danger in this is that when others relate to us in ways that are anything other than positive or affirming, we simply aren't strong enough to handle the situation.

Some time ago, at a large business and networking event, a lady approached me. She had obviously been crying. Her eyes were red and slightly swollen and everything about her suggested fear and defeat. Her name was Barbra. She'd just finished delivering a business presentation to a group of executives on the subject of "company profitability". Barbra was clearly shaken and deeply disturbed. When I asked her why she was so distressed, she explained that, during her talk, a man in the front row had stood up and sharply castigated her before the entire group, exclaiming that the information she was presenting was outdated. He also told her that she was "boring" and "monotonous" as a public speaker. This experience affected her so much that she barely stumbled through the rest of the time allotted to her presentation. She was left feeling totally embarrassed and humiliated, and had been reduced to an incredibly nervous state.

Since Barbra had seen my own presentation that afternoon, prior to her own, she approached me because she was anxious to ask me something. We found somewhere to sit and she asked me what the "secret" was to not being affected by the criticisms of other people; to not allowing the disparagement (even the raw insults of others) to harmfully impact on your performance and how you feel about yourself.

To begin, I explained to her that we should never fully reject criticisms from others as they can sometimes be useful and hold value that can serve us in the form of feedback. In addition, I explained to her that external criticisms can also often have no value at all, and that, when we attune our attention in the right way – when we connect with our deep intuitive insight – we are able to instinctively distinguish one from the other.

When criticism is useful, it almost always comes from those people who hold our best interests in mind and sincerely wish for us to improve, grow and develop as human beings. When criticism is not useful, it invariably comes from those who are envious of us, who wish us harm or have some other ulterior motive or hidden agenda. Naturally, then, a certain degree of discernment is required to know the difference.

More importantly, the facility to be impervious to the words of others – even if such words comprise the form of total insults – rests not on the relationship we have with the people from which the insults originate, but, on the relationship we have with ourselves. When we maintain a relationship with ourselves that is based on the foundation of deep self-acceptance – abiding and unconditional self-love – then even the harshest of insults thrown in our direction really carries no weight. It simply doesn't affect us or cause us distress. And this is because, if our self-love is strong and authentic and holds no condition, it will always be greater and far more sustaining than anything anyone could say to us; so much so that maintaining composure and remaining unshakable in the face of such a verbal affront is completely effortless.

I want to tell you about a particular dream that I experienced in the hotel room I stayed in during my visit to Bahrain. I had been especially flown out there to entertain a group of guests at a well-known venue. That night, after my show, I had a dream I'll never forget – not because of the imagery within the dream itself (although that certainly had pertinence too), but more so due to the level of awareness that the dream emphasised and brought light to.

> Insults and criticisms from others only affect you when you deem the words of others to be more important than what you believe about yourself. But when what you believe about yourself is greater than any insult anyone can throw at you, you become uninsultable. You literally become unable to be insulted. And the only way to truly reach this level of awareness requires you to cultivate a relationship with yourself that is unconditionally loving and unconditionally accepting.

At that period in my life, this dream served almost as a clarification of what my personal attention had been specifically focused upon. That's why it had so much impact on me. It was a reflection and a conformation of the thoughts that had already been predominant in my consciousness. They were thoughts that were central to my entire understanding of what it really means to live and operate in the wakefulness of true self-acceptance; the kind of integral gratitude and deep interior welcoming that is genuine and nourishing of the spirit.

In this dream I was in a foreign country. I was walking through a crowded and busy marketplace, somewhere in the Middle East. I held in my hand a bag of nuts. I ate the nuts from the bag as I strolled along.

The market was enormous and seemed to go on forever. The place was totally alive. There were thousands and thousands of people around me: men and women of all ages, bartering for goods and eagerly exchanging them for handfuls of coins and pieces of gold. I could smell the aroma of cooking meat, and the fragrance of exotic spices. From time to time the smoke from a sizzling barbecue would blow into my eyes, causing them to momentarily close, as I waited for the slight stinging sensation to subside. I could see beautiful hand-made tapestries and the finest silks of every imaginable colour that were lavishly displayed on stalls that extended out as far as I could see into the distance. There were live animals, tables of ornate painted pottery, snakes curled up in wicker baskets and street performers dancing through the avenues. There were women squeezing fresh mango juice into cups and cobblers selling their leather shoes, whilst others sat at small outside coffee huts, smoking hookah pipes. Music was playing from all directions, some from flutes and other from string instruments. It was a scene that was utterly breathtaking; unlike anything I'd ever experienced. And as I continued to walk through the marketplace – eating from my bag of nuts – I could feel the relentless blistering heat of the Sun beaming down on my face. My clothes were drenched with sweat.

I looked down at what I was wearing and realised that my clothing was not consistent with the type off attire being worn by everyone else I could see. The people around me were dressed in flowing eastern garments, constructed, mainly, from natural cotton and other similar raw cloths. They were wearing strapped leather sandals, designed to endure the hot climate. I, on the other hand, was wearing a pair of trousers and a contemporary tight fitting shirt. The gold watch on my wrist, and the shoes on my feet, seemed totally out of place within the milieu that surrounded me. I realised, in that moment, that I was in an entirely different era. It was as if I had been transported backwards – several hundred years – into a time and place that was not my own.

Suddenly, the hustling busyness of the crowded marketplace went totally silent. In a single moment, all buying and selling completely ceased. What was, only seconds before, a loud and boisterous environment, was now totally still. Nothing moved. Everything around me went quiet and motionless. All activity had come to an absolute standstill. And, when I looked around at the thousands of people that were present, all attention was now fixated upon *me*. It was as though I were a trespasser on their sacred land, and I had finally been spotted, recognised and singled out.

There I was, standing in the centre of the marketplace, like a "stranger in a foreign land". Every pair of eyes now focused on me and me alone. The people began to point their fingers right at me, uttering phrases in a language I was unable to understand.

However, in spite of the situation – a situation which, to most, would have been sorely intimidating; even terribly frightening – there was a difference to it all that made it unmistakable. This was because my response to what was going on was one of internal control, not fear. You see, in spite of what was taking place, I felt totally calm. I did not feel any pressure or discomfort. I was completely at ease. I felt no need to defend or explain myself, or to do anything I wouldn't ordinarily do. Even though there were thousands of people jeering at me, there was a sense of composure throughout my body. It was stable and powerful. I felt an inner comfort; a sense of quiet contentment. Even though I had been "singled out", and so much attention was focused upon me, I still remained unaffected. I did not languish or lose my centre. It was like nothing had happened.

Not only did I feel unaffected, there was even a sense of pleasure within me: a warm and pleasurable sensation of knowing that I was perfectly fine, and that I was protected by something profound. It was an incredible awareness. I could feel an intimate and abiding connection to a source of power that was deeply sustaining. It was a knowingness – deep within me – that I was okay, and that nothing needed to change.

And, as I stood there, in that sweltering marketplace – eating from my bag of nuts – I decided to simply walk on. So I began walking onwards, not even bothering to turn around or to see what others were doing. It simply didn't concern or interest me. I just stayed on my path. And those nuts I continued to enjoy tasted just as salty, and just as delicious!

This dream, although unusual, is perhaps the most cogent exposition I can offer you that really speaks to what it means to live and breathe through the wakefulness of total self-acceptance: the ability to feel com-

> To stand boldly in the world – fully embracing every aspect of who you are, without excuse and without apology – is the greatest expression of power you can generate, and one that enriches your life in ways that are astounding.

fortable and rested in the knowledge of who you are; the capacity to honour your fundamental essence and to know that who you are is far greater than your immediate surroundings or the beliefs others have about you. It's knowing you are connected to a power that never leaves you.

There is really no "secret" to being this way. There is no complex arcane procedure associated with it, nor is there anything about it that is esoteric or mysterious. It's not something that is within the capability of some, but not within the reach of others. It isn't something that is reserved only for a "select few". It is simply a *decision* that you make. It's an intentional choice that flows from the willingness to accept all that you are, regardless of circumstances. It includes the capacity to forgive and make peace with yourself – despite what you have done or said in the past – releasing those failures, mistakes and regrets that you've been hanging on to. It's simply making the decision to totally let go of everything that stands in the way of you feeling the vitality of your presence in the here and now, and the pervasive and irrevocable connection you have to the very power that brought you into being. It's allowing yourself to come to rest inside of the potency of this inherent strength, knowing that there's nothing else that you will ever need.

TRUE SELF-ACCEPTANCE IS KNOWING YOU ARE ALREADY COMPLETE

"Love yourself first and everything else falls into line. You really have to love yourself to get anything done in this world."

–Lucille Ball

At a deep level of awareness, we know that self-acceptance ultimately has nothing to do with exterior factors. It has nothing to do with how we look – the particular details of our exterior physical appearance – because we all know and have met people who are vastly overweight, or especially unattractive (at least by conventional standards), and are still supremely confident individuals. People such as this engage with the world through a grounded appreciation of their inherent value, knowing that this value has absolutely no connection with what they look like; the shape of their nose, the size of their breasts or the specific measurement of their waist. This is because they have accepted who they are in a totally unconditional way. They have secured their connection to authentic power: the unchanging solidity that comes from aligning to a locus of control that is inwardly and internally present, and not reliant upon external conditions.

There are also many people that we know who are extremely attractive – exhibiting all of the facial and bodily features many would associate with astounding good looks – and, yet, are still deeply insecure. Countless examples of such men and women can be found in the media. There's an abundance of actors and "celebrity figures" we could point to who fall into this category. In spite of all that they have, they still cannot seem to make their lives work in a way that allows them to feel internally satisfied and at ease. They seem to have everything going for them. They have all of the proverbial trappings of "worldly success" – extreme wealth, global recognition and even incredible outward attractiveness – but are still deeply uncomfortable with who they are.

This tells us that self-acceptance *must* extend far beyond what we look like, and far beyond what we own. It tells us that having all of the external factors of "attractiveness" or "beauty" in place is not enough. We are not out bodies anyway. Our physical bodies – what the late Alan Watts referred to as "bags of skin" – are just the containers within which our spirits reside. And it's, in fact, the essence of our spirit that stands for all that we are, and our relationship to great power. Our outward appearance – in the larger scheme of things – actually stands for much less than we believe it does.

We believe that we have "imperfections" – the physical features which we're not entirely "happy" with – but these are actually the elements of us that add to our unique nature. Dōgen Zenji, a renowned Buddhist teacher, said that "To be in harmony with the oneness of life is to be without anxiety about imperfection." Your "imperfections" (if they can even be called imperfections) are actually the unique and individual characteristics that make you perfect. If you take the word "imperfect", and look at it more closely, you see the words "I'm perfect". The perfection of you is just as it should be, including those things about you that you consider not to be!

Holding on to who we are in a world that tells us that it's not okay to be ourselves can, at times, be remarkably challenging – there is no question about this. There are distractions and persuasions being peddled

> To never let go of who you are – and to move through the world in the magnificence of your uniqueness – means to live your life the way you were designed to be!

at every corner. However, never losing sight of our individual gifts – and never ever letting go of them – is a commitment of tremendous strength, and one that undoubtedly enriches and enlivens every second of our lives. If this is the standard through which we decide to engage with the world, amazing things are possible for us that would not otherwise be possible.

But – to endure the journey – we must be strong enough to withstand challenges, and pull through them each and every time. We must be absolutely committed to staying on the path; the path that is entirely our own. And, at times, these challenges can seem immensely tough. Not surprisingly, they can arrive from all directions. What's more, they even come to us from the people that are supposed to love and care for us the most: our parents.

As children, it was not uncommon for our parents – our sole providers and caregivers; the people that we looked to for support, guidance and comfort – to say things to us that alluded to the idea that we should be more like others, and not more of who we were. But, at the time, we were too young to see the fallacy of this logic, so we simply believed what we were told (after all, parents are supposed to know everything!) and therefore made to feel uncomfortable about operating in a way that was, for us, totally natural.

We've all been in situations in which we've witnessed a mother or father reproaching their child for something they did or said. And we've all heard parents – in the typical authoritative tone we've grown so used to hearing – bellowing such imperatives as, "Oh Richard, why can't you be more like your brother?" Or, even, "Sarah, why can't you take after Carla from school? She is so different from you!" Remarks such as these, although they appear innocuous on a surface level, can be more disempowering than most would care to imagine. What could be more emasculating than a parent sending his child signals that tell him that it's not okay to be himself, and that he would be far better off, and more accepted, being like someone else instead? Do you see how fundamentally damaging this can be to a young boy or girl, especially in those crucial early stages of learning and development?

And often, the parents who said such things did so with only good intentions at heart. It's not that they wanted to case harm or distress to their

> No one else in the world can express their uniqueness in the same way that you can.

children, it's just that they often didn't know what else to say in their attempts to instill the values of "obedience" and "good manners" (often because they were merely just parroting what their parents had said to them when they were children, without stopping to consider why those things were ever said to them in them first place). They just didn't appreciate the full implications of what they were communicating. They thought that they were being exemplary mothers and fathers – in their effort to impart the virtues of "discipline" and "moral rightness" – but did not fully appreciate that part of what that means is allowing their children the room to simply be who they are.

So, if your parents ever said such things to you, know that they didn't mean to cause you confusion or to lead you astray. They simply didn't know any better at the time. They weren't aware that there existed healthier and more discerning strategies to employ in encouraging a path of distinctiveness and individuality. They didn't realise that obligating you to be more like that other boy in your geography class, or your cousin, or the girl down the street – instead of more of *you* – was a mistaken and misleading message in the upbringing of a young child. They didn't realise that it was more important for them to allow your uniqueness to blossom and flourish – and to let you feel good about being this way – than for them to be concerned with what other children were doing (partly because they were worried about their own "reputation", and what other parents would think of them). So, as adults, we have to learn to not only forgive our parents for conveying these "ideals", but to also recognise that the content of such messages – which extolled the ostensible importance of trying to "be more like others" – worked contrary to the good intentions they held for us.

In much the same way, when it comes to cultivating and nurturing friendships and relationships, those who try to make you conform to how they want you to be are ultimately toxic. Why would you ever want to be around anyone who didn't truthfully honour your uniqueness? How could that ever be a healthy foundation for a positive and considerate relationship?

The most valuable people in your life will always be those who give you the room to be who you are, without trying to mould or condition you into someone that you're not. The most fulfilling, valuable and rewarding friendships and relationships are those in which those individuals allow you the space to simply be yourself, whilst also reminding you that it's important to allow them the space to be who they are as well. And as a result, there is no contrivance, there is no falsity, and there is no obligation. Instead, what emerges is an exquisiteness in which the essential nature of both you and them can exist in the most effortless way. This is the openness and honesty that makes relationships enjoyable and engaging and authentic.

And when it comes to embracing new people into your life, when you are simply being yourself – without restriction or effort – you will notice that certain people will be drawn to you. It won't even require any effort on your part. They will instinctively be attracted to the energy that you emanate from within you. And there is special magic inside of this because these are the very people that you will naturally be most aligned and compatible with anyway. So align with them. You'll discover that they will be able to bring to you as much as you can bring to them. New and exciting relationships will organically grow and develop. Your natural confidence will bloom and flourish simply as a result of you letting go of the need to impress and fulfill expectations from outside of you, because you'll have chosen to operate from the total acceptance of your core nature. You will no longer feel the desire for others to accept you, because you accept you first!

So be the full, uncompromised, uninhibited expression of you. Stand strong and unshakable in the incandescence of your existence. Sing your own tune. Write your own story. Mark out your own unique path. Contribute meaningfully. Act from inspiration. Engage others with openness and compassion. Share who you are with joyful abandon. Let your light shine. Welcome every element and every aspect that comprises your incomparable essence in the world. Commit to nothing less than living out every moment through the potency of this wakeful power, and you will embody the greatest most cherished gift you could ever express: the celebration of your very spirit.

> *People yearn to feel significant, not realising that the significance they crave is inextricably ingrained into the very fabric of their existence.*

–Julian James

CHAPTER TEN

You Fit In Perfectly

"You cannot be lonely if you like the person you're alone with."

–Wayne W. Dyer

I have a simple game of visualisation for you. Play right now, as you read along. Picture what I'm describing inside your mind:

Imagine you are standing in a kitchen. You can feel the hard floor beneath your feet. You are holding in your hands a china vase. It's a beautiful and expensive hand-crafted vase, fashioned out of the finest materials – the type you'd only find in an exclusive boutique. And you're just about to smash this vase to pieces!

You throw the vase down on to the floor, hearing the smash of the china below you! You can see the vase broken up into numerous pieces. The vase has broken into sixteen different pieces. Some are small pieces, some are larger pieces, and some of the pieces are very tiny. But, nevertheless, there are exactly sixteen pieces in total. Obviously, these are the *same* sixteen individual pieces that formed the complete vase, just before you threw it.

You reach down and pick up every one of the individual pieces, placing them onto a table. And, one by one, you carefully glue them back together. You take some time to do this, but, slowly, bit by bit, you glue all of the pieces perfectly back into position, exactly where they should be. The vase is now once again whole and complete, just as it was.

That's the end of our little game. Now let's examine what just happened, and what it means. If you did in fact glue all of the pieces back together in the way that I described, you would have to agree that there would be no missing pieces. There would be no pieces left over. *There would be no pieces that didn't fit.* The vase would be a vase, just as a vase should be. It would be complete and whole. There would be nothing missing from it! Remember, the vase was whole and complete before you smashed it to pieces. And, after you had glued it back together again, it was once again whole and complete, because all of the components were in place.

And so, do you see that every piece of the vase was just as *necessary* and *significant* as every other piece in order for the vase to be whole? The larger pieces were not more important than the smaller pieces – or even the very tiny pieces – because even the tiniest pieces needed to be in place for the vase to be complete! There were no unimportant elements!

FUNDAMENTAL BELONGING

The statement, "I don't fit in", is one I hear from people again and again. It's a personal declaration that is spoken from the mouths of men and women of all ages and all backgrounds. What's more, a lack of self-confidence and personal command is often attributed to *this* very belief: the idea that one does not "belong". You've probably met people yourself who believe that, in some way, they are a "misfit". For many individuals, they feel as though there is an acute disconnection between them and the rest of the world. They feel as though everything is taking place around them, without them being integral to it all. They feel "out of place". They feel awkward and ill at ease. They feel uncomfortable in their own skin. They feel separate. And this essential idea – the idea of how we fit into the larger system – is absolutely crucial, because it addresses the nature of our very existence. It speaks to our fundamental presence in the world.

Consider this: how is it really possible for you to be "out of place" when the fact that you are *present* and *alive* consolidates the very notion that you're an essential part of the universe? If you were not intended for this time and place – if it were any other way – you would have no consciousness. Quite literally, if true *belonging* was not your essential nature, you simply wouldn't be here!

Creation doesn't create pointless creations. If you were not intended to be part of the magnificent unfolding of the universe – to breathe in and be sustained by the air that flows through your body and to be present to the boundless potential that surrounds you – you wouldn't be around to even question the fact! Your very *consciousness* confirms the indisputability of your place here. Your very *aliveness* confirms that you belong. Your very energy and spirit makes your presence in the world solid and unquestionable.

> Creation doesn't create pointless creations.

It isn't possible for you to not fit in to a universe in which you are extant and alive and inextricably connected to the same life force that sustains everything. It isn't possible for you to not be a vital component of this ongoing experience if everything around you is confirming that you're living proof of the essential gift of creation!

Humans have a deep yearning to *belong*. We see this yearning acted out in countless ways. People become members of clubs, associations and social groups so that they can feel a sense of belonging. People subordinate themselves to religions so that they can have this same sense of belonging. People proudly brandish their country's designated flags to reaffirm the notion that they belong to a particular region of the world and can therefore be patriotic about that as they are supported by their fellow countrymen. In the same way, a core motivation for people actively supporting football teams is to attain this very same feeling of belonging – it allows them to express allegiance to their chosen group, and be able to garner the support and encouragement of others at the same time.

All of these types of behaviours are rooted in people's need to feel part of something worthy. When they feel part of a worthy cause, it allows *them* to feel worthy as well. And although there is nothing at all wrong with many of these activities – joining groups and institutions, and establishing connections with others in the context of organised community structures – feeling that you *need* to engage in any one of them serves to confirm the idea that they are necessary to sustain your sense of worthiness. But this is a lie. This entire belief simply isn't true. Why? Because you are *already* worthy. Because you *already* belong. You do not *need* any of these things because your belonging is unconditional. You belong to the universe just as intimately as the stars. And when you live through the power of this truth, there is no longer any yearning or longing. Instead, there is a feeling of deep connectedness to everything. You feel as though everywhere you go is just a different manifestation of the *same* benevolent and dynamic energy of the universe. It allows you to be able to walk into any situation, in any country in the world, regardless of who's around you – even if you're in totally "unfamiliar territory" – and *still* feel this integral and irrevocable sense of worthiness, and true belonging. This is because you realise that – beyond the illusions of separation – there really is ultimately only one fundamental source, and we are all part of it.

Once we refuse to accept anything other than the idea that our very existence is a divine treasure – once we embody the power of this truth within every cell of us, and within every thought that we have – all feelings of self-doubt and unworthiness drop away. They are overthrown and overshadowed by the resounding nature of who we are in the most authentic and primal way, because who we truly are is *beyond* separation, it is *beyond* insignificance, it is *beyond* limitation. Who we truly are speaks to the unity of everything.

> It is impossible for you not to fit in to a world of which you are an integral part.

When we live through the wakefulness that we are an essential and inextricable part of the universe – when we allow this primal energy to pervade all that we do – our effortless nature is to feel complete, to feel significant, to feel confident. There's nothing else we need. Like this, our innate power resonates from within us. We feel comfortable in our own skin. We feel at rest with ourselves. The illusion of separation no longer fools us. We see the deeper truth of the universe. We realise that we belong here, unconditionally.

The condition of *belonging* is not something reserved just for a select few – it's true of all of us. The fact that we are all intimately part of this universe is as indisputable as the energy of the Sun and the presence of the oceans. True belonging is not something that applies just to some people and not to others. It is the truth of you and it's the truth of me, and it's the universal truth of all humans. In spite of however it may "seem" to the contrary, it cannot be any other way. It's no less impossible for us not to be a vital constituent of the world as it is for an apple tree to suddenly begin to bear oranges. Everything has its own purposeful place in this immense design. And, by virtue of the fact that everything has been created by the very *same* source of intelligence, the validity of our existence is not up for question – it is rightful and intended, just as it should be. There are no exceptions.

"Your life, because of who you are, has meaning."

–Barbara De Angelis

In our exercise with the "broken vase", you'll know that the vase could just as easily have been broken into several thousand pieces. Yet, each part would have *still* "fit in", because each part would have still originated from the same *whole* – the same expression of completeness. It isn't possible for any part of a larger system to not "belong", simply because of where it originated!

The danger is that we are present inside of a society – a mechanism of control structures – that attempts to convince us that there is no place for us *unless* we buy into its rules: its conditioning, and its "ideas" of how we should be. We are made to be fearful of there not being a "place" for us here, unless we succumb to this deviousness and duplicity. It offers us "support" and "acceptance"; but only after we have given up who we truly are. It uses the possibility of "loss" to control us and to keep us afraid of not conforming. But these illusions do not invalidate our divine nature. They never can. We still belong – and we still "fit in" perfectly – regardless of the lies we have been told about who we are, and our relationship to the larger system that contains us.

You are not a small, separate self. There is nothing "missing" in you. You are not a product of insignificance. You are not borne of lack or restriction. The reason that the universe is the way it is, in any given moment, is partly because *you* are part of its unfolding. You are not just *in* the universe, you are *of* the universe, and the very fact that the universe created you speaks to its design for *your* place here. The validity of your place here needs no approval, nor does it need to be authorised by anything exterior to you. Your inherent value in the world is unconditional – totally and unquestionably.

ESSENTIAL COMPONENTS

When my grandfather was alive, he would occasionally bring me something from his marvellous London workshop. He was a jeweller, and would surprise me from time to time with unexpected gifts. Sometimes it would be a gold chain, or an old coin or ring. Sometimes he'd bring me a pocket watch or even a large wall clock.

I was always fascinated with the intricate workings of things. I wanted to find out what was on the *inside*. I would take things apart, eager to discover the mechanisms that made them work. And so, these gifts from my grandfather were very welcome indeed. I would get very excited whenever he told me that he was going to bring me something from his workshop.

On one occasion my grandfather gave me an old fashioned wind-up pocket watch. It was shiny and pristine, crafted from sterling silver. And if you've ever looked into all of the components that comprise the construction of even a simple pocket watch, you'll know the delicate and subtle intricacy that I'm speaking of.

I remember sitting at the kitchen table and, with a butter knife, carefully lifting away the thin round silver plate at the back of the watch, which protected its inner workings. It revealed before me that exquisitely precision engineered mechanism – an interconnected world of metallic magnificence – that was at the heart of it all. I marvelled at its meticulous arrangement; all parts resting purposefully in their own special place. It was a complete spectrum of countless pieces. There were balance springs, crown wheels, hairsprings, balance screws and banking pins, not to mention the regulator, the escapement wheel, the winding wheel and numerous other wheels and components of all sizes. Together, they all adjoined and integrated to create a cohesive and beautiful working system, which allowed the hands of the watch to turn in perfect rhythm. Each part had its own place; its own function; its own purpose. No parts of the watch were there for no reason. There were no unnecessary elements. Every part fit in to the entire encompassing system. Every part was intended. Every part was significant.

There are no unimportant parts in this universe. Nothing that is a manifestation of the universal creative force is insignificant. We could look at an insect like the honey bee, for example, and declare it to be small and of no consequence. But, the bees, like all creations of the world, all "fit in" in the structure of our planet in their own unique and essential way.

It's actually been corroborated by scientists that bees are vital in sustaining our ecosystem. In fact, almost eighty per cent of our plant life is dependent upon the work that bees carry out through pollination. If the honey bees did not exist, they would be unable to pollinate our crops, and we'd therefore be unable to grow and produce the essential food supplies that are harvested and made available to us for our survival. Einstein said, "If the bee disappears from the surface of the earth, man would have no more than four years to live. No more bees, no more pollination, no more men!"

Throughout the course of your life, you will never know just how many lives you touch – just how much value you bring to the world and how much possibility you open up to others – simply by *being* who you are. And, many of these moments you won't even be aware of. You'll just be doing whatever you'll be doing, and, at the same time, you will be spinning wide pools of influence, from yourself, out into the larger system. So don't ever believe that you're not having an effect on the world. You are *always* having an effect on the world.

I remember once receiving an unexpected email from a mother of a teenage boy who had come to see one of my shows, several years prior to her writing to me. In this message, this woman explained to me that her son had sat with her in the front row of my presentation at the Magic Circle, and was so inspired by what I shared with my audience that he soon after made the decision to spend the rest of his live studying the art of magic. She told me that, since that moment, he had become totally devoted to the art form, and was well on the way to being a professional. She thanked me for being such a deep source of inspiration to him.

And yet, at the time, I had *no idea* this was even taking place! As far as I was concerned, I had delivered my presentation. I just did what I did. I was totally unaware that my performance, on that particular evening, had served as a crucial catalyst for the future direction of a young person's life. And this is the kind of benevolent power we all contain – the power to touch the lives of others without even knowing it.

There can also be great subtlety in such occurrences. A few words that you speak, a certain gesture, or even a simple glance from you can meaningfully affect another person's life in ways you can't even begin to imagine. And none of these things would be possible if it weren't for you being who you are. None of these things would be possible if it weren't for you being part of this huge encompassing system. And that is why you are important and and essential.

In the unified and beautifully interrelated structure of this world, all of its elements are different, yet *all* are important. There are no irrelevant facets to life. Each and every part has purpose and significance, and *you are a facet of this significance.* You are an individualisation of the same sustaining force that brought you into being. You are an integral part of the unfolding of the universe. And one of the most powerful things you will ever do is to remember to stay grounded in the realisation that you're present in the world because you have been bestowed a place here that is special, and meant only for you.

YOU HAVE A PLACE HERE THAT IS EXCLUSIVELY YOURS

As far as your beliefs concerning exactly *how* you came into being are concerned, it actually matters less what you believe, since – whatever your particular standpoint happens to be – it has no choice but to lead right back to this singular truth: that *you are inherently powerful,* because you are intimately connected to the very power that created you.

If you believe that you are a creature of God, and that God created you through God's infinite power, you will certainly know that all of God's creations are sacred and divine, and that you are therefore an inextricable part of God's almightiness.

Further, should your beliefs about human creation be more evolutionarily based, you will know, according to overwhelming and sustainable evolutionary proof, that there is a totally uninterrupted path (a long and progressive chain of events) that extends back millions and millions of years – of the ongoing advancement of one organism to another and another – all the way up to *this* present moment. You will also know that this evolutionary process would only have been possible as a result of a powerful governing intelligence. And this trajectory, which encompasses these millions of years of human development, leads directly to *you* – in this moment of space and time – because you are literally right here, right now! This means that *you* are the living embodiment of the very spearhead of evolution. It means that you are the greatest, most sophisticated, most intelligent, most advanced and extraordinary form of life that there has ever been. So how could you be anything less than truly magnificent – at the core of your existence – when all that you are now, and all that has led up to the moment of your creation, confirms this very truth?

It doesn't matter which means of rationalisation or contemplation you decide to employ in approaching the consideration of you how you came to *be* – religious, scientific or otherwise – because, in the same way that multiple rivers or streams eventually flow into the same ocean, all such approaches inevitably follow back to the same singular truth: the indisputability of your extraordinary and essential nature.

There is nothing you lack. There can be no lack in you. The only lack you will ever experience is the "idea" that you are separate, and not connected to the power that brought you into being. But as soon as you realise that being separate is just an idea you hold in your mind, you can let it go, and replace it with the recognition that who you are is complete and whole and divine.

You are *never* not special. You are *never* not complete. You are *never* not extraordinary. These are the permanent and inextricable qualities that make up who you are. They never change. The only thing that can change is your *awareness* of the divinity within you.

Think of the eternal presence of the Sun. When there are no clouds – and the Sun beams brightly – you can feel the warm dance of the Sun's rays as they caress your skin. But on days when there are lots of clouds in the sky, and the Sun isn't visible, you don't stop believing that the Sun is there, even though you can't see it. You know that it's always there – always. It isn't visible to you, but your knowing of its existence is all you need. And this is what's it's like to stay connected to your own internal power, even when great difficulty and great challenge show up in your life.

> You are not separate. You are not isolated. You are not disconnected. There is a place here that is exclusively yours; it is meant for no one else.

Rumi, the great Sufi poet, said that "You're not just a drop in the ocean; you're also the mighty ocean in the drop." You are part of *everything*. You cannot be "separate" if you are part of everything. You are one with all that there is. You share unmistakable unity with every other person, and all things, because *all things are one thing*. All things have originated from the very *same* source of creation. Everything in existence is indelibly and intimately connected to the same mighty intelligence that brought it into being. And you, too, are a part of this very power; it is impossible for you not to be.

You have confidence in yourself because you have confidence in the boundless power that created you. You have security in yourself, because you are secure in the knowing of this truth. You have certainty in yourself because you have certainty in the extraordinary force that brought you into being, and that sustains you in every moment of your existence. You express yourself without reservation, because you are a unique expression of absolute creative power. You are present to the unfoldment of your life with total assurance because you have assurance in that same vital essence that gave you life, as it flows through you endlessly. It is inside of you always. You are unified with your source. This dynamic power resides at the centre of your being.

Understand that you are priceless. Understand that you are a treasure to the world. Understand that your place here is intended and perfect and complete. And know this to be true of you in every moment. Know that you fit in perfectly, because you cannot exist separately from the power that created you – the same power that flows endlessly through you and permeates every cell of your body.

There is no one else on this planet who will ever be able to bring to the world *your* uniqueness; *your* specialness; *your* distinct presence – only *you* are capable of doing that. Your uniqueness is unprecedented. This is precisely why – within the grand design of this incredible and ever expanding universe – you fit in perfectly!

Settle into this truth, and be powerful in the world.

"*There is absolutely nothing you need to make you complete that isn't already within you.*"

–JULIAN JAMES

CHAPTER ELEVEN
Authentic Power

"You are powerful beyond measure because the very source from which you came is powerful beyond measure."

–Julian James

If you only realised just how powerful you are – and carried this truth through all the moments of your life – you would never again feel empty, unworthy or afraid.

It's not possible for your existence in the world to be anything less than immensely powerful when you are – at every moment – connected to, interacting with and surrounded by that which is replete with infinite potential, possibility and power.

When you stand on the sands of a beach and gaze upon the breathtaking immensity of the ocean, observing the graceful coordination of the push and pull of the tide – knowing that beneath the surface of those waves exists an astonishing aquatic dimension replete with creations and life forms that are yet to even be discovered – the *same* force of creation that shaped every aspect of that immeasurable energetic vibrancy is the very *same* force of creation that brought *you* into being.

When you look up into the sky at night, witnessing the lustrous radiance of billions and billions of stars that glow in stunning cosmic arrangements – soaking in the ineffable luminary vastness that shines down from above you – know that the *same* organising intelligence that created each and every one of those stars is the very *same* organising intelligence that endowed you with the gift of life that endlessly flows through you and within you.

REALISING YOUR IMMENSE POWER

You operate from authentic power the moment you awaken to the knowing that this *power* is the fundamental truth of you. You function this way the moment you accept nothing less than your extraordinary presence in the world. You become powerful when you welcome and embrace the dynamic force within you – that is never not within you – because it *is* who you are.

You are so much greater than you have been taught to believe. You are such a remarkable and astounding creation that it would astonish you to discover just how much power you really do possess. Power is your primal essence. There is nothing you need to do, there is nowhere you need to go and there is nothing you need to acquire in order for this to be so – it is *already* so. And the very moment you come to see – truly *see* – that your deepest essence is *already* powerful, *already* complete and *already* extraordinary, is the moment you stop searching for ways to find completeness or security outside of you. You stop searching because you realise the search isn't necessary. You realise that what you're searching for is already exactly where you are.

Being like *this*, you understand that you need nothing external to you. You come to honour the divinity of your existence. You see that your true strength draws from the *centre* of you, because there – eternally present at your core – resides inextricable greatness. *This* is authentic power.

"Power", in the way that I'm using the term, is *not* associated with the meaning that most people typically ascribe to it. Most people think of power within the context of having power *over* others, or even *against* others. Most people conceive of power in relation to bolstering or aggrandising oneself, whilst diminishing another person. But that is actually not what authentic power is at all. In fact, this type of orientation (which can very convincingly "appear" to be power) is actually a manifestation of fear; since only those that are fearful believe they need to exert "power" *over* others, because they're not awake to the power they already contain. And those individuals that understand true power know that the need to disempower others is a redundant notion, because, ultimately – at the deepest level of our experience – we all share the very same power anyway.

Men and women who wish to control others, and set out to change them according to their will, do so because it's much easier for them to focus on controlling the people around them – and forcing them into submission – than it is for them to harness control for themselves. But the people who have a solid and stable awareness of who they are don't need or even desire to impose control over others, because they know that their control comes from within them. They realise where their true power resides.

The next time you see someone engaged in the process of trying to enforce control *over* another person, stop and begin to see what's *really* going on. If you pay attention, you will begin to see what's actually taking place, underneath their effort to assert superiority and dominance. Much of the time, you will recognise that this person's ardent attempt to control a fellow human is really his own struggle against his own perceived sense of inadequacy. It will become clear that he does not already believe himself to be a powerful being, because real power does not need to exert control to know that it is powerful. If he was at one with his true nature, he would have no desire to manufacture perceived feelings of control through undermining others. There would be no chasing for what he believed he lacked. He'd know that extraordinary power was *already* within him.

People who emanate authentic power know that inadequacy simply isn't the truth of who they are. They don't buy into inauthentic beliefs about themselves, for they know that they can never really be "inadequate". They know it isn't possible for them to be incomplete because their essential being has no connection to insufficiency or lack. Powerlessness only comes out of a lack of recognition of the power that is inherent in all of us. As a result, when we know there's no deficiency to try to compensate for, we don't feel compelled to resist the illusion of inadequacy. Instead, we can be open to settle into the awareness of who we truly are. Being *this* way, only power is present. Being *this* way, we feel there's nothing missing in us. Being *this* way, we resonate the full potency of our life force energy.

We are *all* immensely powerful individuals. There are no exceptions. Our uniqueness is undisputable. We are precious and special and astonishing. We possess unbounded possibility; our creative potential is immeasurable. *Power* is our fundamental truth. And this never changes, never falters and never diminishes.

Our sense of power only becomes diminished when we buy into the "idea" that we're not powerful. After all, we can only feel inadequate when we choose to believe that we are. So this sense of "inadequacy" – at best – is merely an idea, a notion, a free-floating concept that's cognitively processed. It only *seems* to be real, to certain people, because they have decided to buy into the belief that it's true. And when a person invests enough belief, energy and awareness into *any* idea, it seems very real to them, even to the extent that it becomes utterly compelling and unquestionable. Yet, just because an idea "seems" to be real, doesn't mean that it is.

You know this because there are countless things that – in the past – you wholeheartedly believed to be true, which later turned out not to be. You would have even defended those beliefs with your life, had it been necessary to do so. And then you went on to discover that you'd been "living in the dark", convinced you could see, not realising that your vision had been obscured the entire time. And in the moment of revelation – in that single decisive moment when everything changed and everything shifted, and you finally discovered the truth – the illusion was irreversibly destroyed, and a fresh reality opened before your eyes. It transformed something deep within you. You finally came to embrace what had been waiting for you all along, because you were then internally ready for it to be so.

So what's required of you to accept the power that is your innate and fundamental nature is to stop believing ideas about yourself that aren't true, and to stop manufacturing the kind of impoverished patterns of thought that reinforce these apocryphal perceptions. This seems like a simplistic idea when you consider it; perhaps almost too simplistic. Yet some of the most potent ideas in the universe are also the most simple. There is enormous power in the simplicity of unconditional giving. There is enormous power in the simplicity of compassion. So don't be fooled or misguided into thinking that what's required needs to be any more complicated than this: *powerful people simply accept their power, their value and their worth; and they do so unconditionally and unapologetically!*

> Ultimately, being authentically powerful is about accepting your own worthiness.

The embodiment and expression of authentic power is the pervasive awareness of your essential self. It's knowing that you are the ultimate authority in your world. It's choosing to live your life through the wakefulness of total potential – total possibility – so that you function without being paralysed by fear, or restricted by self-loathing. It's about accepting that you are fundamentally and inextricably connected to the same miraculous force that brought you into being, and that you cannot be anything less than divine and miraculous and extraordinary. It's realising you are the ultimate controller of your life. It's realising you have an astonishing ability to create. It's feeling the vibrancy of your vital energy undulating through every cell of your body, and knowing that your presence in the world is an extraordinary and priceless gift. It's feeling the sheer aliveness of your spirit. Authentic power is about living from your *fullness* – the integral completeness of who you are – instead of living from the perception of lack. And when you hold this truth intact – and refuse to allow anyone or anything to stand in the way of you maintaining this sustaining awareness – the only way you can be is deeply secure and deeply confident.

"Magic is believing in yourself, if you can do that, you can make anything happen."

–JOHANN WOLFGANG VON GOETHE

The illustrious writer, Erich Fromm, said that "The lust for power is rooted not in strength but in weakness. It is the expression of the inability of the individual self to stand alone and live. It is the desperate attempt to gain secondary strength where genuine strength is lacking." And this "lust for power" that Erich speaks about stems from the inability to recognise and connect with the power that is endlessly present within us.

This perceived sense of lack is what I refer to as *ontological ignorance*: an ignorance of the inherent power of our divine spirit. It's the inappreciation of the gift that is our birth-given uniqueness; our birth-given worth. It's the unrecognised awareness of our right to *be* in the world. But when we decide to take hold of our unconditional worth – without excuse, without compromise and without apology – authentic power is our natural resonance.

As humans, we carry the need to feel significant and confident and connected. And the truth is that when we are operating out of this sense of authenticity – this natural resonance, in the way that I've described it – the more effortlessly we *already* feel significant and confident and connected, without needing to do anything other than simply be who we are completely. And being this way is our primal state. It's as closely connected to the omnipotent source of our very existence as we can be. And what's magical is that when we are like this, no force or resistance is necessary. We just flow – we just *are* – and it feels perfect.

"ORDAINED POWER" IS NOT TRUE POWER

Ontological ignorance (the unawareness of one's intrinsic power) results in the desire to search for feelings of strength and security through extrinsic sources. People who feel a sense of inward lack rely on factors outside of them to generate the sense of adequacy and worthiness. And many people draw this form of external personal validation from the structure of ordained power.

It is important that you do not confuse *true power* with *ordained power*. People will often try to pass off ordained power as authentic power, but it is not the same by any measure.

Ordained power is a sense of power or authority that is bestowed upon an individual from an external source – a job or professional role, for example – but, outside of that role, the authority or power is not present. Put simply, the power is totally dependent upon the position in order to sustain it.

In contrast to this, a person who possesses authentic power operates from a sense of deep integral command – an awareness of self-worth and significance that is beyond circumstance and beyond limitation and not dependent upon external factors. It is a sense of inherent value that is unconditional. It's a powerful awareness that emanates from the very core of who they are. Others feel it as *presence* and they know that it's real. Ordained power does not have these sustaining qualities. Ordained power is impermanent, dependent on circumstance and always subject to change. Authentic power draws from the core of a person; ordained power comes from a source that is exterior to an individual.

One of the most characteristic examples of ordained power is the authority that is assigned to the role of a police officer. Members of the police, in a particular sense, have power and authority. This is unquestionable. By virtue of the very nature of their work, exercising "power" and "authority" within the circumstances that they encounter is a necessary component of what they do. There are regulations in place that sanction the power for them to direct and command other people. However, such power is ordained power; it is not the kind of authentic power I am speaking of. It is a form of authority that is conditional because the position must exist in order for the authority to continue to exist. This type of power is only present by virtue of the "position" or the "role" the individual is fulfilling. In the same way, government officials, airport security personnel, politicians and CEOs of large global corporations have all been granted certain authority and power. But this is not authentic power, because the power only lasts as long as the job lasts, or as long as the shift lasts. If the "position" goes away, so too does any power that is associated with it.

In the case of the police officer, as soon as he finishes work – and as soon as the all-important emblematic uniform comes off, and the shiny silver badge and the threatening looking truncheon and the handcuffs are placed away – people no longer recognise this person as a figure of power. As soon as he emerges into the world, devoid of his symbolic uniform, he instantly loses that perceived authority. People respond to him as a "regular" person, instead of the towering pillar of authoritarian control that many people associate with members of the police force.

So it's important to appreciate, then, that this "authority" and "power" wasn't really coming from the core of this person – it wasn't coming from his true essence – it was coming from his *role*. It was coming from other people's perceptions of the position that he was playing into. His authority was completely dependent upon the job that he way carrying out. And the truth is that, behind the "smoke and mirrors" – behind the *display*, the *appearance*, the *symbolism* – that's all it really is: a *societal role* which a man or woman plays into, that serves a particular function in a particular time and place.

The same is true for people that work in high level governmental positions. A *director of defence*, for example – who orchestrates army deployments, and commands groups of troops within war zones – is a person with significant ordained power. But if this person were to grow tired of doing this and decide, instead, to become a plumber, the same degree of authority would *not* be in place. The person himself, of course, would be the very same person. But, due to the change in his societal and professional position, his "power" would be considered almost insignificant compared to that of his previous role.

> The societal or professional roles that people play into are not the foundation of authentic power.

The power that is associated with all social positions of "authority" – and all other roles that we have been conditioned to hold in such lofty high regard – is a false concept. This is because: *we are not our jobs and we are not the roles that we play into.* (This doesn't mean that our roles in society can't have importance or great value, it simply means that we are not what we do.) We are fundamentally so much more than could ever been contained within the descriptions or the enactments of a social position, which others subconsciously value – or do not value – according to the public opinion marketplace. So how could our power ever truly come from a "position" (which, even though we play into, essentially exists *outside* of us) that is purely notional and subject to change at any moment? This is what artificial power looks like. You see, when we view the constructed world from *this* perspective, it becomes easy to see the foolishness in buying into these illusory belief systems.

But there are so many people who cannot see beyond the veil. There are so many people who can't see through to what's really going on, without being blinded by the alluring illusions that tell them that they can only feel strong and powerful once they've gained the utopian position they've been making sacrifices their entire life to reach. These are the people who think that the only way they can really feel a deep sense of worth is to strive harder and harder to attain the cultural "status positions" they believe are going to fulfill them.

It's no wonder, then, that there are droves of men and women, of all ages and all backgrounds, desperately trying to climb to the top of "ladders", which don't really exist, driven by the fear of not wanting to feel inadequate. They are essentially running away from the fear of their own inadequacy. They don't see that their true power is separate from what they do, how others perceive them or how they stack up against others in the constructed world. They don't see that if they were to just be still – and settle in to who they really are – they would begin to open to the awareness that the significance they so desperately want to experience is already present within them, without needing a particular description or "title" to give them validation.

Everyone has status; but not everyone claims their status. What we refer to as "social status" is actually a description of the perceptions and conclusions people arrive at about who they think we are. These conclusions may be true or untrue. But, regardless, they are still the thoughts of others. True status is knowing you have value without needing the perceptions others have of you to be a certain way so that you can feel secure. People who are concerned about their social status are constantly on the look out for how they appear to others. They are constantly trying to uphold an image and a reputation of themselves that is the image they know other people will accept and approve of. True status is leaving the need for this acceptance behind so that you can embrace the potent essence of your real nature. True status is living through the awareness that your fundamental power never leaves you.

> Authentic power is totally unconditional. It is present *regardless* of a person's role, rank or social position. It transcends the limitations of social hierarchies. It is pervasive and unchanging. This is true power. If a person only feels significant, worthy and accepted when he or she is fulfilling a particular role or job in society, that person hasn't yet connected to the source of their true integral strength.

I will always remember the old lady who owned a small bicycle shop near to where I lived. Her business, by comparison, was a very humble one. She sold bicycles (used and new), offered a repair service and also sold confectionary at the front counter of the shop. She was short and diminutive in physical build. There was nothing about the way she looked that indicated any of the typical characteristics of a "powerful person". In fact, because of her age, she exhibited many signs of infirmity. However, this lady exuded a self-respect that was hard to ignore. The way that she interacted with her customers was unmistakable. She just moved and flowed with a powerful presence and an abiding assurance of who she was.

No one would ever try to take advantage of this woman, because they instinctively felt the internal command she emanated. It was not supercilious or aggressive, and it was not overbearing or threatening; it was just a deep and resounding projection of her own intrinsic strength. It was clear that she knew her worth as a human being. To observe how she operated was an experience that had great wisdom inside of it. It was clear that she was connected to the true source of her power. It was clear that her social position had absolutely no bearing on how she felt about herself. She allowed nothing to undermine her – and all of this from an old lady running a small bicycle shop! *This* is the kind of unconditional authority and self-awareness I'm speaking of. *This* is what it means to operate with deep personal strength. *This* is authentic power.

"He alone is great and happy who requires neither to command nor to obey in order to secure his being of some importance in this world."
–Johann Wolfgang von Goethe

There have been some interesting research projects which investigated people's motivation and desire to enter into the police force. These projects, through extensive interview processes, examined, in depth, the reasons that people chose this particular profession, as opposed to any other profession. The findings revealed the ideas of "job security" and an "attractive pension" to be among the primary incentives. However, what stood head and tails above even these reasons – as the principle motivations for these individuals wanting to become police officers – was the desire for them to be *respected* by others, and the desire to be in a "position of authority".

There are no surprises here. As humans, we instinctively want to feel a sense of significance. So the outcomes of these investigations ultimately only really served to confirm what we already know. But they also confirmed something deeper than this – they confirmed that there are lots of people who believe that they aren't *already* powerful and significant, and that the only way they believe they can feel powerful is to take on a position that offers them a sense of power they would otherwise be unable to generate for themselves. (Obviously, this is not true for all individuals that pursue, or wish to pursue, a career in the police force. There are clearly countless men and women who are both fully connected to the real source of their personal strength, whilst also carrying out honourable and rewarding work as police officers. I certainly in no way disparage these people; neither do I devalue the profession itself. With this said, however, there still remains a definite pattern, which has emerged as a result of these findings. It's a pattern that is so observable and so cogent that it cannot be ignored.)

RETURNING TO YOUR TRUTH

Most of the people you think of as "authorities" can only really be authorities with your permission. In other words, they can only be authorities if you first decide and agree that they are. So, if this is true, who then is the authority making *that* decision? That's right! That authority is *you!*

The truth is, of course, that we don't need to assume roles so that we can feel worthy and significant – this is just a trap that society has very cleverly led us in to. We have been conditioned to think that in order to have any significance in the world we must first meet the criteria that society has told us we need to meet in order to stand a change of being anyone. We buy into the idea that we have to meet the standards that have been set for us. This is one of the greatest lies of our time. We can feel significant in spite of these external factors, in spite of what we do and in spite of our societal roles. Why can we feel unconditionally significant in this way? Because we are!

But when people don't recognise their power (ontological ignorance) not only will they feel compelled to take on roles and positions that offer them the power that they think is missing in them, they will also, in some instances, abuse the ordained authority that these roles grant them.

There are countless pieces of CCTV footage that have captured – in real time – police officers perpetrating totally unjustified and ruthless attacks of violence upon members of the public. On many occasions, these assaults have comprised several policemen against one single man! We've also all witnessed unscrupulous and less than honourable "doormen" or security staff – the appointed "gatekeepers" to night clubs and other venues – unnecessarily pushing and shoving people around (and, in many cases, viciously beating them, and relishing every moment). This topic has been the feature of many television documentaries. It's the classic abuse of authority. It's nothing other than unjustifiable and inexcusable barbarism of the most ruthless kind. These people are told they can use "reasonable force" in certain circumstances – when it becomes absolutely necessary for them to do so – and this is translated into permission for them to become dehumanised, robotic and emotionless tyrants with carte blanche to throw arms and fists around on a whim and fancy. (I call these people "professional playground bullies".)

Exerting totally unnecessary violence upon others gives such individuals an even greater illusion of power. They experience – and almost become addicted to – the surge of adrenalin that accompanies these kinds of merciless attacks, not to mention the hard-hearted encouragement from their co-workers. But underneath the uniform, and behind the official appearance of the stealth-like earpieces, the walkie-talkie radios and the printed jackets, what's the *real* motivation? What really drives these people to abuse the small amount of "authority" they've been presented with through their assigned roles? What does it allow them to feel that they wouldn't otherwise be able to feel?

Not surprisingly, considering these questions brings us right back to the very same idea I've been speaking of all along: it's because they don't already believe that they are worthy, capable and significant beings. They are disconnected from their own power. They are unaware of their unconditional worth.

True power – pure, genuine, sustaining personal power – needs no effort, no exertion, no force. It doesn't rely on "certifications" or "titles" or "official badges" in order for it to be present. It does not come from being a dictator or an oppressor. It isn't based upon controlling and commanding others into submission. It requires no bullying, no deception, no struggle and no pretence, because it emerges from a much deeper source.

Authentic power is already endlessly and unyieldingly present within you. There's nothing you need to do to get it there because it's already the fundamental essence of your innermost being. This has never *not* been true of you. Power is endlessly at the core of you. Power is the nature of your spirit. Power is the flow of your life force energy. It has been all along. It has been ever since the moment of your very creation. So the only real question is whether or not you're willing to fully embrace what has been yours the entire time. And when you do, you will have come home to your truth.

"

Powerlessness occurs in the struggle against a perceived sense of inadequacy. Power is knowing that such inadequacy doesn't exist.

"

–JULIAN JAMES

CHAPTER TWELVE
The Magic of Living Without Rejection

"A truly strong person does not need the approval of others any more than a lion needs the approval of sheep."

–Vernon Howard

You meet a person at a social gathering, and you find yourself very attracted to them. You instantly warm to their energy and personality. You can feel a connection between you. It turns out that you both share many of the same interests and philosophies. So after a wonderful conversation, you suggest meeting for coffee. But the person immediately becomes cold, aloof and indifferent, saying to you, "I'm sorry but I really don't think that's a good idea!" They then promptly walk off, leaving you standing on your own.

You are on a sales call. You've been speaking to a man for some time about the value of the product you're offering. You have even taken extra measures to ensure you've given him all of the right information, and in just the right way. You feel absolutely certain that this man is going to be a great and valued customer. So at the perfect moment, you ask him if he would like to go ahead and make the purchase. He pauses for a moment or two, and then sternly declares, "No, I'm not interested. I'm going to have to leave it!"

You find out that a special party has been planned by a friend of yours. Drinks, a buffet meal and a live band have all been arranged. However, you soon discover that, although almost all of your closest friends and colleagues are going to the party, you have *not* been invited.

You are working on a new project with several other co-workers. Every person in the team has been asked to put their ideas forward with regards to how they think the project should be approached. You work hard for several weeks, putting together some brand new concepts. You even stay up late to complete your proposal. You feel really excited about the contribution you have made to the project. However, when the final presentation is delivered, you discover that, although everyone else's ideas have been integrated into the plan, not a single one of your ideas has been taken on.

You go out to an exclusive hotel lounge for drinks, with a group of friends. When you arrive, one of your friends recognises an old acquaintance, who comes over and speaks to the group. She then goes over to the bar and returns with a round of drinks for everyone – except for you!

You begin a new job. You're happy with the working environment, but you get a feeling that a certain woman in your department doesn't like you. You just sense it in your bones. You know there's nothing you've done to warrant this, so you try to make conversation with her. But every time you do, she ignores you almost completely.

The scenarios I've just described are all examples of what most people would refer to as "rejection" – the awareness that we haven't been accepted, liked or approved of in some way or another. For many, to be present to this kind of realisation is something incredibly challenging to endure. It seems that people will go to great lengths just to avoid even the remote possibility of an individual, or a group of people, not accepting them, their ideas or the kind of work they do.

I want you to know, right now, that as you begin to embrace and internalise the concepts I've been sharing with you throughout this book, you'll start to really see that when you are operating from a place of *inner completeness* – the embodiment of your essential power; your inescapable truth – the "sting of rejection" almost never arises, regardless of whatever the specific circumstances happen to be, because the elements that would have been necessary for you to feel rejected by others do not form the constitution of your self-awareness. Being this way, even on those rare occasions when you do feel it, it doesn't have the same impact. It just doesn't carry the same weight at all. You simply return to your stable centre, remember what's true of you – beyond anything outside of you – and move forwards.

When you live your life from the awareness of your fundamental birthright – the pervasive and interior sense that you are *already* approved of, that you are *already* complete and that you are *already* significant – approval from anyone else becomes unnecessary. This doesn't mean that you can't or shouldn't enjoy the admiration or praise from other people when it comes along; it simply means that you don't *need* it in order for you to feel good about yourself. In this way, there is little you require from others in terms of acceptance since you know that you are already accepted. You are already accepted because you have been welcomed and accepted into the world – unconditionally – from a source of creation that is powerful beyond measure. You know, deeply, that your presence in the world is already divine and special and unique, without any factors from outside of you being necessary at all. When you know that you're already perfect and complete – just as you are – how could it be possible for someone else to make you feel anything less?

> You can only feel "rejected" when you give others the power to make you feel that way.

The real reason that most people cannot deal with any form of rejection is because they make their sense of self-worth *conditional.* They place what is needed for them to feel significant outside of their domain of control and into the hands of others. They make feeling worthy conditional upon the beliefs and thoughts others have about them. They give others ownership of their sense of security. This is being *externally referenced:* the way a person organises themselves such that their sense of internal security is derived from the circumstances that take place outwardly. And, of course, being *externally referenced* will always lead towards perpetual dissatisfaction, because it's centred around giving away your power. People who require exterior approval in order to feel comfortable and at ease are only able to have a feeling of self-worth as long as the approval is present. When the approval isn't there, they collapse.

Being *internally referenced*, on the other hand, is about allowing what's *inside* of you – the awareness of who you really are, and your unique interior qualities – to form the basis of what makes you feel secure in the world. And this is the cultivation of a personal foundation that stands strong in the face of whatever circumstances, challenges or setbacks you encounter along the journey of your life! This is about connecting to your raw and essential truth, and coming to know yourself in the deepest and most sustaining way.

Self-worth is just that: *worth* that comes from the *self!* So if we allow our worth to be derived from others people's opinions about us – or the comments and criticisms they throw our way – then, by definition, it cannot ever be true self-worth!

DON'T MAKE OTHERS' OPINIONS OF YOU MORE IMPORTANT THAN YOUR OWN OPINIONS OF YOURSELF!

The attitudes and beliefs of people who have great self-confidence are totally opposed to those of people who lack such confidence. They are totally different paradigms; two entirely separate spheres of consciousness. People with a strong sense of who they are perceive their life, and their relationship to everything, from a position of abundance, deservingness, fullness and possibility. But those who are terrified of the world, and become alarmed when they encounter the disapprobation of other people, look at the universe through a myopic lens of lack, worry and separateness.

This is an expression of the attitude of someone lacking confidence: "I don't feel a sense of completeness inside of myself, so I need validation from people and situations *outside* of me to provide me with my sense of worth. I'm afraid of even the thought that someone doesn't approve of me. I need people to demonstrate that they accept and like me, before I can feel significant, secure and internally strong."

This is an expression of the attitude of someone who has great confidence: "I live my life in such a way that I embrace what is unique about me, without fear. I do the things that bring me true personal fulfillment. I'm not afraid to ask for what I want, and, regardless of the outcome, I'm *still* going to feel good about myself. I'm not going to become immobilised when someone tells me that they don't want what I have to offer, or if they disapprove of me in some way. I don't allow other people to determine how I feel. My value as a human being is unconditional; it isn't based on the ideas others have about me. My real worth is derived from the awareness I have of being a divine and irreplaceable individual, with a uniqueness that only I can express. I embody great significance because I am intimately connected to the same source of creation that bestowed me the gift of life. I realise that I possess unlimited potential, and the awareness of the potency of my very presence in the world guides me through every moment of my existence."

> You cannot be made to feel inadequate if the very essence from which you operate is borne of unconditional self-acceptance.

The magic of being *internally referenced* is that it's the source of true personal power and freedom. It allows you to move through the experiences of your life no longer being afraid of others not approving of you, or of "saying the wrong thing", or of not matching up to the expectations other people have of you. You become much less concerned with the "critical reviews", the "observations" and "opinions" that spew from the mouths of others. And you can be fearless in this way because you no longer require anything from outside of you in order to feel significance and satisfaction. Instead, your sense of fulfillment comes from the place within you that is changeless.

SHIFTING INTERPRETATIONS

Once you realise that what you have previously thought of as "rejection" is really nothing more than an *interpretation*, the entire frame of reference from which you operate radically shifts. In *this* way, you can ask for whatever you want, you can speak to whomever you wish, you can embrace your passions and desires, and – regardless of the results – you know that you'll feel complete whatever happens. It opens before you a totally new horizon of possibilities for your life; and in ways that will continue to inspire and delight you!

Rejection is the state of feeling unwanted, unworthy, lacking or "not enough" in response to another person not accepting something about you. But once you truly begin to operate from the awareness that you are already unconditionally worthy and that you will always be "enough", it becomes very difficult to feel rejected. You stop over-thinking everything that happens around you. You stop fearing the words of others. You just regard the things that others do and say as simply things that are about *them*, without them having to mean anything about you.

When you present people with your services, your ideas or your talents, don't expect *everyone* to embrace them – everyone won't! Just always ensure that you're being the very best that you can be at whatever you're doing, that you're giving the greatest value to others, and that you're being authentically *you*. Do this and you'll always eventually arrive at the best outcome for yourself – even if it's an outcome that you didn't expect – and gain valuable insights and lessons along the way as well.

When it comes to asking for what you want, becoming comfortable hearing "no" will separate you from so many others who are so petrified of hearing the "N-word" that they sabotage opportunity after opportunity for themselves. The word "no", in its most basic form, is just a *sound* that emerges from someone's mouth – nothing more than that! This sound, in and of itself, has no power or influence over you. It's what you do with it – and how you decide to respond to it – that determines how you feel, and, consequently, what action you take. Yet, this single two-letter word is something that literally causes others to shake, tremble and lose composure and confidence. It's as if, for most people, the word "no" is like a wooden baseball bat that swings at them out of nowhere, knocking them to the ground, dazed and powerless. But it doesn't need to be this way for you. Instead, you can choose a response that is grounded in resolute strength.

Once you make the decision to do whatever it takes to become absolutely comfortable hearing the word "no", then you can ask for *whatever* you want. Yes – you can ask for *whatever* you want! Just imagine what would be possible for you if you committed to this alone! Just think of what you'd be able to make happen in your life! What's more, the more "NOs" you're comfortable hearing, the quicker you'll begin getting what you really want, without even feeling the "rejection" most others are trying so desperately hard to avoid.

If someone doesn't oblige your suggestions or requests, or doesn't want what you're offering, just recognise the inevitability inside of this. Know that you will always encounter both "NOs" and "YESs", and know that it's necessary for you to experience *both* of these polarities. It's impossible for you to receive *only* "YESs" or *only* "NOs" – there must be balance and diversity. Nature has this quality of polarity built into it. The Sun never stays risen. It rises, and then it sets, just as it's made to. The winter brings snow and cold air. The summer climate warms our skin. And we know that it never *stays* winter, and we know that it never *stays* summer, because all elements are in continual change, and they are also intimately connected. And so, "acceptance" and "non-acceptance" are not disconnected – they are just opposite sides of the *same* experience. The "YESs" allow your requests to be actualised, whilst the "NOs" allow you to learn from the experiences that don't unfold in the way you initially wanted them to. The "NOs" also allow you to sharpen your capacity to move in new directions, to generate new solutions and to develop resolute centredness. There is value in both outcomes, so always be thankful for *both*.

"Demanding that people love us because we cannot love ourselves is an iron-clad guarantee of further rejection."

–Judith Viorst

It's also important for you to realise that the people who are most concerned and afraid about "being rejected" are the very people who most attract rejection to them! (It's a concept that has to do with the way personal energy is discerned by others.) What they are frightened of causes them to function in such a way that almost guarantees that the people around them have to respond with non-acceptance and disapproval. What they most "don't want" is what they most get, because their desperation to avoid being disapproved of is so acute that it creates an energetic resonance that instinctively impels others to disapprove of them!

This is a phenomenon I've recognised in people again and again, within all types of environments. It's counterintuitive, and something which isn't understood by most, yet it's a pattern that "reveals" an individual on multiple levels. What's central to this is that it emphasises the significance of releasing the need for the acceptance of others, whilst fortifying your own internal stability. As a result, you can ensure that you'll never be in such a position, and, instead, allow yourself to remain oriented towards what really matters.

DON'T MAKE THE THINGS THAT ARE ABOUT OTHER PEOPLE ABOUT *YOU!*

Never fall into the trap of making everything that takes place around you, *about you*. Very often, it isn't! If a person that you're attracted to doesn't accept your offer to join you for dinner, it doesn't mean that you are not a worthy person. It doesn't mean that you are not interesting or attractive. It may just mean that this person isn't yet able to appreciate the qualities within you that are special and unique. It may just mean that they don't feel adequate enough within themselves to get to know someone new. It may be that they fear what you'll think of *them* once you find out more about them. Do you see how this kind of situation is often more about what's going on for the *other person*, and much less about you! Do you see how what we call "rejection" is just *one way* of interpreting what something means, when it could just as easily mean so many others things!

From this moment forward, stop thinking of what you have previously thought of as rejection as being that at all! Instead, view all of these experiences as opportunities! As soon as you stop thinking that rejection should be something to avoid, and instead, see it as something *beneficial* and *valuable*, it no longer has any control over you. When you shift your awareness towards finding the *learnings* inside of these experiences – to allow all of the moments in which you're not accepted to function as tools to strengthen your character – they instantly become opportunities for inner growth! And the more of these opportunities you have, the greater the confidence you'll possess in being able to face whatever comes your way.

So welcome these experiences. Invite them. Embrace them. See each and every one of them as an opportunity to demonstrate that, at your very core, you're robust enough and unshakable enough not to languish and weaken in response to the utterances of other people, or the circumstances that you find yourself present to. See them as ways of letting you remember that your true sense of security is *internally* organised, and doesn't need to be validated by external factors.

In a presentation delivered at Stanford University, the late Steve Jobs, CEO of *Apple Computer*, made the following statement: "Don't let the noise of other people's opinions drown out your own inner voice." And what a powerful and rewarding value to live by: the ability to boldly tread the path of your own unique life, despite the disapproval, discouragement and disparagement from others.

Consider this: in order for me to have been able to compile and publish the information you're reading right now I had to fully accept and become completely comfortable with the notion that certain people will read my writings and not support my most cherished values and personal convictions – the very beliefs that I stand for and support. This is something I just have to embrace as a reality of the world. I have to be fully willing to allow others the freedom to criticise and oppose my ideas without allowing those responses to affect or compromise who I am.

Studies have corroborated that the greatest fear a writer faces is the fear that his work won't be accepted. And this is also the same reason that many writers come very close to finishing their work before they abandon it and never take it to the final stage of publishing. As a result, there are more unfinished books in the world than you could ever conceive of. For many writers this is a *subconscious* fear; they don't consciously understand why they aren't able to bring their work to the marketplace. They just have a sense that they cannot, for "some reason", follow through to completion, not realising that what prevents them from doing so is an inveterate fear of their ideas being ridiculed. In fact, for *anyone* to put their personal ideas into book form, and then make that collection of thoughts available to the world, is an act that places them into a position of great vulnerability – it makes them vulnerable to the harsh and uncompromising eyes and minds of the public. And many people simply cannot handle this, because it opens the floodgates to the very real possibility of scorn, refusal and opposition. That's why a true foundation of strength needs to be present, because only a strong individual can be internally stable enough to allow himself to be vulnerable in this way and maintain composure regardless of what happens.

> Real power is being able to fearlessly stare criticism in the face, smile, and move forward, without even a hint of hesitation or uncertainty.

When you live your life like *this*, no longer is there any rejection – there's just information and experiences that serve your ongoing personal and spiritual journey.

When you know that you are inherently significant – and that there's nothing anyone can do to alter this truth – you stop looking for ways to derive your significance from the value judgments of others. When you know that you have unconditional value – and that there's nothing you need to do to "earn" your worth – you stop worrying about trying to prove yourself to the people around you. You let go of the anxiety in thinking you have to make a "good impression". When you operate in alignment with your highest values – and remain centred at the heart of your personal honour – you realise that you don't require the approval of *anyone*, because you are already approved of. The universe approves of you unconditionally, because the universe approved of you enough to bring you into existence. And *you* approve of you, because you realise your inherent worthiness, and you feel the internal resonance of this knowing deep within you.

From this way of functioning – from this fundamental state of awareness – you know there's absolutely nothing you "need" in order for you to be whole and complete. Like this, rejection doesn't exist. Like this, rejection has no room to breathe. Wholeness is the essential nature of your being. All that you need – and all you will ever need – is already present within you in abundance. It flows through all that you are. It saturates and pervades the depth of your spirit.

You are *already* perfect. You are *already* complete. You are *already* the embodiment of pure divine essence: the formless and fearless aspect of you that never changes. And to function from the core of this truth is to access a power that transcends all limitation. It's a power that is astounding. It's a power that is *you*.

> *"Give up who you think you need to be in order to please the world."*
>
> –Julian James

CHAPTER THIRTEEN
Escaping the Venom of Cultural Conditioning

"The Dark Ages still reign over all humanity, and the depth and persistence of this domination are only now becoming clear. This Dark Ages prison has no steel bars, chains, or locks. Instead, it is locked by disorientation and built of misinformation ... We are powerfully imprisoned in these Dark Ages simply by the terms in which we have been conditioned to think."

—Buckminster Fuller

Have you ever heard of the Inland Taipan? If it's a creature you're not immediately familiar with, let me tell you a little about this fascinating reptile:

The Inland Taipan, which is native to the arid regions of central Australia, is the most venomous and deadly snake on earth. Even the tiniest amount of its venom is capable of stripping a grown man of his very life, in some instances, within less than one hour! Its venom is of the neurotoxin variety, which means that it begins to directly attack the functioning of the brain and nervous system as soon as it enters the bloodstream. The effects are numerous: abdominal pain, uncontainable panic, muscle tremors, drowsiness, nausea, vomiting, intense perspiration, irregular increase (or decrease) of the heart rate, paralysis of the neck musculature, inability to swallow, hallucination, confusion and coma. And the result – ultimately – is total respiratory failure, leading to certain death.

If I held a syringe in front of you, and told you that the syringe contained 10ml of fresh venom, which had been collected directly from the glands of an Inland Taipan snake, would you allow me to insert the needle into your arm, press down on the syringe and send the deadly venom surging through your bloodstream? Clearly (unless it was your intention to terminate your life incredibly quickly) you wouldn't allow the deadly poison anywhere near you! You would stand well back. You would keep as far away as possible. You'd do all you could to distance yourself from the potentiality of having any contact with the venom. So, if this is true – if there was no way you'd let into your body a substance that was totally toxic – why would you allow toxic thoughts, ideas and belief systems to enter into your consciousness and affect the very nature of how you relate to yourself?

In many ways, the playing field of Western capitalist culture – the assault of *conditioning* that is imposed upon us from all directions of the consumer-driven society in which we operate – is just as toxic and insidious as the venom that seeps from the glands of the Inland Taipan. If we do not engage life at a higher and more awakened level of awareness – if we do not see through the illusions born of negative acculturation and indoctrination – this venomous conditioning bleeds into our very perceptions and understandings of who we believe ourselves to be. In many ways it's just as deadly, debilitating and destructive as the serpent's lightning attack. Actually, it's even more deadly, because, for most people, it operates on a level that is invisible.

Throughout this book I have been touching upon these venomous cultural illusions – the *impositions* of the world – the lies and distortions that keep us controlled, anxious, inhibited and afraid. These are the mechanisms which attempt to pull us away from owning and expressing our fundamental truth. And so, it's now time to delve much deeper into the jaws of the serpent, to examine these illusions more closely, and to uncover them for what they really are.

CONDITIONING AND BELIEFS

"Spiritual growth basically means going beyond mass thinking to a point where you have so much confidence in your reality that you can stand alone."

–Stuart Wilde

Why do you believe the things that you believe? And why do you hold *these* beliefs as opposed to any other beliefs that you could hold?

Do you realise that many of the thoughts you have are not your own thoughts? And I don't mean this figuratively; I mean this very literally. In the most literal way possible, many of the conceptions you hold inside of your consciousness – all of the mental images and sounds that comprise your internal experiences – are not your own! They are *not* your own thoughts, and yet you're convinced that they are. What's more, these thoughts are directly affecting the relationship you have with yourself. They are literally determining how you think and feel about yourself, and the value you place upon your very existence in the world.

There is a significant distinction between thinking and "having thoughts". Having thoughts is what happens when you give yourself over to the conditioning that engulfs you. It's what takes place when ideas and conceptual frameworks, which are not designed for your best interests, enter into your consciousness from sources outside of you. Having thoughts is allowing others – your family, your peers, political dogma, religious codes of practice or the systems of belief generated by large institutions and multinational corporations – to be the predominant determinants of your cognitive and decision-making processes. It's allowing these exterior domains of information to be greater influences to you than you are to yourself. It's allowing these ideas to be imposed upon you, so deeply and so overwhelmingly, that you lose the capacity to reason and think for yourself. It means to subordinate your own source of personal intuitive wisdom to the ideas presented to you from the outside.

Thinking, on the other hand – *real* thinking – is about having the wherewithal to generate patterns of ideation with great specificity and great intention. It's about accessing your deep intrinsic insight (that aspect of you many others want to subdue) and allowing that to operate as the principal guidance force for your life, because it's from there that your inborn wisdom and creativity flows. This is true autonomy. Most people are not actually thinking autonomously; most people are just repeating what they've been told. But this isn't real thinking; this is being a parrot!

Of course, we can never be totally independent of the influences that external ideologies present to us. In order to operate in the world we are required to interact with others inside of a huge diversity of contexts and social frameworks. We will therefore always be present to an array of paradigms and elements of compelling persuasiveness, some of which will be for our highest good, but many of which will not. So, unless we choose to withdraw into permanent hiding, we will never be completely divorced from the presence of these influences. They will always be around us. However, what we can always control is the *degree* to which we allow our character and our values to be shaped by them. And, when we refuse to let go of who we are – when we make the resolute decision to keep our deepest essence solid and intact – we function from a position of enduring authentic strength. This strength is absolutely required by us to sustain our journey – if what we want is a journey that has purpose, heart and soul – because the conditioning will always be at work. The force of it will be there incessantly, night and day. It will never surrender; it will never retreat. This makes our personal quest extremely challenging, but, at the same time, rewarding in ways that are boundless. We have to be prepared to do *whatever* it takes.

Social conditioning is essentially about the formation of beliefs within a specific cultural context. *Belief*s are concepts and ideas that we hold to be *true*. And just because we have beliefs, doesn't necessarily mean that these cognitive interpretations *are* universally and empirically true – that they're sustainable and verifiable for *all* people, in *all* conditions and in *all* contexts – it simply means that we represent them to be true according to our own subjective experience. We also attune our awareness – the filters of our perception – to search for additional evidence that will support our existing beliefs, whilst overlooking evidence that opposes them. This further strengthens them through time. This subjective experience becomes our individual map of the world – how we make sense of the things around us. And, of course, the elements that contribute towards forming this internal map exist in the very environment that we're born into – our culture.

It's interesting to note that part of the definition of a *cult* is any process of indoctrination that discourages individual thinking, and instead, only encourages thinking that is aligned with the doctrine of that particular belief system. And there's a reason, of course, why the word "cult" comprises the first part of the word "culture".

We enter into existence without beliefs or conditioning. We arrive from the totality of pure possibility. And, although it is true that our genetic constitution can carry some bearing upon certain human tendencies, which lead to the way ideas and behaviours are processed, formed and exhibited – referred to by psychologists as "predispositions" – it has been concluded through countless biopsychological research studies, including the notable work of Abraham Tesser, that environmental factors take precedence over hereditary biases. These research initiatives found no sustainable evidence to support the theory that specific genes are responsible for the existence of specific belief structures. A substantial report in the *Journal of Personality and Social Psychology* provides further conclusive verification that effects from the environment, in determining attitudes and beliefs, heavily outweigh those of heredity across the board.

It still holds, therefore, that beliefs are not genetically inherited. We are not born with beliefs. If we were born with beliefs, then, from a fundamental biological standpoint, identical twins (monozygotic twins) would consistently share the very same views, opinions and attitudes. Yet, in light of this theory, many pairs of identical twins have been conscientiously interviewed – in tremendous detail, covering a diverse spectrum of topics – revealing that many of the individual twins hold very separate and differing viewpoints on an entire range of issues, including political, religious and emotional matters.

No child is born a republican, a democrat or an anarchist. No child is born an atheist, and no child is born believing that a rabbit's foot brings good luck. No child comes into the world with the belief that euthanasia should be made legal, or that the colour green is prettier than the colour orange. No child is born believing that mermaids exist or that it's more honourable to be a Catholic than it is to be a Protestant. No child is born believing that he is a "failure" or that he is unworthy. All of these are *ideas, points of view* and *interpretations* which are formed and cultivated *after* birth – not before.

Beliefs are generated as a result of the information that we assimilate – through a conglomeration of early parental influences, the words of "authority figures", contemplation, observation, personal study and cultural osmosis – which form our individual defining paradigms of the world around us. All of our beliefs are programmed or installed into us (with varying degrees of intention and conscious awareness) through time. As we gain experiences, interact with others and gather information from a multitude of sources, our beliefs are shaped and developed. And many of these beliefs are formed and reinforced *outside* of our conscious awareness. In other words, we hold beliefs and attitudes about ourselves – which we're not immediately aware that we have – because they've been present for so long we've forgotten where they initially came from, and also *who* they came from. And we're unaware that many of the things we hold to be "true" are actually not true at all – at least from a universally objective position – rather, they are the result of a conglomeration of deeply inveterate belief systems.

Do you fancy a dog sandwich? Some nice slices of dog, on white bread, with mustard? If not, why not? Don't you like to eat dog meat? How come? What are your *beliefs* about what's acceptable to eat, and what's not acceptable? And where did you learn these "rules"?

For the majority of Western civilisation, the notion of eating a dog is firmly rejected. Yet, in Taiwan and Indonesia, as well as many other countries, the consumption of dog meat is normal – it's an every day reality. It's as banal as a cheese and pickle sandwich, or a steak pie. So what's the difference? The difference is beliefs! There's no "right" or "wrong" here. Instead we're dealing with beliefs about what is "acceptable" and what is "not acceptable". And such beliefs are culturally formed. These beliefs originate out of cultural stipulations. A large portion of Eastern culture embraces eating dog flesh as an acceptable practice, and, to Western culture, it is violently forbidden. In most European counties, killing a dog for consumption would meet with severe legal consequences. But, in Korea, you could impale a whole dog on a barbecue spit, roast it, and invite your friends over for dinner. This is the power of cultural conditioning.

Most cultural beliefs have been handed down from generation to generation. People just blindly accept them. Most of us don't give thought to how our beliefs are actually formed. Most of us don't question the ideas we hold. We simply go about our day-to-day affairs acting as if these conceptions are universally true. Yet, if someone injected you with a substance, you'd most certainly want to know what that substance was, and what it was doing to your mind-body system. So why do we not question the beliefs that have been "injected" into us? Why do we not ask ourselves *how* our beliefs were formed initially, and *how* they are affecting us right now? Why don't we set out to banish the toxic beliefs that are causing us to feel less than we are? Predominantly, it's because we're living in a culture that doesn't encourage us to do this. The people around us, and the large institutions that want to control us, would rather we stayed docile, confused and afraid. That way, keeping us controlled is a much easier task!

So, what we believe, what we don't believe, what we know we've been led to believe and what we don't even realise we've been conditioned to believe are crucial notions to consider in regard to the fundamental perception of our reality. The beliefs we hold are responsible for what we stand for and our understanding of our very presence in the world. Our beliefs – what we hold to be true – are the components that affect everything that we do!

So, in light of all of this – since you know that much of the conditioning you're present to is not designed to empower you, but rather, to suppress and emasculate you – I want to ask you a question. It's an absolutely vital question because it pertains to everything I've been speaking of thus far: *What has the world around you impelled you to believe about who you are that may in fact not be true?*

THE DISCOURAGEMENT OF INDIVIDUALISM

"You were wild once. Don't let them tame you."

–Isadora Duncan

Since the beliefs we have about ourselves – and about who we are in relation to the world around us – determine how we operate and function, doesn't it make sense to ensure that the beliefs we hold serve us, support us and enrich us? Doesn't it make sense to desire only those beliefs that are conducive to deep personal satisfaction and authentic confidence? Doesn't it make sense to only hold those beliefs which serve our highest good?

Things are not so straightforward. We are being bombarded, from all directions, with messages that have been specifically and expertly crafted to cause us to question who we are and to make us feel helpless, worthless and hopeless. This web of conditioning implies that our only hope to be anyone is to do exactly what we're told to do, and then, maybe, we'll be "free" and "happy". We are offered ideals about who we "should" be, and who we "need" to be in order to feel fulfilled. And it's these very messages that are really no different to that venom from the Inland Taipan snake I mentioned at the beginning of this chapter. Why? Because these messages are actually designed to make us feel empty, unworthy and afraid. This way we become victims of perceived inadequacy, and can more easily be sold the ostensible "solutions" on offer. This is the poison that pervades the society in which we function; and we've been living with some of these poisonous myths for almost our entire lives, totally unaware that they are limiting and restricting us, and totally unaware that they simply aren't true!

In this constructed society we are not encouraged to be unique. There are exceptions to this, of course. But, for the most part, we are impelled to feel dissatisfied and discontented with who we are. We are not encouraged to embrace and celebrate what it is about ourselves that's truly special. Instead, we are encouraged to be like others. We are encouraged not to stand apart, but to join the social collective and to blend into the crowd – to become homogenous. Any person who stands apart from the crowd (the "herd") is considered strange, unusual and even contemptible by others. People who stand apart threaten the status quo, and extreme measures are taken to encourage against this.

> The most subversive and limiting lies you will ever be told are that you are "not enough", that you need to change and that you are not whole and complete just as you are.

When you were a baby, you had absolutely no feelings of unworthiness or lack whatsoever. You were fully alive and flourishing. You felt whole. You felt complete. Life was wondrous and fascinating. You were too busy exploring, creating and enjoying yourself to feel any way other than perfect. You exuded a natural effortlessness that was magical and captivating to others. You fully embraced the gift of being you. And then, after a few years, you entered into society, and society beat it out of you!

There's no question – growing up as a child is not an easy task. It's a fascinating journey – yes – but it's in no way easy. Humans don't emerge from the womb with a set of instructions. As a result, our parents – wanting the very best for us – bring us up according to how they believe we should be "disciplined". They do this according to their beliefs about how they think we should be nurtured, and many of these beliefs are simply picked up from their own parents, without any regard to how these ideas came to be in the first place.

Being a young child was, in many ways, very confusing. A lot of the time, it just didn't seem to make much sense at all. In the evening – when we were having such a fabulous time with our colouring books, our building blocks and our toy cars – we were suddenly told that we had to put our toys away and go to bed. And, of course, we didn't want to go to bed because we were too busy making pictures in the colouring books and expressing our creativity. Things were too good to go to sleep! But our mother or father told us that it was now "bed time" (whatever that really meant) and that we needed to stop enjoying ourselves and go and lie down in bed. We were naturally confused because we didn't even feel tired, yet we "had" to go to bed and force ourselves to sleep. Surely it would have made more sense to go to bed when our body told us that we needed the rest? So we were made to feel "wrong" about the occurrences in our life that seemed so natural and so effortless. We were made to feel wrong for doing what brought us the most enjoyment and fulfilment. Of course, as far as our parents were concerned, they were just "doing their duty". However, for us – at a deeper level – something else was taking place.

This is a very debilitating set of signals to receive as a child, because we learn, through time, that doing what fascinates us, and following our passions, is not good for us. We begin to learn that it's more important to listen to the people around us than it is to look within ourselves. And this impedes our true nature; it stifles our inherent creativeness. This belief perpetuates so strongly – it becomes so deeply ingrained – that we eventually reach a point in which we stop looking inwardly at all. We stop listening to those interior guiding signals. We stop listening to our deep intuitive wisdom. We start to ignore our deepest truth. Instead we grow to learn to pay attention only to the people around us who claim to know better than we do.

So years later, as adults, we often feel a sense of guilt about doing the things we really enjoy because the conditioning we were imbued with at such an early age is still running the way we function and operate. We're unable to transcend that internal inhibiting pattern. It's so deeply imbedded in our consciousness that we've forgotten it even exists. This is why we see so many adults who appear to be totally stripped of any vitality or vibrancy. They move through life cut off from that effortlessness they once had. They move through life as though they are already dead.

Parents naturally want their children to be protected and safe from harm. This, of course, is a primal parental response. But an overwhelming number of parents protect and confine their children much more than is actually necessary. As a result, many mothers and fathers employ a method of rearing their children that involves restricting and reprimanding anything new or unfamiliar the child attempts to engage in. It becomes an incessant barrage of redundant restrictions and injunctions: "Don't touch the dog because it's dirty"; "Don't go near the front door because someone might come along and snatch you away"; "Don't talk to that man because you don't know who he is"; "Don't go near the pond because you might fall in"; "Don't go out of my sight because we might lose you"; "Don't say anything unless I tell you to or you'll get into trouble!"

The underlying message being communicated to the child is that the world is abounding with threat and danger and that everything's a disaster waiting to happen. So the child becomes excessively fearful and sees things as a threat, even when no threat is present at all. Threat, then, becomes the default perceptual filter for the way that young person engages life. He sees the world through the eyes of fear. The child begins to associate anything new with a sense of "danger" and the fear of being reprimanded. Over time an aversion to the unfamiliar becomes established and the child becomes far less willing to do anything he hasn't already done. This is impoverished learning. Naturally, there are times in which it's absolutely necessary for the child to be told not to do something for his own safety. But, in many cases, such overprotection is excessive and unnecessary and only serves to perpetuate cognitive and behavioural patterns which keep the child withdrawn. It also serves to restrict organic growth and self-learning. It doesn't allow him to develop the astuteness and wherewithal that comes from entering into the unknown and handling situations as they arise. So when the child reaches adulthood it's no surprise that he feels the very same sense of fear in relation to doing anything new. Because of this, he rarely ventures into new experiences – he hesitates to speak to that woman he's attracted to at the party, he fears asking for a pay raise at work and he's terrified of getting a gym membership for concern of being criticised. He lives life far below his true potential.

In an experiment that was conducted with a control group of young children, small recording devices were worn by the children, which recorded the interactions and conversations that took place over a period of several days. At the end of the test period, when the audio recordings were examined and analysed, an unmistakable pattern came to light: it was observed that the children were told "no" many more times than they were told "yes". The children were told that they "couldn't", far more frequently than they were told that they "could". And this speaks directly to the kind of restrictive conditioning that infants are subjected to – day after day – during the crucial developmental years of their lives. When a child is told "no" again and again and again, that essential message of restriction and limitation becomes the predominant paradigm for how the child operates and sees the world around him.

When we are children, for the most part, acts of *obedience* and *conformity* are rewarded, whilst behaviours that are contrary to expectations and instructions are criticised and punished. As children when we didn't want to put our dirty clothes in the washing because we were having too much of a good time playing on our bike, we were made to feel bad for not doing what had been requested of us. And if we didn't do what we were told to, we inevitably had to face some kind of punishment, either through verbal admonishment, a sharp smack around the legs, the restriction of pleasures such as favourite foods or enjoyable activities, or even being sent away to our room (ostracism) for several hours to "think about our actions" and to not come down until instructed. As a result, we began to equate subservience and conformity with love and acceptance, because love was only expressed to us when we followed orders. And since love and acceptance were what we wanted from our caregivers, we knew that we had to do as we were told in order to receive them. This, of course, is classical psychological conditioning; it leverages reward and punishment as the prevailing factors of control. So we started to associate our more instinctual and creative tendencies – those behaviours that were falsely labelled as "bad behaviours" – with fear, punishment and potential abandonment. We learned very quickly that the way to stay loved, cared for and appreciated was to just do as we were told to do, to not question anything and not do anything "out of the ordinary".

We then bring these tendencies and beliefs into adulthood, still thinking that as long as we just do as we're told, and remain in a state of willing subservience, things will somehow work out for us. So, when we enter into a place of work, everything seems familiar. There is a boss – the leader of the tribe – who tells us exactly what to do. And by this time, of course, we're very used to being told what to do! We're told when to arrive, when to leave, when to eat out lunch and even when we're allowed to go to the toilet. And we think that this is how things "should be" because conforming and blindly following orders, without thinking to question them, is what we've been conditioned to believe is the "right way to be" ever since we were small children.

THE VENOM OF THE SCHOOL SYSTEM

"I have never let my schooling interfere with my education."
–Mark Twain

The school system is not exempt from perpetrating the very same processes of repression and emasculation. It is not entirely corrupt, however – there is some good to be found. For one thing, school brings young people together in such a way that they're able to develop relationships with each other and learn the values of friendship and loyalty. There is certainly great value in this. There is also, of course, undeniable value in the learning of key competencies such as written language and other foundational skills. However, woven deep into the fabric of the school system is a succession of insidious underlying structures and practices that do little to empower. Rather, the process of schooling is primarily designed to programme and indoctrinate. It's designed to generate – over and above all else – the prevailing responses of obedience, conformity, submission and the worship of authority.

It's all too common for parents to say to their children, "You must go to school so that you can work hard and make something of yourself!" But such a statement serves to consolidate the idea that we are not already "something", and that "being someone" is something we have to strive and work for. So we enter into a contrived environment – an environment that operates from a foundation of control, punishment and reflexive obedience – and "work hard" so that we can attain the personal value we've been made to think we don't already embody.

We have been led into believing that schooling, and formal education, is absolutely critical to our "success". We're told that we should set our minds towards getting "good grades". Secondary school qualifications, degrees and other titles and certifications are glamorised and romanticised and made to appear as the magical elixir for all of our problems and concerns. They are presented to us as utopian goals – goals that, should we reach them, will somehow guarantee comfort, fulfilment and make our lives complete. We're told, "Just get good grades and you'll be okay!" Yet we know this isn't true because thousands and thousands of young university graduates, every year, are unable to find work placements that specifically relate to their specialist subject, despite the fact that they've spent three or four years working hard to obtain their qualifications. So much emphasis is placed upon pleasing the teachers and striving towards obtaining "exemplary marks", yet some of the most creative, talented and successful people in the world dropped out of school early. Many hardly had any schooling whatsoever.

Richard Branson left school early, yet he's built a worldwide brand and empire no one can ignore. Michael Dell also dropped out of education, yet went on to build one of the largest technological corporations in the world. Steve Jobs didn't even complete college – he stayed for only one semester, then left – yet Jobs was regarded as America's most powerful businessman. The list of highly successful people who rejected the traditional model of "education" would astound you!

The school environment made us believe that so much of what we were taught was crucial and essential. But it really wasn't at all. Since leaving school, have you ever had to calculate the angles of a scalene triangle? No – of course not! But, back then, it was all so "very important", wasn't it? And, at the same time, other essential skills, which would have been significantly more practical and valuable – such as the skills of effective negotiation, or learning about what is now referred to as *emotional intelligence* – weren't even mentioned, because it wasn't part of the "curriculum"!

Going to school is apparently about "education". Yet, if we examine the etymology of this word, we discover that "education" derives from the Latin *educare,* which means "to draw out of". Therefore, by definition, true education is about *drawing out* of us our unique essence – our individual gifts – the qualities within us that allow us to grow into the fullest expressions of who we are. It doesn't mean having information and beliefs *forced* into us!

For the most part, however, this is precisely what modern education is about: having ideas *forced* into us, many of which do not and never will, serve us in any positive way. The school system trains students to repeat information in "parrot style" – everyone blindly regurgitating the very same words, like some kind of mass incantation. And when asked a question, we are trained, not to give the answer that we believe is right, but to give the answer we have been told is correct. This allows little room for individual and creative ideation. And, only after we have said the "right thing" are we rewarded (either through reassuring acknowledgement or in some other manner) as a way of further solidifying the habituation of reflexive conformity. This ensures that we are even more likely to respond in the expected manner the next time we are asked a question. And this conditioning process continues, on and on, in much the same way, for the entire span of our educational lives, which, for most people, is between 12 and 20 years!

Predominantly, the modern systems of education have emerged out of a structure that is actually Prussian in origin (Prussia being part of the region we now call Germany). And, put simply, this model of education was never designed for the benefit of the individual – it was designed for the benefit of the government. In the eighteenth century, the kingdom of Prussia was the first to introduce a compulsory system of education. In 1806, Napoleon defeated the Prussians, and it was believed by the Prussians that the reason they had been conquered was due to the fact that the soldiers were thinking far too independently whilst on the battlefield, instead of rigorously following orders.

As a result, stern measures were put in place to ensure that nothing of this kind would ever happen again. What came out of this was a system of education that upheld blind subservience – the submissive following of orders – as the most prevailing principle. This was done in order to create unassuming workers for the mines and compliant civil servants for the government, to train men for the military, and to cultivate docile workers for jobs in the industrialised world. It was all about compliance and servitude! This Prussian model of schooling eventually became prevalent throughout the world. It became the "standard" way of leading young minds through a process of indoctrination that masqueraded itself as "education". It did everything it could to stamp out independent critical thinking in favour of the process of reflexively obeying commands without questioning them.

"It is the mark of an educated mind to be able to entertain a thought without accepting it."

–Aristotle

Philosopher and German nationalist, Johann Gottlieb Fichte, was a man recognised as being the predominant catalyst in the formation of the Prussian model of education. Fichte stated unequivocally, that "Education should aim at destroying free will so that after pupils are thus schooled they will be incapable throughout the rest of their lives of thinking or acting otherwise than as their school masters would have wished ...". Fichte also delivered numerous addresses to the German nation, which underscored his beliefs about supreme dominance. Adolf Hitler was known to have consumed all of Fichte's writings, and the content of this body of work went on to become the central tenets of Nazi philosophy. So it's unsettling to learn that the man who imparted such significant influence upon the development of our current school system is the very same man whose fundamental values were adopted by Nazi Germany – a foundation of oppression and relentless totalitarian control!

The entire school structure essentially says to us: "There is only one way – *our* way! And if you don't act in accordance with our rules, you will be punished!" This underlying conceptual structure and methodology, of course, is no different to organised religion. Organised religion is principally built upon the notion that there is only one "ultimate truth" and that anyone who questions or deviates from this rigid and myopic interpretation of our human existence is wrong, or even "sinful", and therefore needs to be punished. I hardly need to mention the barbaric and unspeakable ways people have been mercilessly tortured and bludgeoned to death – all because they didn't believe what they were told to believe. How's that for a way of living that is supposed to be "heavenly" and "divine"? (Personally, I refuse to embrace or espouse *any* belief system that threatens me with eternal damnation if I choose to think for myself!)

At school, a very specific and intentional system of conditioning was at work. Healthy, self-governed decision-making was discouraged, and often criticised, at most opportunities. Fear of ridicule and humiliation in front of classmates virtually ensured that almost all of the information taught was not questioned, and simply accepted. After all, during class, there was great pressure. The way our learning environment was structured supported this pressure. No one wanted to appear silly or to be laughed at. So the easiest thing to do was to simply keep quiet, be told what to think and not question anything. At least that way, we weren't made to feel uncomfortable or singled out by the adult standing at the front of the room. This further consolidated the process of looking outside of ourselves – to the supposed "authority figures" – who were apparently all-knowing and who apparently never faltered. The teachers were presented as omniscient superior beings whose primary objective seemed to be to mould us into powerless and obedient robots – for us to "sit down, shut up and listen!"

Just consider the nature of the typical teacher-student relationship: when a teacher instructs a child to do something, and that child questions the instruction, the teacher castigates the child, bellowing harsh and daunting imperatives such as, "Don't answer back to the teacher!" or "Just do as I tell you and stop talking!" This kind of predictable teacher-student exchange engenders and supports the idea that it's not okay to have your own ideas and that proposing an alternative to what is being dictated, or challenging the status quo in any way, are acts of defiance and insubordination. And if this happens often enough, the child starts believing that it's wrong to have his own views.

One of the first things we learned at school was that we are not in charge of ourselves. Instead we learned that others are in charge of us. Our autonomy was intentionally stifled in lieu of a regimented military-like indoctrination. We were conditioned to subordinate ourselves to the God-like figures standing by the board. Even when we wanted to go to the toilet, we had to first ask for permission. Doesn't it seem totally crass to have to ask for permission to urinate? Yet that's exactly what we had to do – we had to ask someone else if it was "okay" for us to engage in a necessary and primal human activity. We were made to believe that the functioning of our bladder required sanctioning by another person. "Please sir, may I go to the toilet?" What a ridiculous thing to be trained to ask, especially in front of a room full of your peers! But, once again, this was all part of the subordination process. We weren't even allowed to speak when we wanted to speak. No! We had to raise our hand into the air, like an obedient and conditioned robot, until we were given permission to say something.

We were never really encouraged to express our own unique ideas about things. Instead, we were conditioned and moulded into the patterns of thought and behaviour that were imposed upon us. What's more, if we didn't act in accordance with the rules of the system, we were undermined, reproached and even subjected to humiliation. For most teachers, the use of intimidation was standard protocol. Our vulnerability and lack of worldly experience was taken advantage of. Most of us have had the unpleasant experience of being scorned or laughed at, by a teacher, in front of the class. This, of course, was negative reinforcement, and it only served to encourage the very conformity that was intended of us all along.

As a result, over time, we learned to trust that which was *outside* of ourselves more than we learned to trust what was *inside* ourselves – our own intuitive wisdom – that priceless inner resource that resides at the core of who we are. We learned to listen and pay attention only to the information we were impelled to focus on, and nothing else. Quite literally, we were trained to ignore and suppress those essential signals from own internal experience which are at the heart of our uniqueness and human liberty.

For most people, this trained pattern of personal inhibition carries over into countless areas of their professional lives. Just take a look at the world of job interviews: going for a job interview is not about speaking from a position of authentic truth – it never has been. The art of being successful in a job interview, we are informed, is to give the employer the "perfect answers" – the answers they most want to hear – but not the answers that are necessarily true for us! These answers, of course, have usually been rote memorised out of a book entitled something like *201 Answers to Tough Interview Questions*, regardless of whether or not such responses are truly aligned and congruent with what we sincerely stand for. Therefore, the most successful individual at any job interview is the candidate who can lie the best under pressure. There are even expensive weekend seminars devoted to such a skill, where job seekers pay money to learn "strategies", "tactics" and "techniques" designed to make them even more efficient liars, as they compete in a swarming marketplace of men and women willing to do and say whatever it takes, as long as they get the job! And this further ingrains into us the idea that our own truth is not enough – that it is insufficient and incomplete – and that we have to look outside of ourselves in order to seek that which we're told is missing in us. And, because the school system is ultimately designed to craft us into "perfect employees" – befitting the commercial working world – this same pattern is fed into us, in the classroom, as early as possible.

So the result of all of this insidious conditioning is the gradual dampening of our inherent creativity and aliveness and uninhibited self-expression. Our unique essence is forced and bullied into hiding. But this is where our real power resides – our divine gift – our fundamental truth. And this is why our schools want to deaden this aspect of us as much as they can, because doing so makes it easier for us to be controlled. After all, it's very difficult to control several hundred pupils who are all operating from the heart of their inspired uniqueness. Doing so would be too overwhelming for the system to handle. It would be far too much of a challenge. And so creating "rules" and "procedures" that stifle our distinctiveness is the easiest option.

In order for us to be free we need to reawaken our power, and know that it is the truth of who we are. We need to re-learn to trust those internal signals that resound from within us – those signals we've, for so long, been encouraged to reject. We need to allow this wisdom to guide us powerfully in making crucial decisions for our lives, so that we can live the life that is truly our own, instead of the life others want us to live.

"Disobedience is the true foundation of liberty. The obedient must be slaves."

–Henry David Thoreau

Imagine a young child in his first few years at school. He's sitting on a chair in class, and the teacher is speaking at the front of the room. There are twenty or so other children in the classroom as well, all sitting at desks, facing the front. And this child has a true gift for drawing. He's totally fascinated and enamoured by putting pencil to paper and creating images: action figures, animals, silhouettes, cartoon characters and a whole range of other marvellous artistic creations. Doing this is a skill that is absolutely natural for him. So the young boy is drawing on a sheet of paper with a pencil and things are literary coming to life on the page. For someone so young, what he's creating is absolutely astounding! He's drawing sea creatures and dinosaurs and technical three-dimensional images that would amaze even the most critical of eyes! The sheer detail of them is simply stunning. They're of the quality one would expect from a professional illustrator. For him, drawing is as effortless as breathing; it's the type of effortless creation that is synonymous with genius. This is his gift. This is his extraordinary talent. This is his innate inspiration. This is part of his unique expression as an individual.

The teacher then suddenly notices what he's been doing all along. He rushes over to his desk and yells at the child in front of the entire class. He scolds and criticises the boy, immediately tearing up the sheet of drawings, furiously scrunching the torn pieces into a tight ball. In this moment the teacher takes the very article that stands for so much of the child's unique and individual expression, and ridicules and disdains it. He looks down at him with an intensity that's too frightening for such a young boy to handle. The boy's face flushes. He literally trembles at the teacher's imposing gaze and the volume of his bellowing voice. He feels completely attacked by this imposition. It puts his body into a state of immediate shock. The experience leaves an impression on him that isn't easily forgotten, both cognitively and somatically as well. It is an emotionally charged event that impacts on him severely. And the child learns – through several similar instances of this – that doing what he loves so much is "wrong". His interior creative energy gradually becomes subdued. He becomes less and less willing to express his gift until it virtually ceases to emerge at all; fearing what will happen to him, fearing the humiliation, fearing the threat.

So, in the first crucial developmental years of our lives, the onslaught of doctrine that's designed to restrict and inhibit our divine individuality is immense and impactful. It shows up in numerous menacing ways. It is utterly toxic. It has no value other than to reaffirm the importance of rigid conformity and submission. It is just another mechanism of control.

I can point to instances of this type of structured subordination in my own schooling. Fortunately, I made every effort I could to not yield to the conditioning. Doing so was challenging; it landed me in perpetual trouble. But I knew – deep inside of me – that I wasn't going to give myself over to a system that was built upon a foundation of blind compliance and homogenisation as its principal incentives. Many would say I was "famous" at school – I became recognised as being an unapologetic non-conformist. This never bothered me. I always went my own way. It was the only way I was prepared to go. I even established my own special group, which attracted other non-conformists. It was essentially a "club" for those who shared similar ideas to my own. This was great fun. I even had t-shirts screen-printed, bearing a distinctive logo, which we wore underneath our school shirts. These t-shirts would make special appearances during PE classes and at other times as well. For a long time the teachers wondered what it was all about. No one ever told them!

On another occasion, I purchased several hundred whistling devices, called *Bird Warblers*, from a novelty wholesale outlet. These were small devices that, when placed onto the front of your tongue and blown into, allowed you to imitate the chirping sounds of birds. I started selling these to the other students. I also employed a trusty gang of people to sell them for me as well. This made break time extremely entertaining. At one point, I had seven different people offering the whistles for sale all over the playground and in the dinner hall. My venture was an instant success. Many times, I almost wet myself laughing! I would walk out into the playground and all I could hear – issuing from all directions – were the mating calls of indigenous birds!

When the headmaster found out about my enterprise, a letter of warning was immediately sent home to all parents imploring them to destroy the whistles, should they find their child to be in possession of one. As punishment, I spent an entire week doing my school work on a solitary desk positioned outside of the deputy head's office. I used this special opportunity to eat and drink, something you couldn't easily do during regular class. So, whilst my classmates were being "educated" in a totally different part of the school, I sat upon my very own throne, enjoying all manner of different confectionaries, listening to my Walkman and creating new magical effects with playing cards. A great week it certainly was!

Very often, I would find myself standing in front of the headmaster – in a darkly lit room filled with stale cigar smoke – being told that I was too "disruptive" and that I needed to be more like the other students who did as they were told. But I never languished. I never surrendered who I was to the system that tried to repress me, and it's the greatest personal value I've ever lived by.

"Fears are educated into us and can, if we wish, be educated out!"
—Karl Menninger

My schooling was varied indeed. I spent the first nine years of education attending a private all-boys preparatory school, the next three years in a strict Catholic school (which is fascinating, because I'm not even Catholic!) and the following two years in a state school. So, in a sense, I've had a very "good education", and it's taken me many years to get rid of it!

Not all teachers, however, "play the game" like the others. Occasionally you come across someone who hasn't let go of their capacity to engage with students on an authentic level, beyond the artificial teacher-student relationship. I was fortunate enough to have such a teacher; a very special person indeed. Her name was Anne Horne. She taught me drama and media studies. But Mrs Horne wasn't just a regular school teacher – she was so much more. She was a true individual, and a delight to be around. She made lessons seem like they were a pleasant getting together of good friends. She allowed me the room to simply be who I was; something exceptionally rare. As a result, I saw her not just as a teacher, but also as a wise friend. She was someone I knew I could turn to for guidance. I often did. It was a gift to have a teacher like Anne in my life.

On the last day of school, Anne handed me a special card – a very poignant handwritten note. In this card she commended my value in staying true to myself – something I thought I'd *never* hear from a school teacher. It's a message that, even to this day, reminds me of how important such a value is. I have kept it in my "box of memories" ever since. Sadly, Anne passed away at an early age. She died of pancreatic cancer. So the card she gave to me is a treasure I'll keep for as long as I'm alive. Each time I look at this card, I choke up a little. I remember all of the special moments at school; moments that were made to be special simply because of the delightfully spirited lady Anne was. (On the page following the end of this chapter, you will find a copy of the actual message that Anne wrote for me.)

THE EPIDEMIC OF SOCIETAL VENOM

"A time is coming when men will go mad, and when they see someone who is not mad, they will attack him saying, 'You are mad, you are not like us.'"

–ABBA ANTHONY

The mainstream media – newspapers, magazines, internet sites, radio and television news stations – fill our consciousness with notions of fear. They also send us messages of inadequacy. But how can we be truly confident as human beings if we buy into a mechanism that is ultimately designed to control us by trying to convince us that we're not okay, that we're lacking, and that we need to become voracious consumers of goods if we ever want to have any chance of feeling good about ourselves?

When was the last time you read a popular men's magazine, or a women's magazine, that told you that you were whole and complete just as you are? When was the last time you read an advertisement that affirmed that your uniqueness is a gift to be fully expressed, instead of something to cover up? When did you last see a television commercial that let you know that you really don't have to change who you are, because who you are is perfect?

What, instead, are we confronted with in this merciless consumer-driven world? We are bombarded with an unrelenting slew of messages eager to steal away our sense of contentment so that we can be sold something that will apparently make us more "acceptable", more "beautiful" and more "desirable" to others! Billions of people, every day, hand over their money in exchange for these little packages of colourfully printed pages which tell us that there's something fundamentally missing inside of us. Is it any wonder there are so many men and women who don't believe that they're worthy and precious human beings? The author John Burger, in his book *Ways of Seeing*, describes this concisely (in regard to the specific relationship between women and advertising): "The publicity image steals her love of herself as she is, and offers it back to her for the price of the product." He also goes on to say, "Capitalism survives by forcing the majority, whom it exploits, to define their own interests as narrowly as possible. This was once achieved by extensive deprivation. Today in the developed countries it is being achieved by imposing a false standard of what is and what is not desirable."

For the most part, these magazines are expertly crafted to make you feel as though you are not enough. Making readers feel inadequate

Billions are spent each and every year by large advertising corporations that want you to believe that you are not adequate, and that only by purchasing their goods will you fill the "void" within you that needs to be reconciled.

is an art form that seems to have become more and more sophisticated over the years. Just pick up any glossy publication of your choice, and leaf through the content. Almost the entire underlying message is about *changing* who you are! It's all about "botoxing" yourself, "lasering" yourself, or "shrinking" yourself into the "perfect" person. And the structure of how this operates is very insidious indeed: the first series of pages feature a range of informational or "educational" pieces that tell you how and why you're broken, and then, once you reach the back of the magazine, where all of the advertisements are located, the ideal "solutions" to your brokenness are right there to be purchased! And even on those rare occasions, when you do come across an article that embraces and sustains the value of true self-appreciation, on the very next page you'll see something that opposes this message entirely. According to these ever-popular sources of media, finding comfort in who you are, as you are, is simply not enough. Instead you are told that you have to find comfort by gaining personal validation from outside of yourself, or by altering yourself in some way. Both, of course, are ultimately flawed concepts.

These toxic messages ripple deep into the fabric of modern society. People buy into these messages very literally. And the result is more and more people feeling inadequate and unworthy, and more and more people looking for ways to change themselves. We are led to believe that having a "million dollar makeover", or some other form of surgery, for example, will be the end to all of our worldly troubles. It misguides us from the core of our true integral strength.

I'm not totally against the practice of aesthetic surgery. It's never wise to be rigidly categorical about such things. In certain cases, and under certain circumstances, it is very suitable and very appropriate. Just because a person decides to undergo a procedure of some kind, doesn't automatically indicate that he or she is deeply insecure. There is a host of reasons why a person would decide to have plastic surgery. Predominantly, however, the cosmetic surgery industry does *not* want us to feel secure and confident in ourselves. It doesn't want us to feel good about who we are. Without unstable, insecure, self-loathing men and women, this industry wouldn't be the thriving cash-sucking business that it is. It actually wants and requires us to lack self-confidence so that it can sell "confidence" to us!

These days we have 13-year-old girls asking their mothers if, for Christmas presents, they can have breast implants! And why would girls of such a young age – who aren't even close to being fully developed – even consider the idea of wanting their breasts cut open and stuffed full of silicone, if it weren't for the profusion of messages, from all corners and all directions, telling them that they'll only be beautiful once they've had a breast augmentation? And how will a young girl ever grow to become truly comfortable with who she is if the preponderance of information she receives about her self-worth and her "place in society" is perpetually convincing her that she's not as valuable and attractive as she "could be"? We really do underestimate how damaging these messages are to young people!

Let there be no mistake – I am *not* against the process of advertising and I am *not* against the process of marketing. I use advertising and various forms of marketing in my own businesses. Using these modalities of communication is part of what's required to disseminate your message out into the world, and into the marketplace. What I'm against is the bombardment of the types of ideas that do not support the inherent value that humans possess, and instead, use ruthless means to convince people that they're incomplete.

This is why a large part of my personal work with clients, within my *Extreme Confidence Breakthrough* mentoring programme, is about de-hypnotising people out of the deep trance they've been placed into; it's about allowing them to cultivate an internal position in which they're able to recognise that they in fact need nothing to feel complete, because they're *already* complete. Then they can feel the magic of moving through the world, feeling the vital resonance of their completeness – their internal unshakeable power – emerging from every cell of them.

We step onto a tube train and we're bombarded with banners that tell us that our inner fulfilment is just a "nip and a tuck" away, and that only by purchasing the latest "shiny new object" (car, house, holiday etc.) will we ever stand a change of being accepted and respected by others. We're made to feel that true internal satisfaction is out of reach – but only just – because we can obtain it by spending the right amount of money on the right external "solution".

I'm not telling you that shouldn't buy nice things. Not at all. Buying quality merchandise can be great fun. I love to make all kinds of purchases. So go ahead and enjoy all of your shopping experiences. If you like Armani, then buy Armani. If your taste is for Louis Vuitton or Prada or Ralf Lauren, then buy these items with cheerful readiness. And if you like Jaguar, then buy Jaguar. My message regarding consumerism is not about the fact that we buy, it's about *why* we buy – it's about those deeper motivations that drive our desire to make such purchases in the first place.

It's fascinating that one of the universal "symbols of success" in our culture is that of the automobile. Most people have no idea why or how this idea came to be so prevalent. Yet, there is a belief in our culture that makes an expensive car synonymous with deserving great respect and admiration. And there's absolutely nothing wrong with wanting to purchase an expensive shiny new car. What's wrong is thinking that your obtaining it is going to change you from the inside out. It won't. It never can, and it never will. But people succumb to this illusion all of the time. They say to themselves, "As soon as I get that car then people will really admire and respect me. Then I'll really be someone! Then I can finally feel good about myself!" So they work harder and harder to accumulate the money to purchase this seemingly utopian object of desire. And when the car comes, it fires them up for a few weeks. But the reality soon hits them: they might own this new car, but *they* feel the same. That deep sense of fulfilment isn't present. They don't feel that lasting confidence they hoped owning the car would bring them.

> You can either live in accordance with your truth, or you can live in accordance with the fiction the world has created for you.

You can purchase as much "stuff" as you want to, just as long as you don't start believing that you *need* these things to complete you, because there is nothing you need from the outside for you to be complete. So if you ever buy things because you believe that owning these items will somehow make you more worthy as an individual, that's where difficulty arises. But when you can engage in consumer activities, whilst simultaneously holding on to the truth of who you are at the most fundamental level, you know that if all of your possessions were to be suddenly taken away, it wouldn't affect your sense of personal value, because you'd know that your value doesn't come from the things that you own. That's true personal power!

Television advertisements are guilty of convincing people that there is a void in them which needs to be filled by the very items being presented. Compared to print media, commercials have the advantage of appealing to our deepest emotional responses through the use of carefully selected music tracks, emotive imagery and a range of sophisticated visual techniques designed to engender inside of us the state of desire. And then, once this state of desire has been evoked, it is seamlessly linked to the product being offered.

I remember seeing a television advert for a particular brand of car. At the end of the advert the slogan message appeared: "Get some character". This type of consumer-based mass-hypnosis is very typical. In this particular case the advert suggests to its audience that we can only really possess true character after we've purchased this car, which will somehow provide us with the personal qualities we are ostensibly lacking and unable to generate for ourselves. And so, in a culture where this type of message is hammered into our consciousness again and again and again, is it any wonder why so many people actually start believing that a new car will finally offer them the end to their suffering, and the answer to true inner peace?

Why do you think television programmes are called "programmes"? Isn't it because they're designed to *programme* your mind? And who's behind it all? In the majority of the countries of the world, the television companies are licensed by the governments of those countries. This same rule applies to radio as well. What's more, some television and radio companies are actually owned by the ruling governmental structures. Doesn't this give you insight into what's really going on?

Although I don't believe that the specific individuals who work within the corporations and institutions which are behind the propagation of these campaigns operate out of vindictiveness or maliciousness – because they, too, desire for their families and loved ones to live honest, fulfilling and purposeful lives – it still stands true that many of the messages that are created as a result of the work that takes place inside such corporations remain very misleading, very duplicitous and very disempowering of human beings.

"Accept no one's definition of your life; define yourself."
–Harvey Fierstein

Walk along any street and peer into the windows of large clothing outlets. What do you see? There you find manikins of "skinny" people. Rarely (almost never) will you find manikins of "average" body types; only those of very slender people, donning designer clothing. And it sends the message to us that true personal fulfilment can only be attained through being just the same as the apparent role models we see before our eyes.

Only those who are extremely slim seem to pass the “good looks test”. You only need to attend a live fashion show to notice the physical frames of the women strutting along the catwalk. There you will see what is presented as being “the way to look”. Simply put – to be skinny! And yet, this entire notion of what’s considered “attractive” used to be totally different. At the time of the Renaissance, plump women were actually the icon of beauty, not skinny women. Countless pictures from this era depict portly ladies with ripples of fat, bulging bellies and chubby cheeks. For a woman to be this way was actually considered extremely attractive. What’s more, fat people were associated with the wealthy elite – because only fat people could afford to buy all of the food that made them fat in the first place – whilst extremely skinny people were associated with poverty. So being overweight actually used to be a status symbol. Doesn’t this serve to further reinforce the idea that our beliefs about what is “real” and “acceptable” are not solid unwavering truths? Doesn’t it bring us back to the fact that it’s ultimately all about beliefs? When we reach this level of awareness we can peer behind the curtain, to what it is that causes us to have these beliefs in the first place.

These days, in relation to the idea of women and attractiveness, things are very different. Studies show that poor people are far more prone to being overweight, compared with people who have greater financial means. Modern society presents us with the idealisation of thinness. More women than ever want to be as skinny as possible. And there’s no shortage of “size zero” role models and “celebrities” (who are supposedly in the know about what it means to be “attractive”) to lead the way, demonstrating that it’s somehow sexy to look emaciated and to have so little body fat that every vertebra of the spine becomes inordinately prominent.

Needless to mention, there are women everywhere desperately trying to lose as much weight as possible – even if they don’t need to – because they’re so eager to become the super-thin size they’ve been programmed to believe they should be. To make things worse, this belief is leading to chronic eating disorders. In the UK, the number of young girls admitted to hospital due to anorexia has experienced a shocking increase. And why? Because, more and more, women are made to feel dissatisfied with how they look. And it’s all because of the “big machine” that controls what kind of information makes its way into our heads!

In terms of how we look and how we dress, have you actually ever asked yourself what “fashion” really is?

> The socially constructed environment imposes upon you a set of values that are not your own values, and then demands that these values are more important than your own.

We go out to the high streets and into the departments stores and we're presented with ideals of the types of clothes we apparently "should" be wearing, because it's "fashionable" to do so. From year to year we see changes in what's considered fashionable. One year something is "in", and the next year it's "out". And, of course, there will always be those people willing to blindly buy up whatever happens to be in vogue at any particular time. These people feel a sense of "missing out" if they don't. And, quite often, such individuals aren't even concerned about whether or not the clothes actually suit them, because their main concern – their biggest priority – is keeping up to date with the latest trends so that they'll somehow feel more "accepted" by the people around them. They're constantly trying to keep up with a game that is always changing. As a result, the game has them under its grip. The game controls them!

So what is fashion really? What is it honestly all about, underneath the surface? Is it really about the clothes themselves? Or is there something else at play?

What we call fashion is, ultimately, a psychological structure that operates as a disguised form of control. Fashion is other people telling us how we should look. Isn't this a bizarre notion if you really consider it? Fashion attempts to make us feel silly if we don't have just the right logo on the side of our trainers or the correct type of jeans. Fashion is essentially about the installation of copycat behaviour. It effectively says to us: "Look how we tell you to look and wear the clothes we tell you to wear, or you won't be as special as those who do! We know what looks good and you don't!" Fashion is other people setting a "standard" – which is, at best, a false standard – and convincing us that we have to live up to it. So, on the surface, what appears to be something that caters to our best interests is actually a devious ploy that tries its hardest to convince us we'll be more special, more attractive, more socially aware and more acceptable as humans if we just follow orders and wear what we're told to. Those who don't think this is a control mechanism are still asleep!

Have you ever stopped to ask what makes something fashionable one year, but not the next? Have you actually thought about who or what is determining, and constantly changing, these "rules"? Because when we get right down to it, what's considered to be in vogue is just being *made up* by people. That's right – people are literally sitting around on swivel chairs and just making it all up! Fashion designers just make it up! They pull these ideas out of thin air! And then – a few months later – people go out to high street vendors and pay money for these very same ideas. And most men and women think it's real. They think that these standards for contemporary dressing are indisputable universal truths. They miss the total craziness and absurdity in it all.

There is absolutely nothing wrong with wearing clothes that are "fashionable", as long as you're doing so because it's an intentional choice you're making, as opposed to feeling as though you *should* be wearing them because others have compelled you to through a sense of obligation. That's why what's far more important that fashion is *style* – true personal style. Fashion is about others telling you what you should wear, but style is about *you* deciding what looks good on you and developing your own unique way of wearing different combinations of clothes that are suited to your own tastes. Surely that's a more authentic way of making personal decisions about how to dress? But large corporations would rather you didn't think this way, because then they'd have less control over your buying habits, which affects their sales numbers.

"Death is not the biggest fear we have; our biggest fear is taking the risk to be alive and to express what we really are. We have learned to live our lives trying to satisfy other people's demands. We have learned to live by other people's points of view because of the fear of not being accepted."

–Don Miguel Ruiz

In a very real sense, the more "fashionable" a person is the more they're demonstrating their susceptibility to being controlled and told what to do. This is why being a true individual is hardly ever encouraged through the multitudinous avenues of the mass media. Instead, what's encouraged is uniformity, conformity and compliance – to be part of the "social collective". True individuals are harder to control. The ruling control mechanisms of the world want and require as much submission and standardisation as possible. But that doesn't mean you have to play their game!

THE MYTH OF "SOCIAL NORMS"

What we refer to as "social norms" – those patterns of thought and behaviour we think of as being "real" and "true" – have all been made up. The philosopher John Searle has written about this extensively. Searle's work speaks to the notion of a "constructed reality" – the idea that the things we consider to be "normal" are really nothing more than constructions people have simply bought into. They only mean what they mean because people have agreed upon that specific meaning, as opposed to any other meaning.

An example, from my own life, is my pattern of sleeping. I do not function at my optimum in the morning. I'm not a "morning person" – I never have been. I have discovered that my creative capacities are at their optimum later in the day, and especially at night. I adore the feeling of working, writing and creating into the early hours of the morning, whilst the world around me sleeps. The deep stillness and silence of the night allows me to focus and produce ideas in a manner very different to daylight hours. Almost all of my creations, of which I'm most proud, have been conceived at night. So instead of struggling against this inherent rhythm – what our culture most certainly demands us to do – I embrace it. I therefore go to bed much later than the "average" person, and I awaken later than the "average" person as well. What's more, I never feel guilty about it!

Instead of allowing those around me to make me believe that I'm "wrong" or "strange" for doing this (because it's not consistent with their understanding of what's "normal") I remind myself that my own individual pattern of creativity is something to cherish, not something to try to hide away or become embarrassed about. Who is it that tells us we have to go to bed at eleven o'clock and get up at seven or eight in the morning anyway? Who made this "rule" up? Once again, it's just another result of this conditioned and constructed world. To me, what's far more important than the time you decide to sleep is the value you bring to the world in the hours you're awake. Why fight against an innate pattern that is at the heart of your creativity? Throughout history, there are countless examples of people who didn't subscribe to conventional sleeping patterns, many of whom have been the greatest and most creative thinkers in the world!

The phenomenal artist, Salvador Dali, sometimes worked for several days without any sleep at all. He would often work zealously and at full capacity for four or five days at a time. He would then retire, doing nothing but sleep and rest for two or three weeks until another creative burst inspired him to fire up and begin the cycle all over again. By conventional standards, this manner of functioning is outrageous; it does not constitute "normal" behaviour. But Dali left behind a body of work that is irrefutably stunning. And part of what allowed Dali to create such incredible art was in his rejection of the social norms being imposed upon him. Dali is renowned for his bold proclamation, "The only difference between me and a madman is that I am not mad." Perhaps what he meant by this is that he understood the world around him to be constructed, and that he just wasn't concerned about following social norms or yielding to the expectations of others. Instead, Salvador went his own way – he followed his own path and embraced his own innate inspiration for creation. As a result, he left behind a timeless legacy of unmistakably original work – the result of profound and uninhibited artistic expression.

Think about how our seven-day-week is structured in Western society: go to work Monday to Friday, and then go out at the weekend. There are, of course, exceptions to this. However, this is the prevailing pattern for the overwhelming majority of individuals. So we've been conditioned to believe that it's somehow not appropriate to stay in on a Friday or Saturday night. We've been programmed to think that it's not "cool" to stay at home. In fact, many people would be embarrassed to tell you that they have no plans for the weekend. But we hardly hear from these people; probably because they're too embarrassed to say anything! And yet, the reason most people can't wait to rush out at the weekend is because they want to forget about the 40 or 50 hours they've spent working in a job they absolutely despise. So they go out at the weekend and drink heavily. It numbs them to the mundanity of their nine-to-five working life. They drink as much alcohol as they can possibly funnel down their necks to temporarily forget that they have to do it all over again once Monday comes around!

"Most people are other people. Their thoughts are someone else's opinions, their lives a mimicry, their passions a quotation."

–Oscar Wilde

This type of existence is not about being an inspired human being – it's about settling for what is "expected" and giving your life away in exchange for the illusion of security. There is so much more to life – *so much more* – than doing work you can't stand in order to pay off a mortgage! But, for most people, if they are able to do just this – and not much else – they're made to believe that they're somehow "fortunate" and should therefore be thankful. So many men and women never truly embrace their deepest passions, fascinations or strengths. We are constantly being warned against an inspired and creative way of living. We have been taught from a very early age that if we do something we truly love, then it's not true work. We've been taught that "real work" is doing something we don't like, so we're made to feel guilty for receiving money by doing things that we love and adore. And this cultural myth – this total lie – has been perpetuated and ingrained into our culture so deeply that hardly anyone thinks to question it. So people go through their lives doing work they don't like, believing that this is somehow more "honourable". To me, this isn't being honourable – to me this is lunacy of the highest order!

> You can either be an "obedient robot" or you can be the divine sentient being that is the deepest essence of you.

A large part of our early upbringing rewarded us, not through doing things that really aligned with our inspired and instinctual gifts, but, instead, by doing what we were told to do. We were only congratulated and made to feel good when we followed the orders of our "authorities". If we asked too many questions, or challenged the reasons behind the orders, we were met with hostility and reproach. So we quickly learned that to be accepted we had to follow instructions, and not follow our inspiration. And, of course, it's no wonder that so many people leave their creative passions by the wayside, not realising that those are the very things that make them flourish and come alive. For many, by the time they reach thirty years of age, they've more or less forgotten about their true gifts and fascinations because they're too preoccupied with trying to live a life that has been imposed upon them by those who apparently "know better".

Countless men and women live out their entire lives this way, never doing what deeply fulfils them – what I sometimes call "work of the heart" – because they're still living inside of the idea that it's more important to do what society tells them is "best" and "appropriate" than it is to bring their uniqueness into the world and live the life that is truly their own. And this inward discord can have serious consequences. It can literally affect a person's very state of physical and emotional health. The repression of deeply held emotional and creative energies manifests as tremendous stress in the body. Countless research studies have concluded that this internal dissonance – brought about by the thwarting of the deep instinctual drives inherent in all humans – very often leads to a staggering range of illnesses, muscle tension, severe migraine, panic disorders and even cancer.

The remedy to these symptoms is not throwing prescription drugs down your neck, and then going back to your doctor to ask for an increase in the dosage. Instead, it's found by aligning with your true and authentic path – by beginning to engage in the work that fascinates you, enlivens you, fortifies you, inspires you and allows you to share your inherent gifts with humanity. Doing so literally strengthens the very cells that make up your physical body. It transforms the way the chemicals in your brain function and organise themselves. There is relaxation, alignment, flow and effortless wellbeing. There has been a staggering number of cases in which very ill people have made the decision to turn their lives around – entrusting their lives to their true authentic purpose – who have experienced remission of the most debilitating diseases. This is because these people finally chose to engage with life in a way that sustained and fortified them from the inside out. Such instances have perplexed the minds of physicians and scientists.

Sadly, many people will never get to this stage. They will never arrive at that pivotal moment in which they realise that everything that's been holding them back is nothing more than a series of stories and delusions that has been imposed upon them. They will never connect to the source of their true power. They will always continue to believe that they are *power-less* rather than *power-full.* They will continue to look for evidence to support and consolidate their impoverished interpretations of the world, and of who they are in the world. They will continue on – staying captive to the illusions that keep them trapped and beset with fear – waiting for permission to be who they are.

"What lies behind us and what lies before us are tiny matters compared to what lies within us."

–Ralph Waldo Emerson

It's for this very reason that I have made it my life's work to inspire and empower as many people as I can. It is my deepest mission to guide people into the fullest expression of their inherent truth – beyond all of the lies and myths and distortions – and really come to rest inside of the power and uniqueness that is their gift to the world. Because this is my divine purpose, I feel absolutely inspired doing the work that I do.

The fully internalised realisation that who you are is – as has always been – perfect and whole and complete, frees you from the illusions of the world. There is nothing for you to do, there is nothing for you to prove, there is nothing you need to acquire, there is nothing for you to wait for. All you need is to return to your truth. All you need is to let go of all of the illusions that keep you afraid, because being vibrantly confident is your effortless nature.

But to get to this level of awareness requires deep personal commitment – the commitment to never surrender. Not everyone will stay the path. Most won't. And this is because the conditioning runs deeper than we think. It's present even in the day-to-day language that we use. We've even been conditioned to speak in colloquialisms which, on the surface appear innocuous, but are actually devastatingly disempowering. Ubiquitous phrases such as "my other half" – a popular term used to describe one's partner or spouse – are more toxic than we think. Using the phrase "my other half" only serves to consolidate the notion that we are not complete; that we are only "half a person" – and therefore not a "full" person – and that we *need* this other person to be with us in order to make us whole. Once again, these cultural myths are just perpetuating ideologies which serve to keep us disconnected from our interior wholeness.

THE DEEPEST TRUTH OF YOU

Truth – real truth – is that which never changes. There is no denying that everything around you is subject to change at any moment, regardless of what you do to try to make things be a certain way. There will always be a level at which you are unable to change external circumstances. But the *truth of you* – your inner truth; who you are at your essence – never changes. Your truth is, by its very nature, changeless.

When you carry the awareness of your changeless truth into all that you do – embracing and embodying it at ever moment – you stay connected to authentic power, authentic strength. This is what it means to be a powerful individual: not to garner a perceived sense of worthiness based on factors which exist outside of you, but to truly rest and settle into that indwelling certainty that resides at your centre, in spite of the elements in the environment designed to pull you away from this fundamental way of being.

And whenever you become sidetracked – whenever you are thrown off balance by the overwhelming bombardment of manufactured cultural ideals; the incessant barrage of lies, diversions and distortions – all you need is to settle within yourself once again, reaffirming your true divine nature, knowing that at the deepest part of you, you are divine and magnificent and complete. And when you make the inner resolution to never relinquish your birth-given right to *be* in the world – to never surrender your deepest most essential truth – every step you tread and every word you speak has no choice but to resound and resonate with the very potency of this.

In his utterly inspiring and life-changing book, *Man's Search for Meaning*, Victor Frankell – a noble survivor of the Nazi death camps in Germany – describes the raw inner power generated from holding onto the deepest and most vital aspect of who you are and never letting go. His message is simple, yet absolutely profound. He speaks about what it really means to hold onto the essence of your human dignity, regardless of the conditions and circumstances that you find yourself present to. He refers to what he calls the "last of the human freedoms". He avows that, "... everything can be taken from a man but one thing: the last of the human freedoms – to choose one's attitude in any given set of circumstances,

> Your divine human liberty – the very essence of who you are – is the aspect of you no one can steal away. When you stay connected to this, you stay connected to a power that is immense and extraordinary.

to choose one's own way." Despite being subjected to the brutal and horrific incidences that took place in those concentration camps, Frankell says this: "Every day, every hour, offered the opportunity to make a decision, a decision which determined whether you would or would not submit to those powers which threatened to rob you of your very self ...".

AWAKENING FROM THE VENOM

When someone tells you that you're worthless, the problem is *not* them telling you this – the problem is you believing them! Whoever said that you had to buy into *anything* anyone ever told you?

In certain parts of the world, such as Marrakech, bartering and street trading are part of the culture. People will "offer" you all manner of things. Just walk out into the street and you'll soon be accosted by all kinds of characters, begging you to buy their wares. They'll say to you, "Buy these shoes" or "Do you want to buy this lovely watch?" or "You must buy my lovely fresh bread", and it's up to you to make a choice – you either buy or you don't. But it's always up to you. It's always ultimately a decision that rests in your power. It's always up to you to accept what they're offering, or to say, "No, I don't wish to accept what you're offering me. I do not want it!" And in the same way that you would say "no" to a street trader, if you didn't want to buy what he was offering you, you can say "no" when the world offers you ideas about who you are that are designed to weaken you, to mislead you, to cast doubt upon your true worth.

This constructed world presents to you many illusions. For one, society parades itself as being utopian, but in truth, it is largely dystopian in operation. And so the illusions that flow from this are poisonous. Do not be fooled by them. Don't get sucked in to the vacuum. See through them. And to be able to remain strong and unyielding in the face of these illusions is not to exit the world but to simply live from an awakened consciousness. All you need to de-condition yourself is to become aware of the conditioning – to simply know that it exists – to see what most people are missing completely!

Never allow anyone or anything to convince you that you are not enough, or that, in some way, you don't count. Don't ever be forced into doing the will of others. Don't ever believe that you need something from outside of you to make you whole. Any such attempt to limit your intrinsic human value deserves to be exposed for what it is! Refuse these deceptions that are being imposed upon you. Recognise them for exactly what they are. Laugh at them! You are not broken. There is nothing missing in you. There is nothing wrong with you. You don't need "fixing". You are pure consciousness; pure potential. Your magnitude is beyond conception. You came into the world unique and miraculous and in a state of perfection. This is who you really are.

When you take a wooden pencil and place it into a glass of water, you notice a curious illusion. Looking down, the pencil doesn't appear solid or complete. It appears broken and separated at the water's surface. But you know that this is merely a trick of the senses – a visual distortion created by the principle of refraction. Regardless of what your eyes tell you, you know that the pencil isn't actually broken. You know that, despite how it looks, it is solid and whole. You know that nothing has really changed. You know that the pencil is solid and complete, even though it's *appears* to be very different. Yes, it's a very convincing illusion, but – deep down – you know it's not real. And deep down you know that there's an aspect of you that is strong and fearless; and if, at any time, this appears to be any other way, know that nothing has really changed. Know that the only thing that's really changed is your awareness.

Just like the pencil in the water, it only appears to be broken and disconnected when you accept the illusion that it is. And *you* only appear to be broken and disconnected when you accept the illusion that you are. It's up to you to say "no". It's up to *you* to maintain your strength. It is up to you to escape the "group mentality", the "sheep mindset", the "collective consciousness". It's up to you to develop the capacity to stand alone, to claim your power and move through the world with fearless reserve. When you see the illusions for what they are, they lose their grip on you. They weaken and dissolve. They dissipate and fall away. And when this happens you experience the freedom to simply be who you are, without feeling the anxiety created by pressure, expectation and imposition. And since who you are is *already* powerful, *already* extraordinary and *already* absolutely whole, you can allow this potency to fill you up – to beam from every pore and to resonate from every cell of you – sending emanations of your dynamic vital power out into the world. Like this, you are unstoppable beyond measure.

In this way, you embody the very fearless vibrancy you were brought into the world to express, and nothing less. The people that want you to doubt who you are, and the influences that attempt to make you powerless – to weaken you, to bring you down, to destabilise you – will stand little chance against the sheer dynamism of the energy you project from within yourself. This is the energy of your truest expression; your fundamental power. Commit to this way of being – fearlessly, perpetually, unconditionally – and you will embrace the greatest gift you could ever possibly possess in the entire expanse of your lifetime: the gift of holding on to who you are.

"Who we are never changes. Who we think we are does."
–Mary S. Almanac

In the film *Labyrinth,* with David Bowie and Jennifer Connelly, a young girl named Sarah is held captive by Jareth – the "Evil Goblin King" – who has stolen away her baby brother, Toby. The only way she can ever hope to get her brother back is to enter the menacing twists and turns of Jareth's labyrinth and find her way to the castle at the very centre.

For the abiding love of her brother, Sarah wholeheartedly takes on the challenge – a testing and trying voyage with unexpected happenings at every corner – a voyage abounding with a perilous miscellany of distractions and diversions. And, at various moments along the way, she finds herself unable to remember one particular line of passage – those few final closing words – from the story in her book of fantasy tales; the book that has unfolded into the very adventure she's now living out.

At the end of the film – after an unimaginable journey of great danger, brave determination and poignant personal discovery – Sarah once again finds herself face to face with Jareth. Having fallen into a vast dark expanse of space and time, she meets with her nemesis, standing on the floating fragment of a concrete staircase – another one of Jareth's insidious illusions.

Jareth gazes into her with piercing, penetrating eyes – eyes that bespeak the longing for only one thing: total and absolute control over her. "Just let me rule you," he proclaims, "and you can have everything that you want." But Sarah has now come too far. She has learned far too much to succumb to the enticing but empty promises of her treacherous tyrant. He is offering her "everything" – the possibility for all of her most cherished dreams to become true – but, in order to have all of this, she must give herself up.

Her voyage has made Sarah grow much wiser. She is too discerning – too resolute, too directed, too purposeful – to relinquish her soul in order to taste the bittersweetness of fleeting fictitious fantasies. A deeper purpose exists within her. She is no longer willing to stay victimised by the domination of this cruel and devious oppressor. Sarah's emergent strength places threat to Jareth's distorted world, because she stands firm within the knowledge of a singular encompassing realisation. She now finally sees the illusion for what it really is, and what it has been all along. She is now strong enough to break through all that has kept her afraid and all that has held her back. She has endured a fresh and enlightening array of experiences. Her journey has fortified her with all she needs to triumph and complete her conquest.

It is finally time to claim back what is truly hers: not just the return of her baby brother, but the totality of her ultimate personal liberty. But, in order to end the illusion – in order to finally pierce the hard mask of deception and allow her deepest strength to emerge – she must now remember to speak the truth she has carried with her for so long. She must now speak those last crucial and decisive words; that final sentence that has somehow eluded her.

As she stands there, under Jareth's ice-cold watchfulness, Sarah's countenance and complexion takes on a new and refreshed sense of fearlessness. Jareth's sharp emotionless eyes helplessly soften under the force of her newly found vigour. Poised in a swirling mass of darkness – surrounded by oracular shapes and floating matter; looking deep into those hollow faithless eyes; seeing past his charming iniquity – she opens her mouth to utter those final momentous words: words that will consolidate all that she has finally come to know; words that will, at last, irreversibly crush the illusion to pieces; words that will shatter the mirror of dark and heartless deceit.

The words finally emerge from Sarah's lips – completely and instantaneously breaking the spell that has imprisoned her up until this very moment – forever dismantling the myth of Jareth himself; hurtling his nefarious figure far out into dark vacuous space. The words she speaks portend the totality of her imminent freedom – words so few, yet so formidable; words so unadorned, yet so utterly potent. Her voice unassailably resounds through the molecules between them: "You have no power over me!"

Dear Julian,

You have taught me such a lot about being an individual and how important it is to hang on to what you are. I've really enjoyed knowing you and hope that you keep in touch even when you're rich and famous.

Be happy Julian

Best wishes

Anne Horne x

In memory of Anne Horne (1956-2011)

> *Ultimately, embodying true confidence is nothing more than coming to remember who you really are.*
>
> –Julian James

CHAPTER FOURTEEN

Endless Connection to Power

"When one tugs at a single thing in nature, he finds it is attached to the rest of the world."

–John Muir

I'm on a journey ... a voyage ... an exploration ...

The relentless afternoon Sun beams down at my feet ... I feel the unyielding glow and the faithfulness of its energy embracing me ... the source of this immense power dances elegantly upon my skin. I peer up at the sky ... focusing upon the Sun's shining splendour ... my eyes squint as the blinding radiance is too much for me to bear with naked eyes. I feel a sense of reverence for the perpetual presence of this mighty source ... smiling on the inside ... there's something about its intensity that comforts me inwardly... an awareness of ineffable connection ...

My eyes blur for a moment or two before coming back into focus ... I notice a bee landing on a lavender plant ... it goes to work ... just doing what it does best ... perfectly ... effortlessly ... elegantly ... simply being what it is ... embracing its special place in the universe ... allowing what it does to bring goodness into life ... to nurture ... to feed ... to nourish. It eventually flies away ... rising up into the sky ... moving onto the next adventure. I shall never again observe this very same bee ... but it leaves behind its gift to the world ...

Picking up my bag ... I set off ... I begin walking ... I'm internally excited by the things that await me ... my awareness of endless possibilities pulls and compels me forward ... I have no concern or worry ... just the pure attentiveness to the experience that is unfolding ... right now ... in this moment ... there's an inner sense that lets me know I'll be safe ... and protected ... because I'm treading a path of my own making ... releasing the need to know exactly what will show up next ... opening myself to everything ...

I walk for a long time ... it seems like many hours ... there are plants and trees all around me now ... a full bloom of life and vitality ... and as I continue forwards ... I notice the rhythmic patterns in my breathing ... the invisible yet vital energy that runs through me ... I begin to become aware of a deep sense of the very life source that allows me to breathe at all ... I realise I'm not breathing alone ... because everything's breathing together ... an incredible and almighty intelligence is at work ... the underlying power that supports everything. I take in another long breath ... feeling the pleasurable essence of the primal force that permeates me ... all the way inside ... then out again ... releasing it all ... back into the universe ... back to the source of everything ... where there is a constant supply ... never scarce ... always plentiful ...

There are leaves beneath my feet ... the fresh organic crunch of the leaves as I step through them reminds me that they were once connected to the branches of the trees ... but are now separate ... and even though they now rest upon the ground ... they are not really separate ... in a way ... they are no less connected ... and no less significant ... they're just simply going through the full range of their life ... from branch ... to ground ... naturally ... as they should ... protecting the tiny insects that move in and through the soil ... giving sustenance to the ants ... sheltering the bugs and the caterpillars ... all with purpose ... all with nature ... all with perfect flow ... there is no resistance to anything ... everything is as it should be ... and the leaves are still intimately connected to the larger scope of all that there is ... because that's the only way they can be ... just as they are ...

I stop for several moments ... gazing upon an oak tree ... much larger than twenty times my physical size ... enormous and expansive ... it stands majestic and strong ... yet still and grounded ... piercing rays of Sun beam through the gaps in the branches ... I notice the rise and fall of my breath once again ... the oak tree is also breathing ... in its own way ... helping to supply me with the very oxygen I'm taking in ... and in return ... taking in the carbon dioxide I breathe out ... a perfect universal exchange ... a dance of primal energy ... everything working together ... perfectly ... experiencing the connectedness between us ... and to everything ...

The gentle wind sways the tree's branches ever so slightly ... moving in rhythm ... flowing back and forth ... I reach over ... placing both of my hands on the trunk ... leaning forward against it ... the dry and brittle sensation of the weathered bark pressing into my fingertips ... the support and stability of the trunk allowing me to rest for several moments ... feeling the eternity contained within it ... the years and years of growth ... and nourishing... and wisdom ... of the countless seasons it's endured ... its roots reaching far and wide ... and deep ... I imagine how far the roots reach into the soil ...

I close my eyes ... keeping my contact with the grand oak ... there is great stillness in this moment ... a sense of rest and quietude ... no tension or resistance ... just allowing the beauty of the moment to unfold ... peacefully ... the more I surrender to it ... the more I share with this oneness. I can't put into words this feeling of connection ... and I realise I don't even need to ... because it transcends this singular moment ... into every other moment ... leading me back to what's eternal and infinite ... to the power that sustains me ... totally invisible ... yet present in everything ... and I feel my own integral part of this totality ... beyond measure ... because I am not separate ... and never can be ...

I turn around and sit down besides the great oak ... placing my back against the trunk ... facing out ... towards the almighty openness that engulfs me ... and it holds me in silence ... total internal calm ... focusing inwards ... I feel the same almightiness resounding in my chest ... and radiating through me ... everywhere. A time for contemplation ... reaching inside ... feeling stable ... and grounded ... like the tree ... continuing to notice my breath ... and the stillness ... sensing the wonder of being ...

It's now fully dark ... the warmth has retreated ... the chill of the sharp night air sweeps over my neck and face ... yet ... there's a knowing I have ... in a deeper place ... that lets me know I'll be okay ... just as I am ...

I open my bag and remove a blanket ... I pull it around me ... drawing it close to my skin. I can hear the elegant trickle of flowing water from a nearby stream. As I gaze upwards ... resting the back of my head gently against the tree ... I behold the vast expanse of the darkness. The white light of the moon has a hypnotic effect ... shimmering from above ... sending me inward ... even deeper ... feeling centred and comfortable ... the timeless intelligence in the sky speaks to me ... offering a message of rest ... of settling ... of recuperation ... and restoration ...

When I awaken ... I open my eyes to the world once again ... breathing in the freshness of the new morning. The Sun that had retreated is once again warming my skin ... faithfully ... as it always does. As I focus my vision ... I notice insects ... and plants ... and the feeling of the ground beneath me. I stand up ... stretching my arms high into the moist morning air ... embracing the new day that awaits. I think of the bee from yesterday ... on the lavender plant ... and I stop and wonder where it is ... right now ... in this moment ... and wherever it happens to be ... I know that we are sharing the very same air ... and that we are being warmed by the very same Sun ... and there's an internal sense of that same everlasting connection ... the immense and irrevocable companionship ... between me and all that there is ... the benevolence of the universe moving through me ... carrying me ... holding me ...

I know that I am never really alone ... I know that I am part of this divine interflow of dynamic encompassing intelligence ... I feel ... deeply ... a sense of belonging to the eternal intimacy of the world ... the grand cosmic design ... endlessly flowing ... effortlessly ... guiding me forward ... in the direction that is just mine ... perfectly mine ... because all of the goodness ... all of the radiance ... all of the wholeness ... all of the power and possibility ... all of the infinite potential ... is already here ... endlessly and eternally present ... for me ... through me ... within me ...

It has been all along.

About the Author

Julian James, leading expert in the domain of personal confidence and charisma, is the creator of the *Extreme Confidence Breakthrough* elite mentoring programme – a year-long transformational experience in which individuals work with Julian, in an ongoing one-to-one capacity, to smash through their deepest fears and limitations and embrace the dynamic powerful confidence that is their birth-given privilege. The result is that his clients are able to engage the world fearlessly – without self-doubt or hesitation – and fully embrace the life they truly desire, feeling inwardly refreshed, composed and enlivened!

Julian is a man with a fascinating background and diverse breadth of skills, which culminate in his unique and unmistakable approach to communicating with people from all walks of life and inspiring them to honour, celebrate and express the gift of their inherent uniqueness.

He holds extensive certification in the fields of clinical hypnotherapy and neuro-linguistics – as well as in a wide array of other technologies for personal growth and empowerment – and is a Master Magician of London's prestigious Magic Circle. As a specialist corporate entertainer, consultant and inspirational speaker, Julian's life mission is to connect people with the foundation of their authentic power, and make this the fundamental essence of how they move through the world.

Julian's presentations for organisations and professional groups weave together enriching messages of inspiration and transformation – conveying ideas that have incredible and lasting impact – whilst also creating engaging moments of wonder that are both memorable and utterly fascinating to behold.

As a life-long practitioner in the ancient art of magic, Julian is in demand as an entertainer for a host of events, and is often seen “working the room” at many private parties and exclusive functions. His West End theatre show also continues to receive enthusiastic and encouraging reviews.

Residing in London, Julian enjoys the richness of city life. He entertains, consults and delivers his programmes and presentations internationally.

To learn more about Julian’s work, and to keep up to date with his adventures, visit: www.ConfidenceExplosion.com

Lightning Source UK Ltd.
Milton Keynes UK
UKOW020650031211

183142UK00001B/15/P